URBAN DEPRIVATION AND GOVERNMENT INITIATIVE

URBAN DEPRIVATION AND GOVERNMENT INITIATIVE

PAUL LAWLESS

FABER AND FABER

LONDON BOSTON

First published in 1979
by Faber and Faber Ltd
3 Queen Square London WC1
Printed in Great Britain by
Latimer Trend & Company Ltd Plymouth
All rights reserved

British Library Cataloguing in Publication Data

Lawless, Paul
    Urban deprivation and government initiative.
    1. Poor—Great Britain   2. Great Britain—
    Social policy   3. Cities and towns—Great Britain
    I. Title
    362.5'0941   HV4085.A5

ISBN 0–571–11337–0

Contents

List of Abbreviations

AJ	*The Architects' Journal*
CCP	Comprehensive Community Programme
CDP	*see* (N)CDP
CES	Centre for Environmental Studies
CURS	Centre for Urban and Regional Studies
DES	Department of Education and Science
D of E	Department of the Environment
DHSS	Department of Health and Social Security
D of I	Department of Industry
ED	Enumeration District
EPA	Educational Priority Area
GIA	General Improvement Area
GLC	Greater London Council
HAA	Housing Action Area
HO	Home Office
IAS	Inner Area Studies
IDC	Industrial Development Certificate
ILEA	Inner London Education Authority
LEA	Local Education Authority
(N)CDP	(National) Community Development Project
NEB	National Enterprise Board
ODP	Office Development Permit
RTPI	Royal Town Planning Institute
TCPA	Town and Country Planning Association
UA	Urban Aid
UDU	Urban Deprivation Unit
UG	Urban Guidelines

Preface

This book arose out of an interest I had developed in the mid-1970s in the stimulating, even provocative, publications emerging from the Community Development Projects and the Inner Area Studies. To someone like myself from a fairly orthodox academic and professional background they presented a completely new vision of deprivation, urban processes and the position and impact of professionals in the city. But nowhere was there any comprehensive critique of the programmes, or indeed of the other projects, which collectively made up the government's urban poverty programme. It seemed to me that there was a definite need for a review of these projects: their origins, objectives, results and influence. I hope this book proves to be at least one stepping stone towards a wider appreciation and comprehension of their efforts.

In writing the book it soon became apparent that two exercises would be required. There was a clear requirement to evaluate the projects in a chronological, or roughly chronological, order. But also as so many assumptions undermining the experiments seemed to persist in a very marked manner (an observation which others have made too), there was a need to extract and examine some at least of these common themes. I chose four. Others would no doubt have selected different ones. But I think they serve the purpose of revealing how misguided, even anachronistic, some initial premises were. And unfortunately that may still be true.

Two apologies are called for. The author is a planner and claims no expertise in sociology, social administration, law, public finance, management, economics and housing, to mention but some of the disciplines or professions which clearly impinge on any evaluation of a programme such as the urban projects. But only a polymath could claim otherwise. From whichever direction the projects are attacked this will inevitably be a problem. I approached them as a planner and the book, no doubt, reveals the weaknesses and strengths of this position.

Another problem is that of attempting to evaluate projects which have not, at the time of writing, completed their final analyses. This

7

is especially true of the Community Development Projects some of which produced their conclusions after this book had been finalised. Again, this is an inevitable difficulty when attempts are made to examine contemporary material. And it is perhaps not a really critical one. Many of the teams had finished or issued interim reports; various radical and reformist positions had been expounded; their vital impact was already apparent.

New publications are unlikely to require major reassessment. I hope that proves to be the case for other chapters too. With most of them this is probably realistic, but with Chapter 8, on economic rejuvenation, changing government policy or indeed changing governments, might alter the position considerably. But again probably not critically, and anyway as an evaluation of the situation in 1976–7 I hope it will stand as a valid interpretation.

Many acknowledgements are due. Officials from the Department of Environment, the Home Office, the Department of Education and Science, the Department of Health and Social Security and the National Enterprise Board gave the advice and information upon which the book is based. Over forty local authorities provided a whole host of reports and minutes detailing the progress of the poverty projects on the ground or their own attempts at reversing the tide of urban economic decline. C. Evans gave valuable advice on the National Enterprise Board and other instruments of national economic planning. J. Brian McLoughlin read the drafts and made helpful comments and criticisms. And Mary miraculously deciphered it all and kept me going.

Paul Lawless
Sheffield City Polytechnic
March 1978

Chapter 1

THE RESPONSE TO URBAN POVERTY

Urban problems are not new: medieval disease and the squalors of Victorian growth, for instance. And now apparently we are faced by massive urban decay. Some of the symptoms of this most recent affliction are not new either: population, for example, has been decentralising from the centres of larger, older industrial communities for decades. But the rate and polarised nature of this recent demographic transformation, with the younger, more skilled and better off apparently leaving has been seen as a major social problem, not least by central government itself.[1] It is, of course, widely accepted that most industrialised countries have entered a cycle of absolute urban decline, but what has worried so many British commentators is the rapidity of this spatial transformation and its socio-economic bias. The latter is accentuated in turn because such large proportions of traditional urban economic bases have either migrated too or have disappeared, thus reducing, very markedly some believe, available employment opportunities for the residents—generally poorer and less skilled—who remain. And they might in practice have little option but to remain, because of inherent rigidities in the housing market which inhibit both spatial and sectoral movements. But trapped in the older cities, faced with reduced employment opportunities, making steadily greater per capita demands on social services of all kinds and suffering from outmoded and inefficient housing, educational and health infrastructures, not surprisingly the urban poor have exercised many an official mind in recent years. Add to this litany the growing financial indebtedness of city government, the increasing tendency to locate public and private investment outside the major cities and the considerably higher capital and labour costs involved in urban redevelopment, and the recent emphasis on the 'inner city' by politicians of all colours becomes perfectly understandable.

9

But not all urban analyses are so singularly pessimistic. A report commissioned by the D of E, for instance,[2] concludes that social polarisation between the inner city areas and other parts of the conurbations is not especially marked, housing standards in inner cities are improving, and employment opportunities may not be as poor there as is sometimes imagined. But if this is the sound of sweet reason, not many have been prepared to listen. The cities have cried wolf, and although the response from central government has, until very recently, been somewhat less than totally enthusiastic or consistent, it has in varying, often experimental ways, been forthcoming.

This positive response in itself represents a massive shift in attitudes. Traditionally British planning has adopted an essentially anti-urban stance.[3] In the 20 years after the passing of the 1947 Town and Country Planning Act the strong negative controls instituted in that Act imposed a planning strategy on the country which fundamentally contained the growth of the larger cities[4] and redirected expansion instead, to the new and expanded towns and, to a greater extent, to small towns and villages within commuting distance of the large centres of employment. The emphasis, in fact, was firmly placed on the decentralisation of population to the new suburban and ex-urban communities and on the control of the expansion of cities. Where too, new planning initiatives were undertaken within the older cores of cities these almost inevitably took the form of extensive residential redevelopments which were, in time, to create their own problems of extensive blighting, industrial decline and social malaise, which certainly by the late 1960s were becoming widely appreciated. Add the problems too of substantial pockets of immigrants within city areas and all the inherent racial conflict that allowed, and it is not perhaps so surprising to find central government so willing to introduce a poverty programme of sorts.

What is more surprising is that no comprehensive analysis has ever been undertaken into the ten or so urban experiments which have been established in the last decade, or into the assumptions and premises upon which these projects were founded. This is an attempt to fill that gap. It is an opportune time to try to do so. Inner city initiatives abound, White Papers emerge, the major urban experiments—the Inner Area Studies (IAS) and the Community Development Project (CDP)—grind to a halt, interest in city affairs has never been greater. And yet ironically, findings from the various experiments themselves suggest that new government urban initiatives and policy modifications which have been introduced in the last year or so may be altogether too late and of a different dimension to those required if inner cities are to be 'saved', and significantly also, that the sorts of isolated urban projects which have been established in Britain over the last ten years may be largely irrelevant to the basic issue of urban deprivation.

But more of this later. Some more immediately pressing issues are those of definition. What is meant in this context by those elusive concepts 'experiment', 'urban' and 'deprivation'? With the possible exception of the largest of the projects, Urban Aid (UA) and to a lesser extent perhaps Educational Priority Areas (EPAs) all the initiatives have had an experimental basis to them in that their specific findings and generalised conclusions were always intended for both the evaluation of existing national policies and the development of new directives. They were to act, in a sense, as local laboratories examining in a 'controlled' environment the shortcomings of existing arrangements and the capacities of new ones. In this respect they were therefore different in function to other central and locally devised programmes which clearly impinge on the dynamics of urban development such as, say, area housing improvement policies, regional aid or major one-off investment programmes in the regeneration of either older areas or older industries in the larger cities of the North and Scotland.[5] Now clearly anyone examining the totality of urban policy would need to invoke all these influences and could not make the, admittedly, arbitrary distinction made here of electing to consider simply the urban experiments.

It can be argued further that it is equally inappropriate to evaluate urban policies within the spatial framework of the city. Wider spatial and sectoral factors need to be examined. For instance a more radical urban perspective would hold that the state's major national purposes 'require the servicing of capitalist interests',[6] notably in the reproduction of both productive forces and the relations of production which, collectively, ensure the continued existence and development of the capitalist system. Operating within this intellectual framework, it becomes apparent that all policies which affect cities, whether they be directly experimental, part of new housing initiatives or inherent in regional planning programmes, are all part of a national strategy designed to guarantee the primacy of existing systems by dampening down or assimilating dissent, by creating optimal conditions for economic expansion and by providing the social and physical infrastructure essential to the continuation of capitalism, but often incapable of being provided by it.

If then attempts to understand, still less ameliorate, urban poverty by analysing policies intrinsic to that scale are inadequate, why then bother with the urban experiments at all? There are four reasons. First, they have been, at least in the case of the major later ones, extremely influential in pointing out exactly this necessity of invoking wider spatial and aspatial processes if urban problems are to be understood. Second, they have presented an enormous amount of detailed analytical and prescriptive material which must provide a major informational input into urban debates at all scales. Third, some of them have examined and to a large extent discredited the basic premises which has underpinned official thought as to the extent and generation of deprivation. And fourth, not everyone who accepts the primacy of national economic forces in attempting to explain urban decay is necessarily committed to eradicating the existing capitalist system. Reform is an acceptable, and after all far more likely, solution. The urban experiments can tell us much about why and how changes can be made at the margins.

Some of the more astute analyses which point out the possibilities of incremental change have, however, emerged from some of the CDP teams such as those at Cumbria or West Glamorgan, areas which are clearly not part of the 'inner city', a constraint which applies to some of the Quality of Life and Area Management Trial schemes too. But perhaps this is not important, since certainly a large proportion of the individual action projects within the ten experiments have been undertaken in what might be described as deprived urban areas, and because anyway what is relevant here is not so much the specific findings of the geographically dispersed teams but their general conclusions and recommendations in relation to the question of disadvantage anywhere in the country—which in Britain, almost by definition, will include urban areas. All of the experiments have in fact had as one of their aims, and normally a very significant one, the amelioration of urban deprivation, either through policy innovation or through the improved management of existing resources. And for most of them too, whether they originated in the D of E, the HO, or the DES, it was always intended that specific and areally unique findings would be collated nationally to become the precursors of more general universal conclusions about deprivation anywhere.

In many instances this has occurred, with one obvious failing: 'deprivation' as a concept has itself rarely been defined prior to the development of an experiment, nor, with one or two obvious exceptions, have substantial attempts been made to explain it later. The result has been that many of the initiatives have been bedevilled by a lack of theoretical framework, an abundance of inchoate, *ad hoc* schemes and a marked reluctance to examine and to expand on the officially approved, and yet in many cases clearly inadequate, models of disadvantage. Ultimately it may well be argued that a substantial proportion of the projects have been essentially irrelevant. This is partly because locally schemes are developed, die and are forgotten —this might not be crucial, since often it had been anticipated anyway—but more fundamentally because so very few of the local action projects have emerged with viable, substantially argued theories of deprivation relevant for the country as a whole.

That failing might seem surprising, but only if it is assumed that the programme has in fact been devised exclusively to develop a wider appreciation of the dynamics of deprivation. In practice motives behind this national programme of urban experiments have been decidedly mixed, even ambiguous—a shortcoming, if it is one, which has done much to give the initiative as a whole a typically spasmodic flavour. And since the initial objectives assumed for each of the experiments were in turn to frame the implementation and direct the conclusions, they need to be understood.

SOME MOTIVES FOR REFORM

1. A genuine concern to eradicate, or at least to ameliorate, deprivation has certainly been present in official circles and should not be underestimated. It had, of course, been assumed that the welfare state set up after the war would provide a universal and adequate provision of social services for everyone in the country as a personal right.[7] But it was becoming increasingly apparent by the mid-1960s that despite 20 years of considerable achievement that goal was still a long way off. Large numbers of people were still existing in areas of acute social disadvantage whose welfare standards, it was clear, would only rise substantially if additional public resources, more than strict *per capita* allocations might allow, were to be granted to them through exercises in positive discrimination. And some of this positive discrimination might best be administered spatially through programmes such as UA and its successors.

Although it was anticipated that most of these additional urban resources would be used for new social infrastructure, both capital and current, it was also hoped that this investment would provide a welcome spin-off in the way of additional local employment, probably of a temporary nature. The Labour government of the late sixties was becoming increasingly embarrassed at the prospect of growing unemployment, and clearly if parts of the urban programme could, besides developing politically desirable social services, create additional employment as well, so much the better. In the event some phases of UA were designed specifically to stimulate additional employment through increased capital expenditure in the regions. Almost a decade later a new Labour government was to do the same thing with capital allocated in the 1977 budget being used to stimulate employment, especially in the new partnership authorities, through a capital works programme. *Plus ça change.* . . .

2. It is, of course, possible to ascribe far more cynical interpretations to any government willing to develop an urban initiative. The whole programme can be seen as an attempt to prop up ailing and under-invested social services by trying to plug the gaps in service delivery as and when these occur. In this view it is not at all the case that additional resources are being provided to deprived people or areas through positive discrimination, but rather that the overall baseline for social services is quite inadequate and has deteriorated historically. Urban schemes such as those devised by successive governments in the United Kingdom are therefore, according to this position, largely irrelevant and failing attempts to paper over the cracks. What is needed is powerful political organisation and lobbying to raise universalist guidelines, not the essentially peripheral tinkering mechanisms of the urban programme.

3. However one interprets the urban programme *vis-à-vis* social service delivery, it seems clear that there have been other motives in its proliferation, based on fears as to what the long-term political and financial consequences of unmitigated urban decay would be. If, as had been widely anticipated, the situation existed in which the costs of urban government continued to rise as the rate base held steady, or even declined, it seemed possible that this might lead to, or at least encourage, actual social and physical disorder. Certainly for one urban commentator it seemed possible that city bankruptcy would promote conditions in which 'discontent will follow in the wake of other manifestations of the social pathology of the under-privileged community'.[8] No doubt central government had similar fears too.

It had considerable evidence to suggest anyway that widespread alienation characterised large sections of the urban population: electoral turnouts remained very low, confidence in local government hardly existed and interest in local affairs seemed muted.[9] It seemed very possible that the already deep divisions, social and economic, which typified much of the country were being accentuated in an era of urban decay. Now the urban projects as they emerged were never going to solve all the inherent financial and political problems involved, but they might help. They would for instance provide some, admittedly limited, new physical infrastructure which would help in the continued running of the city, an important issue when the fixed physical infrastructure of cities was so large that it could not simply be written off. They might encourage just a few more individuals to remain. They might reduce political alienation to an extent by highlighting an apparent concern for older urban areas on the part of central government. And by involving local residents, some of whom would certainly be community activists, in the implementation of individual action schemes there was every reason to imagine that grass-roots political opposition could be co-opted into the formal structures and administration of government and there be defused. Certainly there has been a strong line of thinking, expounded even very recently,[10] that acute political and social pressures exist within urban areas which potentially might encourage social instability, and which need to be reduced through officially stimulated projects such as those found within the urban poverty programme.

4.   Urban initiatives represent exactly the sort of commitment politicians like: minimal financial output and yet major political impact. Total resources devoted to the entire set of experiments over the last decade have in fact been minute in relation to total government expenditure. The funds allocated to all ten projects have amounted to considerably less than £200m. For the entire duration of the programme, total government expenditure in recent years has averaged more than £35,000m.[11] Even then, despite the very limited expenditure on the programme, there have been concerted attempts by central government to restrain spending, to encourage projects with very limited financial outgoings[12] and to curtail wayward schemes.

In fact, of course, by far the most efficient compensatory instrument available to central government is the Rate Support Grant, which allocates resources to local authorities of a totally different dimension to those available in the urban programme.[13] And yet

paradoxically, debates on the Rate Support Grant have been very
muted compared with those relating to the urban experiments, partly
no doubt because of the innovative nature of the latter and partly
perhaps because cities anyway appear to receive more from the Rate
Support Grant than strict *per capita* allocations would suggest.[14]
And yet despite the relatively insignificant sums allocated to the
urban experiments, they have, on the whole, been well received
politically. Almost certainly this is due to the large number of
experiments and individual projects within each of the major initiatives, which tend collectively to suggest superactive government and
also because of the immediate and often highly visible nature of the
schemes. The potential for political mileage is in fact enormous.

Naturally urban commentators have not been slow to perceive
such political advantages inherent in the programme, nor reluctant
to ascribe somewhat less than perfect motives to guiding politicians.
Certainly there is a very good argument that as each national crisis
emerges—race, unemployment, public spending cuts—so another
urban experiment is devised to deflect debate away from these essential issues. For one pessimistic analyst of the CDP, for instance, it
seems clear that 'the problem of devising the right poverty programme
will be shelved until another political crisis occurs'.[15]

5. One of the most recurrent political crises in Britain over the last
decade has been that of racial conflict. As early as 1966 the Home
Secretary had been granted powers in the Local Government Act to
grant additional monies to those local authorities with a high proportion of immigrant children on the school rolls, in order to subsidise
the extra social service expenditure it was considered that this involved. And it is not at all far-fetched to interpret the UA programme
introduced in 1968 as, at least in part, a response from central
government, under the general aegis of Harold Wilson, to the
speeches by Enoch Powell on the consequences of continued immigration. At that time it was in fact stressed[16] that the new urban
initiative was not intended exclusively, or even particularly, for
authorities with severe immigration problems, but nor was it denied
that by the very nature of the indicators selected, most authorities
likely to gain from the new experiment would in fact fall into this
category. Later experiments too, notably the IAS and the CDP,
became involved with both specific problems suffered by immigrant
groups and with the more general question of the place of immigrants in British society. Undoubtedly the urban programme has

been seen as one way in which overt racial conflict might be avoided.

6. Another consistent theme running through the government's initiative has been the need to achieve greater service efficiency with stable or even diminishing resources. Calls for 'co-ordination' and 'better management' abound. Indeed some of the experiments have been based on an initial premise that additional resources would not be available on any substantial scale, but that alternatively a number of avenues might be explored which would improve the actual managerial performance of all public bodies, especially local authorities. In fact as these possibilities were eventually explored, some of the teams, notably the CDP, came ultimately to reject assertions to the effect that deprivation was caused, or at least accentuated, by poor management and instead began to perceive the whole management and co-ordination issue as a smoke-screen, and a damaging one at that.

But it is doubtful if central government has been disingenuous. Certainly over the last five years, for example, it has attempted to co-ordinate its own policy on inner city issues. In 1973 for instance, the Urban Deprivation Unit (UDU) was established within the Home Office and charged with both examining the nature of deprivation and also creating co-ordinated action projects to ameliorate it.[17] With change of government a year later, renewed efforts at improving the organisation of city policy involved the creation of a Minister of Urban Affairs, and long-term experiments on the part of the UDU to find within 'existing programmes the right order of priority so that money is spent in urban areas of acute need rather than in other areas'.[18] Despite the fact, too, that one of the very Labour Ministers then most involved with urban issues was to suggest later that the UDU had been relatively powerless to counteract strong departmentalised resistance in central government departments,[19] in the event the search for a unified response from the centre continued. It was finally to produce a Cabinet Committee, under the chairmanship of the Secretary of State for the Environment, which was empowered to co-ordinate the various departments involved in the administration of urban policy. Whatever the shortcomings of this approach, it is undoubtedly true that central government is attempting to counteract the divisive influence of its own administrative line structure and has charged some at least of its own urban experiments with encouraging the same thing locally. Whether that is the sort of process it should be stimulating is altogether a different debate.

7. There is an argument that central government is not simply trying to encourage 'better management' in local authorities, but that urban experiments allow the entire range of centrally devised policies to be evaluated at the local level. Shortcomings in policy can then be assessed and modifications made when this is thought desirable. In practice the IAS, and especially the CDP, have assumed this sort of function and have provided a steady stream of suggestions for policy changes at the centre based on their own local findings. In the case of the CDP these tended to be of such a radical nature that they have been quietly shelved, but alternatively in the case of the IAS there are strong reasons to imagine that their recommendations were the single most important influencing factor in determining central government policy.

8. Relationships between central government and administration on the local scale, in this case the local authority, can be perceived in a different light. It is certainly possible to interpret the urban initiative as an attempt by central government to placate fears within local authorities that the extent of urban deprivation within some of the older cities was simply not appreciated at Whitehall. By introducing such a varied and widespread initiative which, potentially at least, might lead to enormous benefits in certain urban authorities, it seemed that central government was doing its best to allay the most pressing presentiments of authorities.

9. There are other interpretations as to exactly what the effective relationship has been between central government and the local level within the urban programme. To one ex-CDP member at least, the programme was 'to provide government with information and re-search on how the social and political tensions generated by the pro-cesses of economic decline can best be managed within the frame-work of existing institutions and policies'.[20] And whereas it is difficult to argue that central government set off with such a predetermined intention, it is undoubtedly true that, solicited or otherwise, the IAS and the CDP provided a wealth of information on the local conse-quences of economic decline. Predictably, central government has not been prepared to respond to these findings by undertaking major social, political or economic innovations. That should be a surprise to no one.

10. Many of the urban projects, especially the early ones, were based on the premise that deprivation could be ascribed to community or personal inadequacies; that in some generative manner cultures of poverty were built up in certain areas that inhibited the full societal development of individuals, but instead instilled 'antisocial' characteristics into incoming residents and, of course, children. A fuller examination of this concept, its development and eventual rejection will be given later, but in this introductory context it is important to realise how significant the thesis was in the early moulding of the urban programme. In particular because it was widely felt that cultures of deprivation tended to occur in definite and identifiable urban localities, many of the urban action schemes were sited in exactly these sorts of areas. There it was hoped that the positive 'pump-priming' influence of the projects would counteract unsociable attitudes. At the same time through encouraging self-expression and community help it was anticipated that the local authority would become better acquainted with the social problems of such areas, and that some of the more pressing difficulties might be moderated anyway through the effect of community and individual self-help. And naturally the sorts of lessons learnt within specific action projects might form the basis for more generally applicable ground rules which would be helpful anywhere in urban Britain.

11. But even in the late 1960s, when concepts of cultures and cycles of poverty were strongly in vogue in official government circles, there had already been a strong reaction to the entire thesis in academic quarters. Eventually some of this scepticism trickled through to officialdom too, and later on some of the experiments, notably the IAS and the CDP, began to examine in greater detail the actual dynamics of urban deprivation: its distribution, intensity and contributory causes. In a sense this was clearly late in the day, since one of the main and early functions of any urban poverty programme should surely be to assess how and why disadvantage occurs in the first place. But in practice, in the United Kingdom at least, assumed models of deprivation, particularly those relating to cultures of poverty and social pathologies, had a strong and constraining influence until relatively recently. Over the last few years in fact, there has been a reaction away from this, during which time—somewhat to the government's chagrin—other, more structurally based, theories of deprivation have been formulated by poverty projects. Uninten-

tionally or otherwise, the poverty programme has done much to realign thinking on the causes and generation of urban disadvantage.

12. Whereas problems of race, social conflict and urban decay might have seemed acute in Britain at the end of the 1960s, they were clearly of minimal importance when compared with parallel American experience. There, throughout the previous 20 years, there had been a growing awareness that the issue of the city was about to present enormous and unprecedented problems of an economic and social sort, which were likely to be accentuated in a most disturbing way by the ever present issue of racial conflict. These were problems of a scale and intensity which Britain certainly had never experienced, nor was likely to either. In the event in America, corporate and government response to this potential, and later actual, threat from the cities took the form of a variety of policy initiatives in the sixties. These included the Ford Foundation's 'grey area' experiments and, under Presidents Kennedy and Johnson, other programmes, such as those run through the Office of Economic Opportunity and the Model Cities projects. The details of these very varied and complex institutions have been well documented elsewhere and need not concern us here. But what is relevant from our point of view is the extent to which the American experience influenced British policy makers and policy takers at the time.[21] It is extremely difficult in practice to ascribe social and intellectual trends to specific causes. But in this instance it seems in general that the American programme was well known here, some specific elements of it evaluated in terms of its potential use in Britain, the Head Start programme for example, and some influential civil servants had received first-hand experience of the development of the American programme. Certainly it was widely known that the Americans had an urban poverty programme and, as their problems seemed likely to become ours eventually, there seemed no reason why their policies should not as well.

But quite evidently in retrospect, whereas the fact that the Americans had an urban programme was widely assimilated into official circles here, the problems even then troubling their experiments were largely ignored. Difficulties such as suitable formal divisions of responsibility between community activists, city politicians and funding agencies, the growing realisation that local community projects might contain very few fundamental powers, and the dispiriting appreciation that improved education or training might not actually better the lot of urban residents, were central debates in

America before the British experience ever got off the ground. They were lessons of experience which in time were to be learnt here too.

Social policy evolves out of changing, even contradictory, intellectual and administrative trends. In Britain the urban programme emerged as a result of the very complex aims of central and local government politicians and civil servants. Not all the motives outlined above have operated permanently on all aspects of the overall programme, but in different ways at different times they have all been influential. It is then not at all surprising to find the history of the programme littered with confused aims and confusing conclusions, nor that on occasions some projects have rejected or modified initial guidelines to which they were supposed to work, either because of an intellectual refutation of basic assumed premises or because founding aims were frankly unacceptable. The disparate and unstructured nature of the programme can be ascribed, at least in part, to shifting and even opposing aims. Its history is incomprehensible unless this is appreciated.

THE SCOPE OF THE BOOK

The book is divided into two sections. The first of these examines, more or less in chronological order, the different elements in the overall programme, beginning with UA and finishing with the CDP (Chapters 2–6) taking in the EPAs, the Urban Guidelines (UG), the IAS and a number of smaller experiments on the way. Some description is inevitable in order to expand on exactly what each project was commissioned to do and how it did it, and to fit each of the initiatives into their formal administrative, financial and political setting. But as far as possible, an attempt has been made to concentrate on the relevant debates surrounding schemes: their shortcomings, benefits and consequences. It would, anyway, be quite impossible to cover in detail the descriptive, analytical and prescriptive prognostications of all the experiments, since they have been remarkably prolific especially the IAS and the CDP. What is at issue here is an evaluation of the general conclusions emerging from the programme, and the contributions these have made to the more general issue of urban deprivation.

The second part of the book examines in an integrated fashion some of the premises which have moulded and directed the programme as a whole. Clearly the urban projects did not pop out of a hat; they were rooted in working assumptions about how such a programme should operate, the sorts of problems which should be examined, and even the type of conclusions likely to emerge. In the later chapters (Chapters 7–10) four such assumptions are assessed in detail. Chapter 7 looks at the concept of positive discrimination. Traditionally the British poverty programme has assumed that deprivation occurs in small, discrete and identifiable urban localities. The evidence for such an assertion has come from what might be called commonsensical support, since that is how deprivation may seem to occur, and because guiding theories of poverty and its generation, notably those relating to cultures of deprivation, suggest such a spatial distribution. But in fact there are very solid empirical and theoretical arguments to indicate that urban deprivation does not have a markedly concentrated distribution, and hence that positive discrimination in its narrow spatial sense may be irrelevant.

Chapter 8 examines another and more recent sacred cow: that inner city regeneration will require the massive expansion of manufacturing industry. This may well be true, but the sorts of powers currently available to local authorities and the manner in which they are being used makes it extremely unlikely that substantial increases in manufacturing output will occur in older urban areas. Does this imply that greater powers of intervention need to be created for use both by local authorities and by the regional administrative structures of central government departments? Certainly even the new powers recently granted to authorities will fall short of those many see as essential if manufacturing bases are to remain in urban areas. Perhaps ultimately, of course, central government, despite its apparent concern for inner cities, is in fact reconciled to continuous, even if reduced, economic decline in urban areas. Is it not the case that its largely aspatial industrial strategy will take precedence over all other policies, and if this means in turn the choice between industrial stagnation and urban stability or industrial growth and urban decay, then it is not difficult to see which way things will go.

Chapters 9 and 10 look at two other more traditional premises inherent in virtually all of the urban experiments: that inner city policies need to be better co-ordinated and managed, and that urban regeneration will only occur with the active support of the 'community'. Both of these assumptions have become almost received truths, above discussion. But why? Improved management at the centre or area management locally can be perceived as smokescreens, essentially irrelevant to the needs of inner city residents. Their standards of living are only likely to rise if policy is improved, not the management of existing, and clearly inadequate, policy. And community development, besides meaning almost diametrically opposed concepts to different commentators, has been widely over-stressed in terms of its actual capacity. It need not be a 'good thing'; it too can deflect debate away from more important issues.

Is the urban programme itself desirable? There are those who consider that urban life is becoming to an ever increasing extent a second choice for many people, and therefore, rather than attempt to prop up ailing urban structures, we should be encouraging those who want to migrate to do just that, which will in turn reduce pressures on those wishing to remain. One refinement of this argument is that it is not simply the case that the urban programme has been largely misguided, but also that it is and will remain ineffective. The resources and implementary powers available to cities are simply not of an order likely to counteract prevailing economic forces. Chapter 11 will examine these issues, in the light of alternative programmes put forward by those wishing to see the continued decentralisation of the cities, and of perceived shortcomings in the existing urban programme.

NOTES TO CHAPTER 1
Where titles or other details of works are not given here, these will be found under the author's or issuing organisation's name in the Bibliography (p. 228).

1 For a general analysis of urban trends see D of E, Urban Research Note 10, 1976.
2 D of E, *Study of the Inner Areas of Conurbations*, 1975.
3 R. Glass, 'Anti-Urbanism', in M. Stewart (ed.), 1972.
4 P. Hall *et al.*, 1973.
5 For example the massive investment programme in east Glasgow: Scottish Office Press Notice 799/76, 'Glasgow East End Project', 8, 1976.
6 R. Miliband, 1973, p. 77.
7 P. Marris, Foreword to D. Thomas, 1976.
8 D. Eversley, 1972, p. 366.
9 A point which at least one planning authority considers worthy of expansion: North-West Joint Planning Team, 1974, p. 5.
10 See, for instance, the position of a Conservative spokesman in a 1977 debate on cities, who saw community projects as one way of ensuring societal stability: 'We must look at all proposals aimed at increasing stability within our society', *Hansard*, Vol. 935, 19.7.1977.
11 *Financial Statement and Budget Report* 1977/78, HMSO, 3.1977.
12 See, for example, a recent HO position statement on the need to

curtail expenditure in urban programmes: *Hansard,* Vol. 911, 20.5.1976.

13 In recent years central government grant to local authorities has amounted to about two-thirds of the latter's expenditure. For instance in 1975–6, with an estimated local authority expenditure of £8,100m, central grant covered 66·5 per cent of this sum: D of E, *Rates and Rateable Values in England and Wales 1975–6,* HMSO, 1976.

14 Because of the nature of the needs element in the Rate Support Grant: R. Jackman and M. Sellars, 1977.

15 J. Higgins, 1974, p. 574.

16 *The Times,* 22.4.1968.

17 *Hansard,* Vol. 863, 1.11.1973.

18 *Hansard,* Vol. 878, 29.7.1974.

19 A. Lyon, *Hansard,* Vol. 935, 19.7.1977.

20 I. Harford, 1977, p. 99.

21 P. Marris and M. Rein, 1974; D. Moynihan, 1969; K. Clark and J. Flopkins, 1970; E. James, 1970; C. Sackney, 1973; R. Holman, 1974.

Chapter 2

URBAN AID

Urban Aid is the largest and virtually the oldest of the dozen or so separate experiments which collectively make up the urban programme. It is in fact frequently referred to as *the* urban programme, but perhaps unwisely, since it has been one of the least imaginative, least researched and essentially most peripheral of all the initiatives. Ironically this, methodologically the weakest of all the urban experiments, has been granted by far the largest proportion of total global funds allocated to the urban projects.

Although when it was announced in 1968 UA seemed to represent an apparently innovatory approach to social administration, it seems now more like a classic instance of Wilsonian decision making: immediate, political, ultimately trivial and very reactive, in this case to the implications behind Enoch Powell's notorious speech on race in April 1968.[1] In fact, under the Local Government Act passed two years previously,[2] the Home Secretary had already been empowered to make special provision of additional resources to local authorities if, in carrying out their statutory functions, they needed to undertake additional expenditure because of substantial numbers of Commonwealth immigrants, normally defined as being more than 2 per cent of the school roll. In practice about 70 local authorities have been aided under this Act, to the tune of a few million pounds each year.

But UA was to be an altogether more intensive exercise. For the Home Secretary of the time, James Callaghan, it appeared that, despite a more general affluence, 'there remain areas of severe social deprivation in a number of our cities and towns—often scattered in relatively small pockets. They require special help to meet their social needs and to bring their physical services to an adequate level.'[3] This special help was to be made available through the new

25

UA scheme, which would 'supplement the government's other social and legislative measures to ensure as far as we can that all our citizens have an equal opportunity in life'. In initiating such a programme it was anticipated that as far as financial means could achieve this, the downward spiral of deprivation would be reversed and the cumulative syndrome of poverty and neglect be defeated. A tall order, but the programme went ahead, and was formalised in the Local Government Grants (Social Need) Act of 1969, in which the Secretary of State was empowered to pay grants where additional expenditure was being encountered because of the existence of special social needs in certain urban areas.

The administrative procedure by which these grants were to be paid was, and remains, most unusual, and has given rise to considerable criticism, mainly on the grounds that they placed a premium on the bureaucratic efficiency of local authorities and not at all on urban poverty as such. This was so because UA operated through a bidding process whereby local authorities put in claims for specific allocated resources, advertised in circulars issued by the HO and, originally other departments too, notably the DES and the DHSS, in a series of Phases, 16 in all. The first of these Phases,[4] initiated in late 1968, was different to all subsequent exercises in that voluntary organisations were not invited to make applications (subsequently they were), and rather than all authorities bidding for allocated resources, some 34 authorities, selected on the grounds of residential overcrowding and there being more than 6 per cent of immigrant children on the school rolls, were invited to apply for the first tranche of about £4m, of what was anticipated as being a £20–25m programme over four years. In the event a substantial proportion of this first Phase was granted to local authorities for new educational facilities for the young, notably additional nursery places and homes for children in care. This pattern was to be repeated for virtually all the first eight Phases, but then a separate nursery expansion programme was announced which released far more resources within the UA programme for other sorts of social schemes.

After this first phase new UA circulars emerged about every six months. The second and third stressed the need for 'rapid result' projects which would provide direct aid to areas of particular social need, and the latter widened the geographical scope of bidding authorities to include even rural districts with fairly large towns. The fourth Phase invited all eligible authorities to bid for non-capital projects such as social centres, family planning and welfare agencies and language schools. The fifth Phase, on the other hand, was somewhat different to other initiatives, being part of a national £100m investment programme in capital projects in areas of high unemployment in the Development and Intermediate Areas. Since that scheme in 1971, the Phases have tended to adopt a dual pattern with some, much smaller, allocations being available for holiday projects, and other circulars requesting claims for much larger funds, often 10 times as much, mainly for capital projects. In the former category, notably Phases 6, 8, 10, 13 and 15, authorities and voluntary groups have been bidding for not more than a few hundred thousand pounds, normally less, to go on experimental or pump-priming exercises such as immigrant classes, gypsy schooling projects, summer play schemes and so on. The alternate and much larger allocations available in Phases 7, 9, 11, 14 and 16, for example, have been for capital and revenue projects, and here there has been normally a few million pounds available. Phase 7 for instance, issued in May 1972, and in which about £6m was eventually allocated,[5] requested bids from local authorities and voluntary organisations for capital projects to be initiated in 1973/4, some capital projects for the under-fives for 1972/3 and non-capital expenditure for 1972/3. The circular stressed that priority would be given to projects such as nurseries, social and play centres for the young, old people's homes and welfare and family planning services. In bidding for grants from the global (normally predefined) sum, local authorities were to indicate what the specific needs of small deprived areas were and how these might be met by schemes funded from UA. These poorer areas might be identified, according to central government, by criteria such as unemployment, delinquency, children in care, overcrowding, immigrants, old and dilapidated houses and so on—areas in fact, so official thinking went, where rapid results possible through UA projects would do much to reduce social stress. Sometimes this amelioration might best be achieved directly through schemes implemented by the local authority, but in other circumstances voluntary organisations might be the best agents to achieve sensible improvements.

This administrative pattern laid down in Phase 7 was to a large extent followed in subsequent Phases too. Collectively the 16 Phases resulted ultimately in the approval of literally thousands of small-scale capital and current projects, over 3,000 in the first nine Phases alone, for example.[6] To a large degree, in the early years of the scheme very little research or formal evaluation was undertaken into this proliferation of social experiments, but in 1971 Professor Greve was commissioned to monitor UA as part of a general research project into urban deprivation. Despite the fact that some of the findings of this research were far from universally optimistic, central government apparently remains convinced that the programme should continue, and indeed be expanded. Recent pronouncements have indicated,[7] for instance, that UA will be transferred to the D of E, will provide grants for economic as well as social infrastructure, especially in the defined partnership authorities, and will be increased to about £125m p.a. by the end of the decade, with the possibilities of further expansions, geographical and financial, after that.

But if central government appears satisfied with the actual and potential benefits of UA, many others involved with questions of urban deprivation are not, for a whole host of reasons relating to the administration and methodology of the initiative.

1. Administrative arrangements for the distribution of UA follow certain set procedures: circulars are issued by the HO and are sent to local authorities, which should in turn publicise them, and in particular should inform voluntary bodies likely to want to apply for funding. Both local authority departments and voluntary organisations submit applications to the local authority as a whole, which after due consideration forwards a priority list to the HO. The latter, in association with other government departments, examines priority lists, makes selections and informs local authorities accordingly. This procedure has caused considerable criticisms, especially from voluntary bodies, which have felt much aggrieved at the relatively small proportions of UA which they receive. It has been suggested in this context[8] that local authorities have consciously delayed providing information to voluntary groups, or have altered priority lists worked out by all relevant voluntary organisations, in order to reduce the impact of these claims on the global sum, and alternatively to encourage projects the authority itself wants to run. Certainly with regard to this last point there seems, for example, to be little evidence that, until quite recently, UA has been employed to encourage the massive proliferation of independent advice centres, not normally madly welcomed by authorities, although there have indeed been calls for the scheme to do just that. Holman, for example,[9] wanted the programme to 'facilitate the gaining of power by the deprived by funding their movements'. It would be hard to

envisage central or local government echoing those particular sentiments.

Instead they would argue that local authorities are in the best
position to evaluate the impact of rival, even conflicting experiments;
that this sort of decentralised structure is exactly what is needed to
administer a very varied and complex programme; and that as local
authorities have to provide 25 per cent of the costs of approved
projects, they have every right to vet applications. Moreover, since
Phase 7 was announced in 1972, a specific percentage of the total
grant has been allocated to voluntary organisations, a proportion
which has in fact been growing, although in the first nine Phases[10]
this amounted to only 7 per cent of capital funds and 43 per cent of
the revenue allocations, in all 13 per cent of the total.

Certain reforms have been suggested which might do much to help
voluntary groups without necessarily totally abandoning the existing
administration. These interested bodies could be informed why
applications had failed for instance; there could be much greater
co-operation between local authorities and federal voluntary organisations to select priority lists; voluntary organisations might
well apply direct to central government or be able to appeal against
local authority lists forwarded to the HO. There is no reason, either,
why voluntary organisations should not supply the additional 25
per cent of costs normally provided by local authorities themselves,
which might do something to widen the choice of projects supported
by UA to include perhaps, more community advice, consumer pro-
tection and local political organisations.

2. Some of the initial assumptions of the programme were that it
would provide immediate funding for rapidly implementable projects,
which could not be financed through alternative means and which
might provide unforeseen benefits and desirable multiplier effects.
Batley and Edwards in a review of these premises[11] based on evidence
from a number of completed experiments, have suggested that these
assumptions may not all be true. In particular, projects in their
experience were not normally implemented especially rapidly, 13
months on average even for non-capital schemes, with local authority
initiatives generally taking longer to get off the ground than those
promoted by voluntary bodies. Moreover about half the projects
they examined might well have been carried out anyway without the
help of UA funds. However, on the other hand, they did find considerable evidence to suggest that UA schemes stimulated unanti-

cipated side benefits and that in general 'the multiplier effect of programme projects is very strong, and the long-term pay-off from the initial programme investment considerable'.

3. An additional problem is the idiosyncratic spatial distribution of this 'long-term pay-off'. The first Phase invited some 34 local authorities, selected centrally on the basis of two indicators, to apply for the predetermined global sum. This process inevitably created some unfortunate anomalies, Bradford being 'chosen' for instance but not Leeds. More worrying, however, is the permissive nature of the bidding system in subsequent Phases. In effect authorities need not apply at all if they do not wish to do so. This can have unfortunate consequences, and has given rise to what Holman has called the 'Southwark Syndrome'[12] in which more progressive authorities—and these often tend to be in London—know more about UA, make applications for schemes more readily, and even if they receive a relatively small proportion of their total claim, will still obtain in absolute terms more than equally deprived but less progressive authorities. A central or regional administration might overcome this problem, with resources being allocated on the basis of need according to defined indicators rather than according to local authority prowess. There are severe problems associated with the use of indicators, but their gross conclusions would appear to be more accurate in representing deprivation than the present form of administrative roulette.

4. But even if resources were to be allocated to more deprived localities, would they be on anything like the scale required? Central government pays grant aid at the rate of 75 per cent on the loan charges of capital projects for five years and for costs over five years too, on non-capital projects. At the end of the five years the grant may be renewed, though not automatically. But the actual amount of grant available to UA is very small, both relative to demand and in terms of the absolute total. Evidence from various sources suggests that demand for funding from local and voluntary bodies vastly exceeds available resources. In Phase 9 for example, about £4·5m was apparently spent on 385 projects when total demand was for £21m on 1,300 schemes.[13] In Phase 11 too, demand exceeded supply by five times and in Phase 12 the figure by almost 20.[14]

Obviously the main reason for this discrepancy is the minuscule grant made available by central government. Overall, in the last eight years, about £5m p.a. has been committed to new projects and the annual costs of past commitments has run at about £12m p.a.[15] In fact, relative to other experiments and initiatives in the urban deprivation programme, UA has easily claimed most of the central aid, the expenditure on UA being in fact in any one year probably greater than the global costs of all other projects put together. But this is only a relative evaluation, of course, within what has been a markedly parsimonious programme. Relative alternatively to say, overall programmed public expenditure, Meacher, for instance, points out that for the year 1972–3 UA amounted to 0·05 per cent of this total and to about 0·1 per cent of expenditure on social services.[16] Moreover since 1972, the programme has anyway been a specific charge on the Rate Support Grant, and thus is in practice not a special additional grant paid by central government to local authorities, but simply a means of refining total spatial allocation of central government support to local authorities in such a way that with luck, more deprived areas, with supposedly more applications for UA, will receive more.

5. Discussions about the relative inadequacy or otherwise of resources allocated to UA assume that the entire exercise is worth while and that presumably it will have some ameliorative effects on deprivation. But will it? The evidence is that the objectives of the programme have been, at best hazy, at worst undefined and that the implicit underlying premises upon which the overall exercise has been based are wide open to dissent.[17]

As far as it is possible to rationalise these things, it seems that two sets of objectives have underpinned the project: some more permanent, generally desirable ends, others directly related to the passing socio-political whim of the time. In the case of the latter it might be argued, for example, that the whole experiment was originally 'hastily assembled at the height of the Powellite controversy'[18] and was intended to provide additional resources to immigrant areas to socialise local residents into 'acceptable' behaviour and thus dampen down potential racial conflict. Although this interpretation has always been refuted by central government, it nevertheless remains true that substantial proportions of UA have been directed to areas of high immigration, partly of course, because the recommended indicators of deprivation have included exactly this criterion.[19] Equally it can be argued that the promotion of family planning facilities within UA was essentially a politically inspired initiative aimed at reducing the

B

numbers of children in poorer areas entering the 'Josephian' cycle of deprivation, and also, that some phases of the project, the fifth for instance, have been used to increase jobs in areas and at times where unemployment was rising to politically unacceptable levels. UA has undoubtedly become a reactive project, a political catch-all, whose short-term aims have been switched according to the political problems of the day. And, of course, politically it is ideal: quick, immediately visible, symptomatic of 'something being done'.[20] The relatively tiny global funds available are not, however, overstressed.

But this should not be taken to infer that longer term, more permanent objectives have not been apparent within UA. It can be seen as an instrument for solving, or at least moderating, social problems, as a catalyst for stimulating community development, or as an attempt to fill gaps in usual social service provision. The real operative difficulty is that no substantial efforts have ever been made to define exactly which of these long-term objectives the project should aim for. This dysfunction in turn makes all attempts at long-term planning or evaluation virtually impossible. The experiment has in fact floated on a sea of political and administrative 'ad-hocery'.[21]

And yet despite this lack of consistency in terms of long-term objective, the project has clearly retained a central vision as to where and how deprivation occurs. It is undoubtedly envisaged as being areally limited to definable localities within older urban communities, where processes of cumulative and cyclical interaction mean that large numbers of children being born there will not achieve their potential development because of the deleterious effects of social pathologies working within a sort of culture of poverty. Evidence that this thesis has been a major motivating force comes from a number of sources. In originally setting up the project for instance, Home Secretary Callaghan said that it was 'to provide for the care of our citizens who live in the poorest or most overcrowded parts of our cities and towns. It is intended to arrest, in so far as it is possible by financial means, and reverse the downward spiral which affects so many of these areas. There is a deadly quagmire of need and apathy.'[22] Certainly for Callaghan, and for many others at the time, cultures and cycles of poverty were very real. And to overcome them the UA programme perceived a need to give priority 'to those projects which will provide rapid and direct benefit to areas of special social need',[23] which in practice turned out especially to be educational projects. Parliamentary questions, in 1971 for instance,[24] as to the sorts of projects being sponsored, elicited the response that for the first six years of the project one-third of the grant would be paid to nursery schools and classes, one-third to day nurseries, children's homes, play schemes and language teaching projects, and only one-third to all other miscellaneous social services and to community and advice centres. The clear implication must be that the main impact of the programme was intended, even at an early stage, to focus on children at and before formal early education, in an attempt to break perceived cultures of poverty at their allegedly weakest points and in so doing to direct young people on to the 'straight and narrow'.

It seems evident too that conventional UA wisdom saw these 'pockets' of deprivation as being scattered widely in many older communities. Certainly approved grants have tended to be distributed in a very broad geographical pattern, normally to smaller schemes. In Phase 7, for instance,[25] 60 per cent of all approved projects costs less than £5,000 and only 5 per cent costs more than £40,000, and exactly because of the tendency to spread resources thinly but widely, many local authorities have benefited in some way or another, well over 200 in fact. The programme has obviously perceived deprivation in such a way that its ameliorative role is likely to be achieved through the approval of more and smaller schemes aimed at obtaining rapid results within small areas at vulnerable stages in an imagined cycle of poverty. Irrespective of the problems intrinsic in such an approach, it has been pointed out that the sheer lack of project monitoring, not even required until Phase 7, inhibited any thorough review of exactly how successful this intervention had been.

But more important than the lack of monitoring has been the consistent undermining of these basic UA premises, stimulated as much as anything, ironically, by the outpourings from a later HO offshoot of UA, the CDP. But however the intellectual process has occurred, it is clear that conventional wisdom regarding the origin and operation of deprivation has changed enormously over the last 10 years or so, since in fact UA began. This view, outlined explicitly in circulars and implicitly in the administration of the scheme, was of deprivation as having an areally discrete distribution, which could be defined by indicators such as poor housing, delinquency, large families, overcrowding, immigrant populations, alcoholism, the elderly, the mentally ill, the handicapped and so on. Clearly here, the main focus of attention as to the causes of deprivation is being directed towards personal and community inadequacies as reflected in mental, social

and even physical disorders, but not at all in system-blaming phenomena such as say, basic poverty caused by unemployment or low pay.

Of course, it should be pointed out that attitudes within UA have
changed. An increasing proportion of grants has been allocated to
advice and welfare centres, for example, where poorer residents can
receive information as to rights, benefits and the possibilities of local
political organisation. There are, too, recent suggestions within the
Inner City White Paper that UA should be extended in size and
scope to include industrial provision. The emphasis evidently is
drifting away from personal deficiency arguments towards a methodology which perceives one cause of urban deprivation as being
structural changes within economic, housing and educational
markets. Why this intellectual metamorphosis should have happened is examined in more detail in Chapter 7.

But this changing focus within the UA programme should not be
overemphasised. The continued stress on small-scale, scattered projects suggests that there have been minimal attempts to attack urban
deprivation on a wider front or to encourage national campaigns
aimed at moderating deprivation through, say, increased personal
incomes, higher social benefits, wider public interventionist powers
or stronger political organisation, which are now seen by some commentators as possible channels of action. But because UA retains a
different, somewhat anachronistic, position as to the origin and
generation of poverty, it lends support to those who interpret it as
essentially a political exercise. Of course evaluations as to the efficacy
and functioning of UA have varied tremendously. Holman and
Hamilton have suggested that the initiative can be interpreted as a
'continuum ranging from a means whereby central government can
direct local authority spending, to a regulator which acts to restrict
and control voluntary activity in deprived areas, and on to a radical
tool for transferring resources from the privileged to the deprived'.[26]
But in fact that is far too wide a range of acceptable interpretations;
there are far better ways of controlling local authority spending,
transferring resources and regulating voluntary action. No, UA is
surely the perfect political tool: visible, concrete, widely flung,
flexible to passing whims and really minimal in terms of committed
resources. Townsend's description of it[27] as being marginal and even
diversionary is surely more to the point.

So whither UA? There have been calls for radical changes in its
administration and scope: more resources, directed to most deprived
areas, combined with a bureaucratic willingness to co-ordinate and

monitor all relevant policies within local authorities. Holman, for instance, has stated that 'the weakness of the poverty programme can only be made good by a programme able to assess need, designate priority, allocate a vast range of resources and prepared to act outside of some local authorities by funding voluntary groups or setting up its own schemes'.[28] But if any amended programme is going to mean more nurseries or day classes, in their turn aimed at breaking supposed cultures of poverty, it will not work either. It is not so much that more *ad hoc*, random, unco-ordinated social facilities are required in older urban areas, reflecting the impossible task of attempting to plug gaps in inadequate social service provision, but rather that the entire initiative needs to redirect its attention towards achieving greater collective and individual wealth within an altogether more acceptable aetiology of deprivation.

NOTES TO CHAPTER 2

1 *The Times*, 22.4.1968.
2 Local Government Act, 1966, Sec. II.
3 *Hansard*, Vol. 769, 22.7.1968.
4 HO Circular 225/68, DES Circular 19/68 and Ministry of Health Circular 35/68, 4.10.1968.
5 HO Circular 91/72, 10.5.1972.
6 *Notes of the Urban Programme Legislation*, HO, 4.1972.
7 HMSO, *Policy for the Inner Cities*, 1977, Pars. 63–4.
8 See for instance *New Society*, 'Urban Aid', 1975, where the case of the priority list worked out by Liverpool's voluntary groups and rejected by the authority is mentioned; and *Community Action*, 1972, where various criticisms of the programme are made.
9 R. Holman, 1971.
10 R. Batley and J. Edwards, 'CDP and the Urban Programme', in R. Lees and G. Smith (eds.), 1975.
11 R. Batley and J. Edwards, 1974.
12 R. Holman, 1971.
13 *Community Action*, 1973.
14 *Hansard*, Vol. 881, 21.11.1974.
15 R. Batley and J. Edwards (as 10).
16 M. Meacher, 'The Politics of Positive Discrimination', in H. Glennerster and S. Hatch (eds.), 1974.
17 This theme is developed by R. Batley and J. Edwards in Urban Programme Research Working Paper No. 11. A substantial amount of research was undertaken into the various aspects of UA at Leeds as part of the general monitoring procedure established in 1971.
18 T. and G. Smith, 1971.
19 See, for example, HO Circular 83/74, Urban Programme Circular No. 11, 22.4.1974.

20   See, for instance, M. Burchnall *et al.*, 1975.
21   A point expanded by J. Edwards, 'The Urban Programme', in E. Butterworth and R. Holman (eds.), 1975.
22   *Hansard*, Vol. 774, 2.12.1968.
23   HO Circular 117/70, Urban Programme Circular No. 3, 12.6.1970, par. 12.
24   *Hansard*, Vol. 828, 16.12.1971.
25   R. Batley and J. Edwards (as 10); see also HO Circular 100/75, Urban Programme No. 14, 18.6.1975, where in general it was anticipated that 'only small-scale schemes can be considered and capital projects with building costs exceeding £100,000 will not normally be approved'.
26   R. Holman and L. Hamilton, 1973.
27   P. Townsend, 6.8.1976.
28   R. Holman, 'Combating Social Deprivation', in R. Holman (ed.), 1970, p. 185.

Chapter 3

EDUCATIONAL PRIORITY

Unlike most urban experiments, which emerged, often unwanted and frequently unanticipated, from the depths of Whitehall, Educational Priority Areas (EPAs) can trace their lineage back specifically to the findings of one report: Plowden.[1] The members of that committee were clearly impressed with the Head Start programme then operating in America, which was attempting to provide additional educational facilities for children in deprived areas.[2] To the committee there seemed a clear need to introduce a similar scheme in Britain, since if the fruits of economic development were left to run their course there would be no 'assurance that the living conditions which handicap educationally deprived children will automatically improve —still less that the gap between these conditions and those of more fortunate children will be narrowed'.[3] What was needed, the committee felt, was an expanded educational programme specifically to bring standards within deprived areas up to the norm of those elsewhere and additionally, to quite deliberately make them better to compensate children for poorer environmental and economic standards. Such a policy would best, the committee thought, be carried out through a policy of positive discrimination in which additional resources would be allocated to schools in certain selected areas, to be known as Educational Priority Areas. These resources might take the form of higher teachers' pay, more teachers' aides, increased capital expenditure and wider provision for nursery education. If improvements of this sort were to be undertaken together with policy innovations such as specialised in-service teaching for those working in deprived areas, the development of community schools and a co-ordinated attack on all aspects of disadvantage, the committee remained optimistic that educational deprivation could be reduced and social and economic inequalities be moderated.

These proposals elicited a surprisingly rapid response from central government. In 1967 it was announced that £16m would be made available for school building in deprived areas.[4] It was decided at an early stage that central government would not designate EPAs, but that local authorities would do this, and they were advised to concentrate on areas of apparent multiple deprivation and generally poor physical environment. The £16m was to be spent on the replacement or improvement of old buildings and the introduction of additional amenities or facilities to enable schools to play a larger part in the life of their communities. In the event most of this capital was spent on primary education, with the Midlands, the North-East and London receiving more than £3m each and the North-West more than £4m.[5]

Nor was extra finance to be limited solely to this single lump sum. Local authorities and voluntary groups have been able, for example, to bid for UA funds to go towards immigrant language teaching schemes, youth and community facilities, projects to improve links between the home and schools, adult literacy experiments and so on. Until Phase 9 of UA in 1973, bids were also accepted for nursery education expansion proposals, and indeed in the first five years of UA over 20,000 additional places were provided, many of them in EPAs. But in 1972 the government announced a major increase in nursery education[6] aimed at meeting, by 1982, the recommendations of the Plowden Committee, which envisaged a need for 15 per cent of three- and four-year-old children to attend full-time nursery education, and much higher proportions to attend part time. Education authorities were urged in the new programme to give priority to 'children from homes which are culturally and economically deprived',[7] and of the £34m[8] which was granted to initiate the policy between 1974 and 1976, the Education Secretary gave precedence to authorities with greater social need assessed centrally by reference to income, housing and occupation; the ILEA, for instance, received almost £2m, Birmingham £1m and Liverpool and Sheffield more than £0·5m. Within each authority it was then up to local officers and councillors to define smaller areas of special social need, although the local use of indicators such as the percentage of children receiving free school meals and the lack of basic amenities was advised by the DES.

Another Plowden recommendation which has been implemented was the suggestion that school teachers in disadvantaged areas should receive a special salary supplement. As early as 1968 the Burnham Committee introduced an annual additional payment of

£75 for teachers employed in such localities, a figure which has gradually quadrupled. Initially the scheme was run by the Education Secretary, who laid down the global sum available for the additional supplement and designated the exceptionally difficult schools. Since, however, the global sum (never more than £1m) was so small, it was clearly necessary to exclude many appropriate schools. The problem was overcome, in part, in that LEAs were eventually able to recognise their own difficult schools and could there increase the number of teaching posts. Later, too, in 1974, it was decided to allow the Burnham Committee to recognise 'schools in areas of social deprivation', where efforts would be made to attract and retain able and experienced teachers by offering additional supplements from a global figure of 1 per cent of the current salary bill.[9] This in fact increased the sum available for the scheme from less than £1m to more than £11m.

Other administrative innovations have continued throughout the decade, aimed at understanding and alleviating educational disadvantage. In 1974, for instance, an Assessment of Performance Unit was set up to study the incidence of underachievement, and after the publication of the White Paper *Educational Disadvantage and the Educational Needs of Immigrants*[10] in that same year, an Educational Disadvantage Unit was established to serve as a focal point for the consideration of all questions relating to the issue of educational disadvantage. It itself subsequently set up the independent Centre for Information and Advice on Educational Disadvantage, whose 'main concern will be to help the substantial numbers of children whose education is impaired by socially difficult circumstances'.[11]

Add together, then, these various action initiatives which have begun in the last decade and, bearing in mind the fact that deprived areas can anyway be advantageously treated through the normal processes of educational grant allocation such that they receive more than strict per capita distributions would suggest,[12] it is clear that there is a veritable battery of educational priority instruments available. Nor has the educational priority project ended there. It had always been intended—and this was regarded as an essential part of the experiment—that the scheme would be action-research, in that the various policy suggestions made by Plowden relating to compensatory education would be evaluated by a complementary research team. This was established in 1968, and was to run for three years under the general direction of Dr A. H. Halsey of the Department of Social and Administrative Studies at Oxford.

It was decided to select four areas in England and one in Scotland where intensive local action-research would be undertaken to examine such issues as improved educational performance, parent involvement, and better educational-community links within socially deprived localities.[13] In practice, the five local teams adopted different programmes. In Dundee, for instance, an emphasis was placed on nursery schools, playgroups and primary schools and some of these developments were to be retained later;[14] in Liverpool[15] and in the West Riding, attempts were made to improve educational standards through tapping the inherent teaching and learning capacities of the local community through broader curricula and, in the West Riding in particular, through the establishment of a multipurpose educational centre; and in Deptford in London, the local team concentrated on evaluating the potential of innovations such as reading aids and language work in the nursery.

Clearly the research teams investigated a whole range of potential educational experiments, some of which had a direct bearing on areal priority policies, others of a more general nature applicable to educational theory in general. Over some issues they were equivocal. EPAs for instance were seen as 'socially and administratively viable units through which to apply the principle of positive discrimination',[16] although they were envisaged essentially as frameworks within which more detailed work would need to be done at the level of the school, the family and the individual.[17] Certainly for Halsey it remained essential that 'action should be taken down to the level of the individual if it was to be effective'.[18] Over other questions the teams were more universally optimistic: preschooling could be a very effective way of reducing educational disadvantage; relationships between schools and parents could be fruitfully improved through policies such as home visiting and the community school acting as a local contact centre; action-research as a methodological tool in investigating and proposing policy innovation might be very useful. But on the other hand the teams suggested, and others were to agree with them, that the whole issue of educational priority, both as a generally desirable end and as it was being practised in Britain, begged some very profound questions.

Many of the recommendations from Plowden were not, for instance, being implemented in full, or sometimes not at all. Halsey, for example, found little evidence that increased numbers of teachers' aides were being employed or that many links were being forged between EPA schools and local teacher training colleges, reforms advocated by Plowden. Nor was there much evidence that notions of the 'community school' were being widely discussed. Plowden had suggested that there was a distinct value in creating a 'school which is open beyond the ordinary school hours for the use of children, their parents and exceptionally for other members of the community'.[19] On the other hand, even if the community school had become a widely accepted innovation, it would still clearly have been open to very different operational interpretations. As a concept it begs questions such as the extent to which the community should become involved with educational issues such as curricula, or alternatively the degree to which educational content should be altered to meet the perceived needs of that community. Is the implication behind the idea that such a school should promote social change, if indeed this is possible? Or is it to improve educational standards through involving local residents? And again, is this feasible? The whole concept is also evidently bound up with the idea that education is only one aspect of the totality of problems affecting poorer communities, and hence attempts at positive discrimination in education need to dovetail in with other social services and the innate capacities of the community as a whole. But in practice, attempts to bring together relevant educational, housing and other social service bodies in administration such as, say, Liverpool have usually run into difficulties because they could not prevail against the indisposition of the city authorities to take a total view in any one area.[20]

But it is not simply a question of poor administrative co-ordination that has militated against the development of compensatory education in Britain, lack of resources has been at least as important. According to Townsend, for instance, total resources allocated to schools in EPAs amounted to about 0·5 per cent of the total educational budget in the 1970s.[21] Halsey too, pointed out that the numbers of children in nursery education remained a minute proportion of those anticipated in Plowden. And clearly as Halsey also established, the nationally deficient figures were being mirrored at the city scale too;[22] in Birmingham, for instance, he found that the local education authority wanted to designate about a quarter of its 1,000 schools as exceptionally difficult, but in the event less than a tenth was accepted by central government.

Of course one assumption behind this apparently unfortunate discrepancy is that educational positive discrimination is a desirable policy to aim for, that it is a way of reaching deprived children, that it can reduce disadvantage. But is this true? One of the first problems in this context is that of actually selecting indicators supposed to highlight areas of educational disadvantage in the first place. Plowden, for example, attempted to devise apparently objective criteria by which to designate EPAs in suggesting eight possible indicators: occupation of heads of household, size of family, overcrowding and sharing, benefit claimants, poor attendance and truancy, the percentage of retarded, disturbed and handicapped children, incomplete families and pupils unable to speak English. In fact this list was subsequently modified by a number of later commentators, including Little and Mabey,[23] who tried to work out a more refined means of highlighting educationally deprived areas within the ILEA. The Burnham Committee too, have adopted the use of indicators to select social priority schools where teachers receive additional salary supplements. In this last instance social and economic status of parents, lack of basic physical amenities, the percentage of children with linguistic difficulties, of retarded or disturbed children and of children receiving free school meals are the preferred criteria. Later, in Chapter 7, the whole issue of indicators and their applicability will be examined in greater detail, but here it is important to outline the specific discrepancies which these educational indicators can create.

For a start, some of the criteria which Plowden had wanted to employ, such as incomplete families, could not readily be collected at the time. Other indicators such as, say, children unable to read English, were not definite and incontrovertible phenomena, but clearly relative and heavily dependent on the subjective judgement of the investigator. It can also be argued that some of the criteria proposed by Plowden, such as family size, have a very tenuous link with educational disadvantage anyway. Many of the indicators recommended can be seen as implicitly underpinning theories of community and personal inadequacies. The emphasis was being placed, in fact, on the perceived social and economic deficiencies of residents, and not at all on the deleterious influence of inadequate teachers, schools, or of general structural inequalities. The selected indicators were, in effect, implicitly assuming that deprivation was the result of individual and community social pathologies, and hence that the use of criteria reflecting these shortcomings would in turn reveal deprived children and schools in an apparently objective way. But there was very little evidence to support such a hypothesis, certainly not enough to focus primarily on indicators reflecting this argument. Quite simply, there was no empirically tested theory to support the idea that educational deprivation had a specifically areal distribution, nor that it was caused by social pathologies working within older urban communities. Nevertheless, the criteria suggested for designating EPAs assumed that there was.

Moreover, there was soon a body of empirical data pointing out that areally discrete educational disadvantage was nothing like as marked in practice as had been imagined by Plowden and others, nor that policy contained within such an areal framework was especially successful in dealing with the educational disadvantage that did exist. From a variety of sources there emerged substantial evidence that educational deprivation did not occur in a particularly marked way. Gray, [24] Ackland[25] and Barnes,[26] amongst others presented evidence to show that the concentration of children who might be regarded as educationally disadvantaged was not especially marked; that variations within schools tended to be far more acute than between schools; that in the London context anyway, most children in EPAs were not disadvantaged, but most disadvantaged children were not in EPAs; and that the whole process was in any case markedly arbitrary, since authorities were under no obligation to promote educationally deprived areas, nor central government to approve them.[27] Moreover, even when efforts had been made to designate areas of educational deprivation, evidence from Gray and Barnes indicated that the children who benefited tended to be the more educationally advanced and those from middle-class backgrounds, so even within apparently disadvantaged areas it was the better off, economically and educationally, who gained. Not surprisingly, there has been a concerted call for the emphasis to be placed on helping the disadvantaged child rather than the area or the school.

The value or otherwise of compensatory educational programmes was, of course, supposed to have been evaluated in the complementary research programme. However, there has been criticism of the methods adopted by the teams in their investigations. Rutter and Madge in particular point to the deficiencies of their approach.[28] Not enough care, apparently, was taken over ensuring that baseline differences were collected; tests were not properly random; some information was lost; no assessment of teachers was undertaken; nor were tests carried out on different rates of progress within different groups both inside and outside EPAs. Even then, despite all these failings, some results suggested that statistically there was little evidence to indicate that educational standards had been radically improved within EPAs *vis-à-vis* control groups outside priority areas.

Of course it might well be argued, why should it? Is there any reason to imagine that new buildings, or small additions to teachers' salaries would make statistically significant improvements to children's performance? And even if this did happen in one deprived area, is it not likely to lower standards relatively in surrounding localities?

However, the main line of criticism which has come to dominate thinking about educational priority relates not to the extent to which the experiment has been adequately researched, nor indeed about the results of that research, but rather the relevance of the entire under-pinning philosophy. It seems quite evident that EPAs, as perceived by Plowden, and as implemented, were rooted in notions of cultures of deprivation. That committee, for instance, saw the existence of a vicious circle of disadvantage turning from generation to generation, with the schools playing a central role in the process, both causing and suffering cumulative deprivation.[29] EPAs can clearly in fact be seen to reflect notions of cultures of deprivation which, it was hoped, additional educational resources would break by inculcating 'normal' standards of behaviour in children at a very early age that would be sufficiently strong to counteract latent antisocial charac-teristics inherent in deprived areas.[30] In Chapter 7 the entire philo-sophy relating to cultures of deprivation will be examined as it has operated throughout the urban programme, despite growing doubts and criticisms as to its relevance and accuracy. In the specific context of educational priority, however, certain basic shortcomings need to be mentioned.

Positive educational discrimination assumes that once cultures of deprivation have been broken, children will achieve their optimal development. Such a position evidently presupposes that opportuni-ties are there to be taken. But clearly they are not, or at least not always, and in particular children brought up within older, poorer urban areas are likely, no matter how well educated, to encounter fundamental structural inequalities, especially in housing and em-ployment markets. Education is only one of a variety of influences which affect and define deprivation. Producing better educated children through processes of positive discrimination is ultimately irrelevant if the employment market is incapable of accommodating and retaining job seekers. This more developed view of deprivation holds that it is not that cultural pathologies prevent children from achieving their aims, but rather that structural inefficiencies prevent even better educated children from advancing. To those in this position, improved education is perhaps a necessary but not at all a sufficient condition for the alleviation of disadvantage. It is in fact one of a multitude of community needs. To be fair, the research team evaluating the efficacy of educational priority were quick to point this out themselves. For Halsey for instance, commenting on the EPA idea, it was in practice 'impotent except in the context of a comprehensive organisation of social services in the community', and hence 'no amount of success with work on either the cultural poverty of the home or the educational poverty of the school will result in anything but frustration if socialisation cannot be translated into opportunity in the end'.[31] Similarly, to the Dundee research team it was evident that if radical improvements were required they 'must involve public policies relating not merely to education and "social work" but to social, and with it, economic structure'.[32] Predictably, parallel American experience emerged with much the same sorts of conclusions.[33]

The EPA project differs from virtually all the other urban experiments in that it examined only one aspect of the multitude of factors which might interact with, and possibly cause, deprivation. Many of the conclusions emerging from both the Plowden Report and from Halsey's research teams later would anyway have had a relevance for educational theorists, irrespective of locality or of policies of a real discrimination. To students of the urban programme, the EPA idea will nevertheless remain a focus of interest because it predated so many similar areally based initiatives, and because it assumed a model of deprivation widely incorporated into later experiments. This whole action-research project clearly made tremendous advances: the notion of educational priority came to be widely discussed and, more important, evaluated; locally some community involvement in school activities and new approaches such as home visiting were explored; and the bringing together of action and research has been seen as 'of fundamental importance and hopefully of considerable long term significance'.[34] But on the debit side there are two enormous shortcomings: as Rutter and Madge point out, 'positive discrimination in the form of EPA schools is a very clumsy way of meeting the needs of children from disadvantaged homes',[35] and more basically, educational improvement can only be seen as an aspect, and in many ways a subsidiary one, of deprivation, and that therefore attempts to refine it can only be a useful contributory factor in eradicating urban inequality.

NOTES TO CHAPTER 3

1 HMSO, *Children and Their Primary Schools*, 1967. Some reference had also been made to the existence of severe educational problems in the Newsom Report: HMSO, *Half Our Future*, 1963.
2 U. Cicirelli *et al.*, 1969.
3 HMSO, *Children and Their Primary Schools*, 1967, par. 142.
4 See DES Circular 11/67, *School Building Programme. School Building in EPAs*, 8.1967
5 DES Press Notice, 'Over 150 Major School Building Projects for Priority Areas', 4.1968.
6 HMSO, *Education: A Framework for Expansion*, 1972.
7 DES Circular 2/73, *Nursery Education*, 1.1973, par. 9.
8 DES Press Notice, 'Nursery Building Allocations 1974–76', 10.1973.
9 DES Press Notice, 'Education Secretary Proposes Extra Money for Teachers in Stress Areas', 5.1974.
10 HMSO, *Educational Disadvantage and the Educational Needs of Immigrants*, 1974.
11 Centre for Information and Advice on Educational Disadvantage, First Report.
12 So that by 1973, for example, about £50m had been allocated for the replacement of older, pre-1903, schools in areas selected by local education authorities as educationally deprived: *Hansard*, Vol. 856, 15.5.73.
13 A. Halsey (ed.), Vol. 1, 1972; J. Payne, Vol. 2, 1970; J. Barnes (ed.), Vol. 3, 1975; G. Smith (ed.), Vol. 4, 1975; C. Morrison (ed.), Vol. 5, 1974.
14 Scottish Education Department Circular 11/74, Dundee EPA Report, 7.1974.
15 E. Midwinter, 1972.
16 A. Halsey (as 13), p. 180.
17 A. Halsey (as 13), p. 181.
18 A. Halsey, 1975, p. 5.
19 HMSO (as 3), par. 121.
20 Shelter Neighbourhood Action Project, 1972.
21 P. Townsend, 1976.
22 A. Halsey (as 13), p. 45.
23 A. Little and C. Mabey, 'An Index for the Designation of EPAs', in A. Shonfield and S. Shaw (eds.), 1972.
24 J. Gray, 1975.
25 H. Acland, 1971.
26 J. Barnes, 'A Solution to Whose Problems?', in H. Glennerster and S. Hatch, 1974.
27 A point developed by the North-West Joint Planning Team, 1974, who established that Bootle, probably the most deprived borough in the region, had no EPAs.
28 M. Rutter and N. Madge, 1976.
29 HMSO (as 3), par. 132.

30 This idea is expanded on by A. Halsey, 'Government Against Poverty in School and Community', in D. Wedderburn (ed.), 1974.
31 A. Halsey (as 13), pp. 18–19.
32 C. Morrison (as 13), p. 209.
33 U. Cicirelli (as 2).
34 A. Little, 'Schools: Targets and Methods', in H. Glennerster and S. Hatch (as 26), p. 17.
35 M. Rutter and N. Madge (as 28), p. 128.

Chapter 4

THE SIX TOWNS STUDIES

Peter Walker was in many ways a very active Secretary of State. He it was who began to restructure the Rate Support Grant in favour of older urban areas and, more relevant here, set up the Six Studies, one part of which, the Inner Area Studies (IAS), has been a major instrument in moulding central government thought and initiative in recent years. The IAS, and its allied experiment the Urban Guidelines (UG), were first mooted by Walker in the summer of 1972 when he announced that he intended to carry out two types of study to develop a 'total approach' to the problems of the urban environment.[1] The first of these was 'designed to formulate guidelines to help local authorities apply this approach to the town as a whole. (This was to become the UG.) The second will explore the environmental problems of three inner city areas.' (This was later to emerge as the IAS.)

Walker had not plucked the idea of the 'total approach' out of thin air. Much of the initial thinking on the subject had been developed, and this was acknowledged at the time, in the Shelter Neighbourhood Action Project (SNAP) in Liverpool's Granby district.[2] This scheme, launched in 1969 to improve the social, physical and economic recovery of a very depressed inner city area, came to the conclusion in a later review of progress in 1972[3] that as long as policy was implemented by any number of different ill co-ordinated bodies, attempts at comprehensive renewal would be at the very least extremely difficult. What was needed was a 'total approach' to the problem of such areas, in which all relevant public bodies would be involved, devising objectives and defining common policies. Walker visited the scheme, was impressed by it, in particular the attempts being made to improve co-operation between the various agencies involved and the public, and clearly incorporated his growing

48

interest in this co-ordinated outlook into the 1972 proposals, which in many ways as originally conceived, placed a very heavy emphasis —in the case of the UG almost exclusively so—on the management and organisation of policy. Fortunately, a wider brief and a changing outlook encouraged the IAS in later years to investigate not simply how existing policy might be better co-ordinated, but more fundamentally whether that policy was worth co-ordinating in the first place.

MAKING TOWNS BETTER: THE URBAN GUIDELINES

The earlier, briefer and much less influential parts of the Six Towns Studies were the UG undertaken by consultants in Oldham, Rotherham and Sunderland in 1972–3. Local authority reorganisation was imminent, and the UG were seen as providing practical guidelines to new local authorities to back up the management structures examined in Bains. Certainly the Chairman of the Sunderland report[4] saw the initiative as having most relevance to the District Councils which were to emerge a year later on reorganisation. It was clearly hoped that the new administrations would adopt a 'total approach' to the problems of the urban environment, and to this end the consultants were given a quite specific brief. They were to identify the problems of the selected areas, and to consider their environmental implications and the local authority's policies and programmes in relation to them. At the same time it would be necessary to examine how decision making processes could take into account the needs of people in the area, the policies of other public authorities and the allocation of resources. In the light of these constraints the consultants were to formulate guidelines to help develop a 'total approach', to test these guidelines in relation to the authority's current and future practices, to highlight problems arising from legislation and procedures dealing with environmental problems of the area and, in general, to assess the usefulness of the 'total approach'. The main focus of attention was thus not to be on how functions were discharged by the authority, 'but how they fit together to make a total impact on the environment of the town as a whole'.[5]

Even at this early stage of brief design comment was not entirely favourable. Eddison pointed out some immediate difficulties.[6] The resources being allocated to the projects in the way of time and cash (about £170,000 per project) were so trivial that the resultant reports could amount, he considered, to no more than limited failures. Anyway, it made little sense to encourage a 'total approach' at the District Council level when central government remained so departmentalised, and when so many of the problems arising within inner city authorities were also the problems of the regions and counties in which they were set. He might well have added that a 'total approach' to the administration of environmental problems within an authority, which the brief laid down, might in practice inhibit the development of a 'total approach' within the administration as a whole; and also that this emphasis on examining problems in their totality assumes that a local authority can in fact operate at this catch-all scale. But is this so? Surely even the most energetic of local authorities, even operating in co-operation with other public bodies, simply cannot— they do not have the power to—achieve everything they would want to. The UG, on the other hand, seem to start off with the premise that providing everyone who matters can be brought together and policies co-ordinated, local governance will improve and deprivation be reduced. Certainly with hindsight that seems a remarkably naïve approach.

Despite a detailed brief and the common organisation of the three Steering Committees, each chaired by a D of E politician, there is a striking difference between, for example, the way the Rotherham team approached the task and the method favoured in Sunderland. The former effort[7] has an avowedly physical emphasis, with analysis concentrated almost exclusively on the identification of environmental problems, in the narrow sense of the term, and potential management systems which might ameliorate these perceived difficulties. This somewhat idiosyncratic approach is justified on the grounds of lack of time, and that anyway an analysis of 'the total approach' within one sector of an authority would provide valuable guidelines for other fields too. Subsequently, however, objective commentators were largely to disagree with the selectivity of this approach, and generally the Rotherham Study is regarded as the least useful of the three.

But within this narrow self-imposed commission the consultants, Urwick, Orr and Partners, in collaboration with the Steering Committee, devised a structured management cycle to deal with environmental problems. Initially this approach stressed the necessity of examining both the total physical environment and individual elements within it in order to understand which agencies performed which tasks, how different elements interacted with each other, and the constraints which improvements within one field might create in another. These attempts to understand the workings of the physical environment were to be complemented by efforts to create some sort of 'objective' assessment of the perceived severity of different environmental problems as seen by the public and by elected members. At this stage, therefore, it was anticipated that problems and their interrelationships would be understood, some idea as to who might be responsible for improving them be devised, and an appraisal be made of the relative importance of different issues.

Later the management cycle predictably moved from trying to understand the workings of the physical environment towards how inadequacies within it might be resolved. The team considered that certain steps would be essential: the development of long- and short-term policy objectives, clear instructions as to who would do what, a thorough appraisal of resource investment required with each policy option, direct guidelines from a central Policy Committee to functional committees, built-in consultative procedures with other agencies and the public, and effective monitoring procedures. In all a sort of 'mini' corporate planning exercise, dealing solely with physical environmental issues.

The consultants thought this approach would bring benefits: problems and their interrelatedness would be identified in a more structured manner than before, to the benefit of elected representatives, the public and policy formulation in general; attempts at dealing with intrinsic environmental difficulties would be far better co-ordinated and assessed, and if necessary changed. But against these advantages there was a welter of contemporary criticism. The approach was seen as too remote from the actualities of local government and from the residents it was supposed to serve; there was far too much concern with, as one local politician put it, procedures rather than vision,[8] with analysis of problems and attempts to understand their interconnectedness becoming more important than results on the ground. One reason for this might have been that the consultants were management specialists rather than planning experts, and hence saw the task as being one of improving the efficiency of government, not its end product. One unfortunate side effect of this discrepancy was that many of the recommendations to improve the co-ordination of environmental matters anyway fell within the brief of the planning department as it already stood, and might have been attained with minimal authority reorganisation.

This issue relates in turn to the principal objection to the Rotherham Study: that it represented in a way an antithesis of the 'total approach'. It dealt with one small, and in many ways unimportant, aspect of the total obligation of an authority, and it specifically excluded many social and economic questions normally considered of prime importance in dealing with deprivation. This deficiency was compounded because the report envisaged considerable preparatory analysis being undertaken and organisational structures altered to cater for its very limited scope. In the light of the real totality of the problems faced by authorities, this seems an optimistic appraisal of the ability and willingness of authorities to implement such proposals. Not surprisingly, in a consideration of the three Studies at the time, Hancock suggested that 'it is a poor effort, not of great value to the town or its officers, and less, one fears, to its people'.[9]

The Sunderland effort was very different. McKinsey were appointed as the consultants and produced two documents, a basic handbook and a working guide to aid local authorities in what was anticipated as a period of local authority reform and increasing community involvement, but declining national resources. In such an era it was clear to the team that new management tools would be required, and the report outlined in considerable detail how this might be achieved. Initially it was vital that problems and their relative significance should be identified through a Community Review. This would be an attempt to highlight the totality of problems within an area through, for instance, opening a register, using indicators, canvassing views and examining existing policies and their shortcomings. Having identified the totality of problems, it was envisaged within the Review that problems should be grouped into both areas and departments, depending upon their interrelatedness, priorities would be worked out, opportunities to attack problems highlighted, resource allocations worked out and, where it was clear that problem definition was inadequate or policy initiative uncertain, this would be pointed out and reserved for more detailed later examination. The Community Review would thus be an annual document outlining past and present problems, policies and future directions for the entire authority. For those topics which the Community Review identified as needing further consideration a permanent Community Review Team, backed up where necessary by temporary interdisciplinary Project Teams, would analyse problems and evaluate the range of possible options open to an authority within existing legal and financial constraints.

Clearly the sort of organisation envisaged by the consultants would require a changing role for members, officers, other public bodies and the community as a whole. For members for instance, the report wanted introductory induction courses which would allow elected representatives to use and benefit from the new system, and in particular give them experience of different committees and a greater opportunity to become involved with issues affecting their particular wards. Officers, too, would have to live within a far more flexible structure than normally existed within most authorities, in that the focus of their work would be on problem solving rather than departmentalised functioning.

But it is the arrangements envisaged for dealing with other public bodies, and with the community as a whole, which make the Sunderland report far more radical than the Rotherham approach. In the case of the former the UG Steering Committee considered that a Collaboration Plan was needed, within which different tiers of local government, central government bodies and other interested agencies would outline their functions and responsibilities, highlight problem areas and indicate where administrative arrangements might be bettered through improved collaboration. The whole process was to be encouraged through common management networks, flexibility in staff placement and inter-agency agreements. Certainly the 'total approach', according to the consultants, would require all individual authorities to 'recognise that they share common and highly complex problems which are best tackled through collaboration'. Equally, there was a clear need to enlist the support of the 'talents and resources of local people and organisations in tackling local problems'. This two-way relationship between the authority and its clients could be encouraged through a Ward Secretariat providing relevant areal information to members and residents; through the use of neighbourhood councils which might provide for local forums with some investigatory and supervisory powers, possibly on a formal decentralised basis with seconded officers answering local queries; and simply through better participation, built into formal stages in the Community Review.

The Sunderland approach was thus a far more intensive attempt to deal with the problems of local governance than its Rotherham equivalent: a wider range of problems was covered, a more thorough understanding of the workings of local government indicated, more radical formal arrangements promoted, and operational relationships between the authority, other bodies and the community as a whole outlined. Certainly there has been considerable interest expressed in some of the formal suggestions presented in the report, notably the

Community Review and the Collaboration Study, and it has been widely evaluated as the best of the three studies.[10] But on the other hand there still remain real problems specific to this approach. The community as such is represented as a unitary, consensus-seeking entity prepared to go along with the authority, which is a naïve interpretation of the very complex relationship between governed and government. There is an assumption, too, that what is best for the authority is, first of all, easy to define in that objectives will be almost self evident and, second, that it is best for the area as a whole. These assumptions are at the very least debatable. So too are those which presume that the authority will be prepared to make public all its records concerning contentious issues, such as housing. And finally, because of the very nature and reputation of the consultants, suspicions were voiced as to exactly what the main aims of the report had in practice been. To Rustin, for instance, there were fears 'that the main emphasis of this new approach will turn out to be managerial, aiming at greater efficiency or cost-effectiveness rather than at greater welfare'.[11]

The Oldham Study[12] falls somewhere between the very narrow interpretation of the Rotherham Study and the more comprehensive outlook emerging from the Sunderland team. The Oldham approach is to concentrate on the provision of factors such as building, land, movement, public services and so on, which were to become the responsibility of the new authorities beginning operations in 1974. Within these specific fields the first essential was to identify, and measure where possible, problems such as shortcomings and deficiencies in services, and to understand the interrelationship between them. In fact, because of the wide range of potential interactions between different elements making up the total environment, the consultants, Nathaniel Lichfield and Associates, suggested that the majority of important environmental problems could be examined within key groups of issues, notably those relating to the local economy and housing, and that much early analysis within the overall programme should concentrate on an understanding of these sectors, the interrelationship of problems and the ability or otherwise of the authority to amend matters.

The organisational reflection of this initial analysis would occur within two management systems which the report called Extended Development Planning and Operational Planning. The former would deal broadly with matters contained within the Town and Country Planning Acts, in a 'systematic' manner: identifying problems, evaluating policy options and implementing the preferred choice. This process might place a heavy emphasis on the local economy, indicating how, for instance, the authority itself might act as a direct employer, or how private developers should operate, or on housing, linking together an analysis of deficiencies with policy options such as more improvement grants and improvement areas, new land requirements and so on. This attempt at extended physical planning would thus hope to combine policy consideration normally contained within structure plans with a broader analysis of potential options and means of implementation.

The Operational Planning system, on the other hand, would be akin to forms of corporate planning. Overall objectives would be devised, using a wide range of information based on Programme Areas such as housing. An operational cycle of three to five years would be created, working towards defined aims devised by a central Policy Planning Unit, and functional committees would need to dovetail their aims, and eventually detailed policies, into the resources, aims and phasing operating on the authority as a whole. As the operational process rolled forward, annual reviews of policy would be undertaken and appropriate changes implemented.

The consultants envisaged that their new system of Extended Development Planning and Operational Planning would work more efficiently if advice were to be given to elected representatives, particularly in their dealings with the public, for example through a secretariat providing council and ward information. In any case, general relationships with the public could be put on to a far more effective footing if bodies were to be set up dealing, say, with specific area problems or overall authority issues, and the public were to sit on these. Widespread publicity should also be given to the legally required stages of participation within formal planning procedures. Finally, the Oldham team also considered that certain changes might be undertaken at central government level in order to ensure that more deprived authorities received additional resources to deal with particularly acute problems. This aid might take the form of a more sensitive rate support system, or of a new Urban Renewal key sector administered by a consortium of relevant central government departments.

The Oldham report on the whole has not had the impact of the Sunderland initiative. Partly this may be due to the lack of overall corporateness involved in the approach: splitting development and corporate planning is not likely to achieve a 'total' outlook at all.

But also attempts at participation are really minimal, recommendations lack the precision needed for implementation, and the attempts to create specific 'objective' measurements of problems seem overoptimistic in what is a notoriously difficult process of social policy: measuring deficiencies. The Oldham report is really the middle way; not totally corporate like the Sunderland vision, but wider in its consideration of topics than the Rotherham Study.

There are also general methodological problems raised by the Oldham Study which it shares with the other approaches. Some of these relate to the practicalities of the systems put forward. Local authorities, for instance, are not normally in a position to undertake the sort of additional tasks put forward in these reports and because so many are recommended the whole operation of the system may become extremely complex. As Lomas pointed out when they emerged, they 'are an elaborate set of bureaucratic devices designed to multiply the tasks of dissection, analysis, computation and reconciliation which the Districts are urged to do unbureaucratically'.[13] In fact they pursued a sort of comprehensive rationalism, believing that authorities could intervene effectively in a wide range of issues where in reality they may have little power. Not surprisingly, they have been labelled naïve in the extreme.[14]

And although they were perhaps overexpansive at the level of the local authority and its operations, the whole approach took little or no cognisance of government at the local, regional or national scales. At the local level there was little consideration of how particularly deprived communities within authorities might be aided. Nor was there an adequate development of relationships between authorities and their regional setting and government. And even more important, there was no attempt to balance out 'totality' at the local scale with movements in that direction nationally. The impression remains that central government appointed outside consultants who produced naïve interpretations of what local authorities might do, without any attempt by central government itself either to reorganise its own administration or to find out what sort of evolving initiatives, which had stood the test of viability, had been devised elsewhere.

And finally, at a more theoretical level, the Studies, implicitly perhaps but vitally, proceed on two assumptions: that improved management techniques and organisational systems can create a 'total' approach to local authority administration which in turn will help eradicate environmental problems (and in some cases that covers a very wide field) without additional resources,[15] or even a more effective distribution of resources within authorities; and that the 'community' is a coherent, unitary force which will work with the authority in achieving the latter's apparently 'objective' goals. But in reality are not both of these premises wrong? Additional resources to and within authorities must precede reorganisation and not be supplanted by it, and the 'community' is in practice a complex, transient, conflicting and contradictory force. Of these assumptions, more later.

THE INNER AREA STUDIES

Whereas the first part of Peter Walker's initiative of 1972, the UG, have largely been relegated to the forgotten reports category, his second and much larger concern, the IAS, has been ostensibly quite the most important of the urban deprivation experiments in directly moulding central government thought, and in the last year or so, action. Indeed the White Paper on Inner Cities specifically acknowledges its debt to urban studies on inner city problems, and above all to the IAS.[16]

Of course when they were set up in 1972 their ultimate influence on central and local government could hardly be guessed at. But the brief was sufficiently wide to envisage considerable scope in recommendations emerging from the consultants' findings. The Study teams were, for instance, to promote a better definition of inner areas and their problems, and establish how action projects and area management could be employed to alleviate physical and social inadequacies and the consequences these innovations would have for local authorities. One final clause in the commission widened this brief considerably by suggesting that the consultants should 'provide the base for general conclusions on statutory powers, finance and resources questions and techniques': in effect virtually a free hand to investigate that elusive concept, 'the inner city'.

It had been known early in 1972 that the D of E was intending to undertake an urban initiative, and in consultation with various local authorities the Department eventually selected Birmingham, Liverpool and Lambeth as the sites for the new experiment. It was clear at that time that Walker intended the main focus of the study would, as with the UG, be on the potential of the 'total approach'. Certainly he anticipated that the Studies would 'look at the needs of the study area as a whole from the point of view of the people living in them and . . . derive lessons on powers, resources and techniques'.[17]

In the light of Walker's commitment to this sort of co-ordinated approach, it was not at all surprising to see Liverpool selected. The SNAP project had been operative for three years by then, and had done much to widen its scope from a more detailed study of housing into an altogether more comprehensive look at all inner city problems; indeed there had been direct recruitment of people from SNAP to the D of E, taking with them notions of total government. The local authority itself too, saw much that might be achieved in an exercise such as the IAS, both in improving existing policy and as a means of generating meaningful new programmes of action within the city.[18] In the event the consultants, Wilson and Womersley, who were to work later in association with outside firms of urban economists and civil engineers, were appointed in September 1972 to examine an area with about a 60,000 population in the south-central area of the city, which was chosen partly to avoid overlap with the city's CDP project then under way. Reports emerging from the consultants were forwarded to a Chief Officers' Advisory Group, and thereafter to the Steering Committee of leading members of the District and County Councils under the Chairmanship of a Minister from the D of E.

The Birmingham team, from the Llewelyn-Davies, Weeks, Forestier-Walker and Bor organisation, selected a smaller area of about 36,000 people in the east Sparkbrook and Small Heath area.[19] They arrived at this choice by using indicators from the 1966 census, modified by certain constraints such as the existence of strong physical and community boundaries, local community associations, buildings capable of being improved, a mixture of land uses and so on. A similar, but somewhat more refined, approach to area identification characterises the Lambeth Study. Here the consultants, Shankland Cox, in association with the Institute of Community Studies, employed seven criteria to identify the sort of area they wished to examine, which of necessity, they believed, should contain the main problems characteristic of inner London. In the event they chose the area, Stockwell, on the basis of its size being large enough to reveal most of the problems of inner London, because of the existence of housing stress and other social problems, the presence of large numbers of immigrants, a wide variety of housing types, the existence of several community groups and the coincidence of the project's boundaries with those of other agencies. As with the other experiments, reports were to be forwarded to a Steering Committee, in this case of local GLC, ILEA and D of E politicians, initially through a Chief Officers' group.

The structures set up in 1972 have been responsible for the proliferation of an enormous amount of material on the problems and policies of inner cities, and have produced ultimately what might be called an IAS approach, which certainly has found favour in official circles. Nevertheless this should not be taken to mean that differences in approach and emphasis did not occur between the projects, nor that changes did not occur through time in the methodology of the experiments. The Liverpool Study, for instance, has consistently placed a far greater emphasis on the development of the 'total approach' than other initiatives, both within the authority as a whole and at the local level, there being a much stronger emphasis on area management than elsewhere—a bias which has been welcomed, perhaps to a surprising extent, by some commentators.[21] The Birmingham Study, on the other hand, concentrated initially on a number of smaller projects, many dealing with improved means of implementing Housing Action Areas in the study area. But at the same time quite early in its development the team presented a strikingly acute analysis[22] of the sorts of problems action-research projects such as the IAS encountered: lack of speed and flexibility in the administration of the project, the realisation that many desirable improvements could not be induced at the local area scale, and the need to understand problems as perceived by residents as well as by the authority.

The Lambeth approach is in many ways the odd one out. It placed far less stress on resident surveys, community involvement or getting projects 'off the ground' in its somewhat academic vision of how action-research experiments should operate. The analysis of policy operative at all government levels influencing areas such as Stockwell was the focus of research for the Lambeth team, and if this took them into uncharted or at least unorthodox areas, then all to the good. In developing, for instance, its thesis as to why inner London had declined, the consultants became closely involved with promoting the notion of continued population dispersal from the older urban areas, both because so many people they talked to wanted to do this[23] and because, if jobs and people were to ever achieve a more sensible spatial balance, it was vital that workers should be able to move out more easily (and for some others to move in) than the current housing market allowed. This advocacy of continued decentralisation was not a particularly fashionable notion to be bandying around by the mid-seventies, partly because of the volte-face on the part of the GLC regarding this issue. But on the other hand the TCPA, for instance, welcomed this somewhat idiosyncratic approach since it reflected a regional vision not always apparent in urban experiments, and a willingness to promote decentralisation policies which the TCPA certainly envisaged would in the end create a more attractive London.[24]

And yet despite the differences between the studies, in practice it is quite apparent that one can talk of an IAS approach, partly because the reports themselves have been finalised in a markedly similar way, which is perhaps not surprising in view of D of E involvement on the relevant Steering Committees, and also because the government has within its response to the initiatives presumed a uniformity of problems and policy within older deprived areas. Certainly the reports emerging from the teams have shown considerable similarity both in the appraisal of what inner city problems are and in how they might be ameliorated.

It had originally been intended, of course, that the experiment would be action-research based, with results from local projects being assimilated and, where possible, expanded into broader policy objectives. In the event, although a very substantial proportion of IAS publications relate to the creation and implementation of small-scale projects, the summary and final papers present a more theoretical appraisal than might originally have been imagined. As the Liverpool team admits, 'we moved from our original statement of local issues which gave rise to the action projects to one which raised wider issues of fundamental importance to people's opportunities for housing and a job'.[25] It is tempting to speculate why this should have happened. Certainly economic circumstances worsened markedly during the mid-seventies, which might well have stimulated consideration of a wider vision of deprivation and its causes, especially as government ministers apparently encouraged such a drift. But one wonders to what extent the more intellectually satisfying findings of the contemporary experiment, the CDP, rooted to an increasing extent in all embracing theoretical framework, was influencing the IAS teams by the mid-seventies.

But whatever the genesis of the IAS position ultimately to emerge, it is clear that the root cause of deprivation is ascribed to basic poverty caused by low personal incomes, resulting in part from shrinking and changing labour markets, and poor and inadequate benefits for the old, the unemployed, those in the child-rearing age groups, the physically and mentally disabled and so on. Deprivation in this analysis is envisaged therefore not as a reflection of inadequate personal and community attitudes, but as thriving on the simple and permanent facts of so many people's lives: poverty. The Liverpool team in particular saw low personal income as one of the main characteristics in its area, which in itself created acute problems but was also clearly related to allied social problems such as inordinately high burglary rates in the city as a whole, and to the emergence of a separate black culture as poorer, younger blacks increasingly rejected the apparently limited opportunities offered them in conventional white society.[26]

But apart from the specialised situation within Liverpool and the more general national concern over low benefits and income supplements, most recent commentators on inner cities, including the IAS teams, see the fundamental problem as one of declining job opportunities. As the Lambeth team sees it, 'job opportunities and the ability of residents to earn a living are fundamental. They directly affect people's income and standard of living and hence have a major influence on local resources available for housing, the environment and many services both public and private'.[27] Within London, as these consultants see it, the problem is one more of imbalance between the skills of residents and jobs available, which tend increasingly to be in the professional, administrative and managerial sectors. Alternatively, in Liverpool, the consultants perceive the problem as one of basic decline in job opportunities.[28] Here 'the economic problems of the inner area have been caused directly by the loss of low-skilled jobs in the dockland and port-related industries, some manufacturing industries and the railways'. The problem is accentuated by virtually no investment in the area, extensive blighting by the local authority, a shortage of skilled people, and the siting of new industrial investment in the suburbs of Merseyside, not in the older core.[29] What makes the problem that much more worrying is that so many of the unemployed are young, black and with almost no educational qualifications or industrial experience. This is structural unemployment on a vast scale, and as the consultants see it, a prime cause of decay and neglect.

So too is the housing market. In part, as the Liverpool team point out, inner city rented accommodation has always fulfilled a certain function in providing cheap, easily available housing for transient workers, immigrants and the young.[30] But unfortunately so much of this housing is old, badly maintained and overcrowded.[31] And even within what might be generally inadequate housing there are smaller pockets of especially bad property where overcrowding in both the public and private markets can be very high and physical conditions acutely deficient.[32]

And as the Lambeth team point out,[33] it is not just the condition of housing which is worrying. For many London residents there exists a housing trap. Large numbers of poorer residents are housed by the local authority, which makes it extremely difficult for them to move, perhaps to take up new employment, because transfers within the public housing sector, even within particular authorities, are very difficult. Furthermore, there is hardly any available private rented accommodation, and few can afford mortgage repayments. In effect many are trapped in their existing accommodation, and hence even if employment is available within a sub-region, if this involves residential relocation it remains unlikely that many will be able to take it up.

The teams also point out that it is not just lack of residential mobility which inhibits people entering or moving around within the labour market. Educational standards are generally low,[34] and school curricula are perceived as being irrelevant to children's future job needs. In turn training facilities may be geographically distant and inadequate in scope, and entry may be competed for. In effect the educationally weak may be permanently disadvantaged. And because in turn there may be a proportionately large number needing social services exactly because educational, housing and employment markets have failed them, there is a marked demand for strong and efficient welfare delivery. But overstretched and ill co-ordinated agency provisions militate so strongly against this that, as the Lambeth team says, 'it is very much a matter of chance whether or not those in need of services get any, or if any (get) all the services which could help them'.[35]

Inadequacies in social service provision are mirrored in deficiencies in general environmental standards: limited open spaces, yet paradoxically huge amounts of vacant land, general physical decay, which the London team thinks might well be accentuated by large numbers of children in high-density areas,[36] and overall a sense of despair in the future of inner city areas compounded through insensitive, delayed, and in many cases unnecessary local authority acquisition, demolition and redevelopment proposals.[37] Not that central government comes out much better either. Regional planning policies, for instance, have not helped inner city areas[38] but rather suburban zones in Assisted Areas; and in general too, there has been a tendency to encourage the dispersal of population and employment to new and expanding towns, with only marginal attempts at providing more deprived areas with additional resources. Certainly to the Liverpool team it appears that 'much of the response by government has been of a supportive character and a response to crises rather than attempting fundamentally to change circumstances'.[39]

In the light of these problems encountered within inner city areas it is not surprising that some assume that a 'cycle of deprivation' operates in such a way that the cumulative mass of problems creates a culture, and an ongoing cycle of deprivation likely to enfold within it children born into such circumstances. To some extent the reports confirm this picture, in that a life cycle of poverty did seem to operate, with deprivation especially marked at certain stages, such as old age.[40] But on the other hand evidence from all the IAS teams suggests that other more complex processes operate as well. In Lambeth, for instance, the team distinguishes between housing and income deprivation, which tend to occur in different places to different people,[41] and in Liverpool too, there would appear to be those on the social margins of society, usually vulnerable minorities, and those on the economic margins, normally housed by the authority, but who have lost their unskilled or semi-skilled occupations. In effect, therefore, the reports reject a vision of deprivation based on a transmitting syndrome in which children are imbued with a somewhat antisocial culture inhibiting them from achieving their full development. Instead poverty is seen as the root cause of deprivation. Partly this poverty is caused by low social benefits for the young, old, and those rearing children; partly it is due to an increase in the emergence of poorly paid service industries, especially in London; partly it stems from basic unemployment as older primary and secondary employment either dies or migrates; and partly it is because so many people cannot follow the employment out, since they are trapped within inflexible housing markets. Raise income, the Lambeth study considers for instance, and people enter a 'virtuous' cycle, in which they can widen their housing choice, and ultimately provide additional investment into the private and public sectors.[42]

Clearly, if the prime causes of deprivation are intimately related to basic poverty, any programme intending to relieve this discrepancy should look closely at policies which can reverse low income. And this the IAS do. In one way this might be achieved through improved income maintenance and higher benefits of all kinds. The Lambeth team, for instance, suggests that there 'needs to be a new national scheme for income maintenance, to give more generous support to

C

those who cannot earn or whose earnings have to be supplemented'.[43] Such a programme might be implemented through a tax credit scheme, higher individual benefits or improved central government co-ordination, but however it is to be done, it is clearly a prime and essential prerequisite in counteracting urban deprivation.

But a policy of improved income support is seen as essentially an additional way of boosting inner city incomes. The main advance would need to come from new employment opportunities for residents, or a better balancing-out, in a geographical and sectoral sense, of employment opportunities and demand. Some necessary changes would need to be implemented by national government. A relaxation of Industrial Development Certificates (IDCs) and Office Development Permits (ODPs), for instance, and the introduction of a more refined regional programme to help older urban localities in the Assisted Areas are two persistent suggestions. On a more positive level, training facilities should be expanded and co-ordinated,[44] firms encouraged to second workers, greater financial incentives provided for trainees, more easily accessible centres built and those skills that are in demand taught. To provide jobs for the retrained, the reports consider that there should be more direct central government development initiative in attracting firms back to the inner city, and in nourishing existing concerns. Assistance[45] could take the form of grants, employment subsidies, interest relief loans under the 1972 Industry Act, the creation of industrial improvement grants and areas, all under the general aegis of the NEB, a more entrepreneurial D of I regional structure, or perhaps an autonomous industrial agency charged with aiding inner city establishments through centrally allocated capital.

Of course, the teams suggest, not all the necessary development initiatives could or should come from central government; local authorities would help too. They should, for example, provide land for firms wishing to expand, create a dossier of industrial sites, give advice, introduce more flexible zoning to allow non-conforming industries to survive, encourage transport routes outwards as well as inwards in order to allow inner city residents to seek employment in other suburban localities, and co-ordinate crèche facilities to allow women to work more easily. On a more controversial note too, the Lambeth team suggests two additional policies: to allow more unskilled and semi-skilled people to move to outer London and the new and expanded towns, and to stimulate an educational programme which will more readily fit children to work discipline than hitherto.

If the consultants see employment as the key factor in inner city regeneration, they also envisage changes elsewhere, notably in housing, social services, the involvement of the community, the improved management of existing resources and—vitally—additional resources. In the housing field,[46] for instance, the reports welcome the drift to rehabilitation, which should amongst other advantages reduce amounts of vacant property and allow for the creation of very different-sized units to cater for the widely ranging residential demands of older urban areas. At the same time grant provision for, and the administration of, rehabilitated properties are seen as inadequate, and should be modified to allow for more flexible standards, 'repairs only' grants, special provision for the poor and elderly, and so on. Flexibility within the administration of Housing Action Areas (HAAs) and General Improvement Areas (GIAs), and improved local management, are also stressed by the Birmingham team, since in its study area the local authority has placed a heavy emphasis on area improvement policies.

Although the improvement of housing is considered a vital issue by the consultants, important too, is the question of helping households to enter and move around within specific markets. Cheaper and unorthodox mortgages should be provided by local authorities to help the large proportion of residents wishing to buy.[47] In the private rented sector, the Lambeth team considers that in the London context it may be necessary to allow rents to rise if landlords are to make improvements and repairs to their properties. But it is in the public housing market that most policy modifications are suggested: improvements, in many cases quite minimal, in management[48] and design standards can do much to reduce vandalism and the costs of upkeep, and improved arrangements for dealing with vacant land, rubbish collection and other environmental services can have an effect out of proportion to their very limited costs. Allocation procedures need to be changed as well, the reports conclude, to make for far easier movements between and within authorities,[49] and here a national allocation pool would be helpful in allowing wider scope for workers to move to employment opportunities. The Lambeth team suggests also that many residents, in inner London anyway, want to move out to the suburbs and beyond, and that this should be encouraged, thus helping to reduce the too high population densities in the centre, and allowing workers to find employment elsewhere at the same time.

Although housing is probably the most pressing of social problems for inner city residents the reports suggest improvements are needed in other fields too. The Lambeth team wants improved geographical and functional co-ordination amongst the multitude of public and voluntary agencies involved in inner city welfare delivery,[50] and the teams all point out the poverty of educational standards and facilities in their study areas, which the Birmingham team sees capable of being improved in part through the appointment of educational development officers helping to forge links between the community and its schools.[51] Certain social groups would in addition require specific aid. Single parent families, for instance, would require special financial, housing and educational support.[52]

The changes envisaged in inner city policy by the teams would require—and this is seen as essential in all the projects—community involvement. This might take the form of local residents implementing particular schemes, possibly initiated by seed money from the authority, or being involved in say the management of housing policies or the creation of Community Federations to work in liaison with the Council in the organisation of urban governance. As the Birmingham team suggests, the community could 'progressively take on responsibility for planning its own activities and managing its own facilities, whether they are advice centres, clubs for young people or the elderly, playgroups, or childminding schemes, even small parks or playgrounds'.[53] At the same time the teams are aware of the limitations of local community action. To the Lambeth project for instance, local residents cannot make decisions bigger than their limited collective interests in the area, and indeed, 'consulting the local community is never a substitute for positive decision making by a council which alone possesses final powers'.[54]

And yet these 'final powers' might not of themselves, even when linked to central government initiative, be enough. All three teams have examined this issue, specifically within the context of whether adequate resources are available to deal with inner city problems and if these resources are being managed in a sensible way. The Lambeth team points out that its recommendations might not involve huge additional resources, since some policies would involve a reallocation of funds, and others, for example increased employment facilities, might ultimately provide a net gain. As this project sees it, 'problems are not necessarily solved by spending more money alone. Indeed overgenerous budgeting can lead not only to waste but also to misdirected effort. . . .'[55] On the other hand the Birmingham team is less sanguine about resources and their need.[56] Improved management, reallocation of existing funds and community effort might help, but without the redistribution on a large scale of national funds to inner city areas, 'the chances of making further inroads into the problems of personal and collective deprivation seem fairly slim'.

The Liverpool team would clearly agree with this latter prognosis. It suggests that initially all central government departments with an inner city dimension need to be co-ordinated at the national level to allocate additional specific funds to inner city areas for both economic and social provision, with this 'urban stress' grant being made part of the Rate Support Grant.[57] But any additional capital made available should, the reports advocate, be spent in detail by local authorities according to their priorities, providing, as the Birmingham team sees it, that these priorities can 'be justified by reference to local circumstances and are consistent with the government's decision concerning the overall level of national expenditure on urban renewal'.[58]

At the same time the teams would not want local flexibility to cement the traditionally poor organisational methods found in authorities. As the Birmingham project sees it, the obstacles to getting things done through local authorities can be huge because of poor co-ordination between agencies (public and private), inadequate integration of policies, failure to estimate manpower and financial resources and failure to communicate decisions. These and related problems need to be overcome, not through superficially attractive solutions such as new development agencies, with their inbuilt problems of lack of accountability and local experience, but through better co-ordination within authorities, superior methods of corporate planning, better budgeting exercises and the introduction of tight monitoring devices. These changes ought to be paralleled in turn by more appropriate land use planning covering shorter time periods, involving a willingness to be more flexible with zoning questions and perhaps through the production of a Community Plan worked out by the authority and relevant voluntary organisations on an annual basis, with clear indications of what policies are being pursued how, when and why.

Improvements in organisation at the local authority scale of operation should be complemented, as the Liverpool team envisages, by better and more meaningful area management techniques to deal with local administration and to provide a rapid, decentralised response to local issues.[59] The sort of organisation created might be formal in practice, with Area Consultative Committees recruited from elected members dealing with as many local issues as possible at a decentralised 'mini' town hall. This approach the Liverpool team sees as vital in enhancing local democracy, providing an areal basis for corporate planning and encouraging better welfare delivery. The Lambeth team, on the other hand, would not want such a permanent arrangement, but would prefer the creation of specific inter-directorate co-ordination teams set up as a sort of 'flying squad' to deal with different problems, as and when they crop up. But whatever the details of the organisation envisaged, clearly all three teams see the necessity for greater co-ordination of policy in local and central government. Specifically in the case of Liverpool, there is a very heavy emphasis on 'total government', in which centrally funded and agreed allocations of cash to deprived areas would be administered by one co-ordinated local body attempting to bring together all public and private agencies in order to create a new overriding inner city dimension within which political and financial directives would acquire a specific areal dimension, and within which all interested agencies would work towards regeneration.

This then, very broadly, is the IAS approach. The three programmes differ in detail, and in many ways the Lambeth approach, with its concern for population dispersal, and its relatively limited discussion of management or the 'total approach', can be evaluated on its own, although variations between it and the others may well reflect the idiosyncratic position of London rather than any determinedly maverick spirit. And even then, in methodology it is strikingly similar to the other attempts. Throughout the entire IAS project, indeed, there is a concern for the regeneration of manufacturing industry, improved income maintenance, greater flexibility and co-ordination of policy at both local and central levels, better housing allocation policies and a more structured channelling of resources to poorer, older areas. But this package is always to be accomplished through modification and not radical changes: existing authorities are to be retained and reformed; policies for extensive public control are eschewed; the community still remains outside the political and decision making centre; policies should not be totally abandoned but modified to meet changing circumstances; calls for additional resources are balanced by an acceptance that this might not happen immediately; and a realisation is shown that more in the inner city will mean less elsewhere, and therefore it will have to be fought for. It is, in fact, the social-democratic, reformist position, moulding into and marginally altering official policy; a leader and a follower of government thinking.

And exactly because it has been linked into official D of E thinking it has been widely welcomed, and implemented in part—in a way that the CDP, for instance, has not been. By late 1976 the new Secretary of State, Peter Shore, was indicating an apparently greater concern for 'the inner city' than had been voiced previously. In what have become milestone speeches at Manchester and Brighton,[60] he showed concern, clearly based substantially on IAS findings, for reduced employment opportunities, thoughtless planning policies and inadequate housing, and suggested that changes could be forthcoming on policy governing new town admissions, the retention of inner city employment and land acquisition procedures. Subsequently in Parliament, and through the 1977 White Paper, it became clear that some changes, real or otherwise, were to occur. New towns were to be cut back and instructed[61] to take 'more of those who have retired or are chronically sick or disabled—together with those unskilled or unemployed workers who are willing to move and whose prospects of employment will not be worsened by moving';[62] firms were to be encouraged to remain in inner cities and devices such as industrial improvement areas created to help them; IDCs were to be made more flexible; and greater employment priority given to inner city areas. In circulars and other publications the D of E also stressed the importance of avoiding job losses through residential redevelopment, and emphasised that local authorities could do much in the way of providing advice and infrastructural aid to industry since there was 'a particular need to retain industry and where possible to encourage the location of suitable new industry in inner city areas'.[63]

In an even more amazing volte-face, the Location of Offices Bureau was requested[64] to virtually reverse its traditional policy and attempt to promote office employment in inner city areas and not, as previously, encourage it to leave. The UA programme, too, was to be extended both in amount—from £30m to £125m by 1979/80—and in scope—to cover industrial provision—and transferred to the D of E. The need to co-ordinate policy at both the central and local level and to introduce an inner city dimension was greatly stressed and, specifically with regard to the IAS, special partnership schemes[65] are to be set up within which new, powerful and experimental policies will be devised through joint administrations of all relevant central and local agencies for the varied problems of Manchester/Salford and the Dockland authorities, and also, significantly, Birmingham, Lambeth and Liverpool. Initially, too, these partnership authorities are to submit claims for a large proportion of the £83m of capital expenditure in older urban areas announced in the 1977 budget.[66] Manchester and Salford are to receive £11m in all, the Docklands £17m, Liverpool £11m and Lambeth £5m, with a very substantial emphasis in all the programmes being placed on employment, transport and housing proposals. Later pressure on the Secretary of State was eventually also to allow a limited widening of the partnership arrangements to include Newcastle and Gateshead and Hackney and Islington.[67] Each of these areas will receive £5m out of the funds allocated to inner city construction, and at least £1m will be available to each of the seven partnership authorities by 1978–9. In another 15 areas too, authorities will have powers to declare industrial improvement areas, and to lend capital to viable local firms according to 'inner area programmes' which will not, however, directly involve the participation of central government in their preparation. The latter will, however, obviously be closely involved in the partnership authorities where it is anticipated that large, ministerially chaired committees will be created representing all local, citywide, regional and national interests.

Quite evidently then, the findings and recommendations of the Studies have had a considerable influence on central government thinking, as reflected in the sorts of developments, even reversals, of policy which have been implemented in the last year or so, down even to the specific details of which authorities should become partnership councils. And it is exactly because the IAS present an acceptable, reformist position they have been acclaimed and implemented. But that is not at all to say that their conclusions and methods are acceptable to every one, nor that central government policy based on their findings will succeed. Indeed there has been considerable criticism on both accounts.

Partly this has related to the political organisation of the teams, particularly their close, perhaps too close, relationship with the parent local authorities. Reports to the Steering Committees tended to have to travel through some form of Chief Officers' meeting, and this cannot have helped in the dissemination of more unorthodox or radical proposals. One commentator of the Lambeth political scene, for instance, suggests that the IAS arrived 'on the understanding that they would be able to bypass the council's tedious committee structure in the initiation of their projects, but they appear to have to go through the mill like everyone else'.[68] And anyway, many of the reports finally arriving at the Steering Committees seemed to deal with *ad hoc*, one-off schemes undertaken without substantial attempts being made to outline, even very generally, where the programme as a whole was going. To be fair, this might be an inevitable problem of short-term action-research programmes such as the IAS. Projects have to be brief because of resource constraints; small schemes can dominate the overall direction of the team work out of all proportion to their real importance; changing perspectives as to the root causes of deprivation might emerge from the small-scale projects, but there may not then be time to expand and test these new hypotheses. But nevertheless the impression does remain that much of the earlier IAS initiative was overconcerned with relatively minor experiments such as, say, housing maintenance schemes, which do not seem to have been integrated into an overall thesis testing exercise. Nor either do they seem related, except in the most marginal manner, with the much more theoretical prescriptions which finally emerged in the concluding papers.

Even then some commentators closely associated with efforts to improve inner city opportunities consider that the basic problem of the IAS is that, although they outline the nature of the difficulties being faced by older urban areas, these are not adequately related to the processes underlying their existence.[69] In particular, although the IAS perceive employment and income problems as causative agents in the generation of deprivation, they do not adequately explain why industrial decline has occurred, nor put forward policies which are likely to be sufficiently interventionist in outlook to prevent the continued decline and decentralisation of employment. The CDP, on the other hand, freed from too close a symbiosis with government, has been able to promote and work within a Marxist or neo-Marxist framework which, despite its political unacceptability in general, has provided a far more satisfying intellectual environment within which to place action projects, whatever their apparent triviality.

If any one of the IAS seems somewhat less open to the charge of 'ad-hocery', it is the Lambeth one, which has adopted a much more analytical, even academic approach. This in turn has generated its own criticism on the grounds that this experiment has made little effort to stimulate or even understand community development.[70] Yet because of the strong formal structure of the project, with local and central government representatives heavily involved in its administration, this reluctance to court community activists is not at all surprising. Certainly the present Secretary of State believes in general that responsibility and decision making powers should remain with properly elected representatives.[71] It is very predictable that urban experiments under his aegis should adopt a similar position.

Lambeth's approach has created controversy in other ways too, notably because of its emphasis on the dispersal of semi- and unskilled inner city residents to outer London and the new and expanded towns. This attitude has, not unexpectedly, been well received by the TCPA[72] and perhaps, in a paradoxical manner by central government too, which, although it has reduced the anticipated sizes of some new towns, has also requested that a wider social intake should be accepted into the communities specifically to aid the urban disadvantaged. The real problem about the decentralisation of London, however, is that it needs a change of attitude on the part of outer London boroughs. But there is no sign that their traditional reluctance to take inner city residents has abated. The Lambeth team is knocking on a very closed door.

The Birmingham team has been criticised on different counts. The very choice of the area has, for instance, been attacked by one analyst who sees it as 'too small, too homogeneous, its immigrant residents too inclined to owner occupation, and . . . destined for GIA and HAA treatment anyway'.[73] Another, more detailed examination of the actual operation of this project within the city's administrative structures also suggests that the local authority has not been especially helpful to the team over issues such as the possible establishment of an area management process in the study area.[74] But on the whole the opposite impression remains: that the teams by and large adopted too close a relationship with the relevant local authorities. And yet, ironically, many would agree with Self's evaluation of urban local authorities and would consider them lacking in 'resources, speed, understanding, flexibility and imagination'.[75]

What makes this particular discrepancy that much more unfortunate is that one of the basic *raisons d'être* of the IAS was to test out in practice the 'total approach', which by its very definition requires flexible and imaginative responses from public bodies, especially local authorities. In reality, however, the Studies shy away ultimately from advocating genuine 'totality'. Few references are made, for instance, to public agencies such as transport authorities or to education or health and social services departments—vital to inner city functioning, but unwilling perhaps to play ball? The search for 'totality' assumes in practice that the very many 'traditional line' departments are both willing and able to adopt integrated structures, assumptions which are optimistic at best. Not surprisingly, one commentator[76] at least has suggested that the drive for co-ordination at the horizontal level is too complex for authorities and government to handle, and that existing vertical structures are more likely to succeed.

But attacks on the organisational structure of the IAS should not disguise the fact that there has also been determined criticism over issues such, for instance, as the resources allocated to the project as a whole, and more important, the policy modifications proposed by the Studies. Grants from central government to the IAS have been small, less in fact than £2m[77] together with some additional allocations from the parent local authorities for specific action projects. This sort of global figure has been seen as totally inadequate, by some local politicians for example;[78] but such an attitude surely misunderstands the function of the project, which was envisaged as an essentially experimental and exploratory agent into the dynamics of deprivation, results from which would form the basis of general nationwide initiatives. This has in fact happened, and it is those criticisms levelled at the subsequent amounts of central government aid made available to all older urban areas in Britain which are more valid in pointing out the trivial amounts provided, and their marked spatial concentration.[79]

But policy is what the IAS were set up to examine and to innovate, and there has been no shortage of comment on this score. There has been a steady groundswell of opposition to the IAS approach on a number of vital issues: land, housing, employment and regional planning among others. A number of commentators have pointed out the very peripheral treatment of land typical of all the teams.[80] And yet it is in a sense, the *sine qua non* of any urban planning policy. Few would now argue that the present administration of the Community Land Act is anything like interventionist enough to operate successfully within the historically high urban land costs and to provide sufficient low- or at least lower-priced urban land for development. Certainly the IAS do not in any comprehensive way broach this problem at all, partly no doubt because of central government influence in the running of the projects, a central government in this case consistently back-pedalling over the whole issue of land and its acquisition.

Not everyone is satisfied with the IAS approach to housing and employment either. With regard to housing there is the feeling in some quarters that rehabilitation has been overstressed, and the essential aspects of urban residential redevelopment ignored. The teams seem too to have been acquiescent over issues such as the acquisition of vacant property, the ambiguous role of Building Societies, low improvement grants and inadequate housing resources in general. Suggested employment policies are also seen as unsatisfactory, in that the powers advocated by the Studies for local and central government to intervene in employment markets are not envisaged as providing a sufficiently strong and co-ordinated counterbalance to the decentralising forces of the market. Neither would regional policy as it stands at the moment, a deficiency which is unlikely to change as a result of the somewhat anodyne redefinition proposed by the teams. If inner city areas are to benefit from regional policy, then that policy needs to be both sectorally and spatially far more specific, to allow certain sorts of industries to be encouraged to move to specific locations within regions.

But beyond the shortcomings of particular IAS findings, it seems clear that at a more theoretical level there are those who would reject the entire methodological framework of the experiment. Generalising vastly, but perhaps fairly, they come from the right and from the left of the political spectrum. In the case of the former,[81] the main lines of criticism are that the teams adopt too interventionist an approach, which ignores the innate capacities of residents and the private market to regenerate inner city environments. According to this view the way forward is through tax cuts, the encouragement of community employment, philanthropic powers of business, the release of more land, capital cost allowances, and in general, 'setting people free'. Why these forces of free enterprise, which have to a large extent contributed to inner city decline in the past, should now be party to urban regeneration is not explained.

Predictably there is exactly the opposite response from the various strands of left-wing thinking, demanding on the whole greater powers of intervention than those proposed by the IAS. The lack of a 'black dimension', for instance, is perceived by one former Home Office minister as a shortcoming.[82] Following a similar tack, another reviewer[83] saw the whole exercise as too bland, and suggested that the sort of spontaneous economic revival needed in inner city areas might well be encouraged through greater and not reduced immigration, which would tend naturally to locate in older urban areas. From other left-wing sources too, there has been widespread general dissatisfaction that the 'strategies devised are insufficient to bring about the necessary intervention which could secure an improvement in the economic and social circumstances of disadvantaged areas'.[84]

This sort of policy modifications proposed by the IAS are simply not, then, of an intensity which the left sees as acceptable. Quite irrelevant, in fact: in some views housing markets will still remain very inflexible, with limited opportunities for working-class residents to move around spatially or sectorally, when at the same time huge national subsidies are paid to more fortunate owner-occupiers; and more fundamentally, within the employment market, the IAS propose no new initiatives which are likely to make more than marginal dents in the naturally decentralising forces of the private sector.

How valid are these criticisms? It can be argued that a dose of political reality is exactly what was needed from an urban experiment such as the IAS, and certainly they have provided just that. It is not coincidental nor surprising that the Director of Planning and Development Services at Lambeth itself should praise the Studies on the grounds of 'their common recognition that any quick response must, to a considerable degree, mean alleviation of the symptoms of decline and deprivation rather than removal of causes. . . .'[85] Nurtured as they were by both central and local government, it is only to be expected that more radical prescriptions were not forthcoming. And perhaps that is as it should be, for policy in this country is based on pragmatic incrementalism and not on radical innovation. The IAS reflect this: their recommendations are well within the compass of political reality. But should urban experiments be so parochial and pragmatic? Surely the intention of major urban experiments, which the IAS certainly became, should be to examine the entire range of urban problems and potential policy modifications, to stand on a few toes, to be a little heretical, a bit unorthodox—for after all no public body can stand piously above general accusations of incompetence when it comes to urban decay.

Clearly of course, one cause of the inhibitions which seemed to paralyse more radical spirits in the teams was the very close official supervision of the project, which undoubtedly helped to delineate acceptable areas of debate and, until very late in the history of the experiment, discouraged the formulation of a general theoretical framework. This latter discrepancy was especially significant, since it meant that the characteristics of urban decay which the teams identified were in no way related to underlying processes, and at the other end of the methodological spectrum the small one-off action projects were not integrated into any general operative framework or thesis testing exercise. It is true that towards the end of the programme urban deprivation was being increasingly related to structural changes, especially economic ones, in national and international markets. But despite this, the policy recommendations proposed to counteract these prevailing structural conditions do not seem of an order likely to succeed. Employment decline is seen as the key cause of urban decay, and yet it is impossible to envisage that the financial and spatial rationalisations, mergers, closures and general industrial contraction which characterise the British private sector will be influenced to any substantial extent by the essentially permissive nature of the IAS recommendations; the intensity of economic decline which their own findings suggest necessitates a parallel strong line in policy proposals, which is largely lacking in their concluding publications. It may, of course, be that in a social democracy such as Britain, anything more radical in the way of public control is politically unacceptable, but that is no reason to pretend that the IAS are 'right' or that urban policy based on them will succeed.

Ultimately any evaluation of the IAS must remain ambivalent. They have presented a voluminous mass of detailed findings on urbanism. They have wisely expanded on their original activities, eventually examining the entire range of economic and social issues which impinge on inner city areas. They have presented a whole range of pragmatic, implementable recommendations in the short and long term covering many aspects of urban functioning. They have looked at resources, at management, at national, regional and citywide issues. They have shown, perhaps implicitly, that inner cities are different and may require varying policy responses. But would these work? Would the policies they advance be of an order to counteract the acute processes they themselves identify?

As to the chances for the government's urban policy, so firmly rooted in the findings of the IAS, doubts must remain initially even about the government's genuine willingness to provide a co-ordinated and intensive attack on urban deprivation. Certainly the sums allocated are quite inadequate, and some cities traditionally regarded as having substantial pockets of deprivation will receive no grant at all in the new partnership schemes: Bradford, Leeds and Sheffield for instance. And why, one wonders, is the D of I so little involved in the new urban policy when its controls and powers would seem essential to any new initiative on urban employment? Why, too, are so few actual legislative changes outlined in the new White Paper? Does anyone believe existing powers will suffice? And more specifically, are the very limited positive powers for industrial regeneration likely to encourage meaningful industrial growth in inner cities, which everyone seems to see as vital? What about the question of land, and its artificially high cost in decaying industrial centres? What about the necessary reforms in government financing to ensure more stable allocations of resources to local authorities? Why too, when the government stresses the need for co-ordinated action, do we still have different investment programmes, covering different time periods, for transport policies, housing investment programmes, social services plans and land acquisition proposals—none of them, predictably, temporally coincident with structure plans? What about changes in regional policy[86] to create a more sensitive instrument than the blunt cudgel we have now? What about housing resources, allocation policies, higher and more flexible improvement grants? Relative to the government's largely aspatial industrial strategy for the country, how important is the 'urban dimension'? Not very, one suspects. And that is what matters.[87]

NOTES TO CHAPTER 4

1 *Hansard*, Vol. 840, 10.7.1972.
2 Walker had commented favourably on SNAP in 1970: *Hansard*, Vol. 807, 2.12.1970.
3 Shelter Neighbourhood Action Project, 1972.
4 K. Speed, Foreword to D of E, The Sunderland Study, 1972, Vols. I and II, 1973.
5 K. Speed (as 4).
6 T. Eddison, 1972.
7 D of E, The Rotherham Study, 1973.
8 S. Crowther, 1974, p. 184.
9 T. Hancock, 1974.
10 See, for instance, J. Stewart, K. Spencer and B. Webster, p. 8.
11 M. Rustin, 1975, p. 743.
12 D of E, The Oldham Study, 1973.
13 G. Lomas, 1974A.
14 T. Eddison, 1973.
15 A point made by A. Wood, 1973.
16 HMSO, *Policy for the Inner Cities*, 1977,   par. 1.
17 *Hansard*, Vol. 841, 26.6.1972.
18 F. Amos, *Inner Area Study and Local Planning Making Process*.
19 IAS/B/1, 1974.
20 IAS/LA/1, Appendix I, 1974.
21 See, for instance, D. Hutchinson and S. Gibbs, 1976.
22 IAS/B/4, 1975.
23 A point expanded on in greater detail by a member of that team: D. Jordan, 1977.
24 See, for instance, D. Lock, 1977.
25 IAS, Liverpool IAS, Final Report, 1977, p. 21.

26 IAS (as 25), p. 225.
27 IAS/LA/11, 1976, par. 2.1. Similar sentiments are expressed by the Liverpool team: IAS/LI/12, 1976.
28 IAS/LI/12, 1976, p. 6.
29 A problem also perceived by the local planning department: A. Lees, 1977.
30 IAS/LI/12, 1976, p. 7.
31 See, for instance, IAS/LI/12, 1976; IAS/LA/5, 1974.
32 See, for example, IAS/B/11, 1976, p. 61.
33 IAS/LA/11, 1976, p. 13.
34 IAS/B/5, 1975, p. 30.
35 IAS/LA/9, 1975, p. 11.
36 IAS/LA/11, 1976, p. 17.
37 See, for instance, IAS/LA/7, 1975, p. 67.
38 See, for instance, IAS/B/9, 1976, p. 13.
39 IAS/LI/12, 1976, p. 18.
40 IAS/LA/10, 1975.
41 IAS/LA/11, 1976.
42 IAS/LA/15, 1977.
43 IAS, Lambeth IAS, Final Report, 1977, p. 73.
44 IAS/LA/16, 1977: a point made by many urban commentators. See, for instance, R. Richter, 1977.
45 See, for instance, IAS/B/9, 1976.
46 Largely from IAS/B/11, 1976; IAS/B/4, 1975; IAS/B/7, 1975; and IAS/B/10, 1976.
47 As advocated in, for instance, IAS/B/11, 1976; IAS/LA/11, 1976; and IAS/LA/6, 1975, p. 37.
48 As indicated in IAS/LI/16, 1977.
49 IAS/LA/11, 1976, pars. 5.12–5.20.
50 IAS/LA/14, 1976.
51 IAS/B/8, 1975.
52 IAS/LI/18, 1977.
53 IAS, Birmingham IAS, Final Report, 1977, p. 210.
54 IAS/LA/11, 1976, par. 8.34.
55 IAS/LA/11, 1976, par. 8.17.
56 IAS/B/4, 1975, p. 22.
57 IAS/LI/12, 1976, pars. 3.29–3.40.
58 IAS/B/10, 1976, p. 66.
59 Examined in IAS/LI/3, 1974; and IAS/LI/9, 1976.
60 P. Shore, Manchester, 1976; and Brighton, 1976.
61 *Hansard*, Vol. 929, 5.4.1977.
62 HMSO (as 16), par. 68.
63 See, for example, D of E Circular 71/77, 11.7.1977, par. 24; and D of E Housing Services Advisory Group, 1977.
64 *Hansard*, Vol. 932, 17.5.1977.
65 *Hansard*, Vol. 935, 19.7.1977.
66 *Hansard*, Vol. 929, 6.4.1977.
67 *Hansard*, Vol. 938, 8.11.1977.
68 C. Jackson, 1975, p. 122.

69 See, for instance, The Inner City Working Group of the Joint Centre for Regional Urban, and Local Government Studies, 3.1977.

70 See for instance C. Jackson (as 68); M. Burchnall *et al.*, 1975; and D. Hutchinson and S. Gibbs, 1975.

71 *Hansard*, Vol. 929, 6.4.1977, where the Secretary of State indicated his belief in the prime responsibility of 'properly elected councillors'.

72 See D. Lock (as 24); and T. Hancock, 1977.

73 D. Lock (as 24), p. 152.

74 N. Flynn, 1977.

75 P. Self, 1977, p. 245.

76 *Town Planning Review*, Editorial, 1975.

77 *Hansard*, Vol. 906, 3.3.1976.

78 See, for instance, Liverpool MDC Policy and Finance Committee, 18.1.1977, where politicians within one of the parent authorities move a motion requesting central government to assist the city through direct financial means, since the IAS reports are a 'scandalous waste of time' and have produced nothing new.

79 See, for instance, A. Lyon questioning the absence of a partnership scheme for Bradford: *Hansard*, Vol. 935, 19.7.1977.

80 See, for instance, M. Allan, 1977; and the Association of Metropolitan Authorities, 1976.

81 See Tesco, 1977; D. Lane *et al.*, 1976; and Slough Estates, 1977.

82 See A. Lyon, *Hansard*, Vol. 935, 19.7.1977.

83 P. Hall, 1977A, p. 225.

84 The Inner City Working Group . . . (as 69), p. 11.

85 E. Hollamby, 1977.

86 See, for instance, how existing regional policy is inadequate to deal with subregional distributions in D. Massey and R. Meegan, 1976, where they examine spatial changes in the electronics and electrical engineering sectors and conclude that regional policy needs to be spatially and sectorally far more refined than is the case now, if inner cities are to benefit.

87 But for a more optimistic appraisal, see R. Nabarro, 1977A.

Chapter 5

THE SMALLER MANAGEMENT STUDIES

This chapter examines five smaller experiments initiated either by the HO or the D of E in the period from 1971 to 1974. There are inevitably considerable differences in the approach and conclusions of these projects, but equally so there are some strong common themes. They are all relatively small, for example, both in the sense that limited funds have been allocated to them and also in that each of the five separate experiments was conducted by no more than a handful of individual action teams. Furthermore, they were all envisaged very much as exploratory pilot projects setting down, it was hoped, guidelines for wider national programmes to follow; significantly, that now seems very unlikely. And finally and essentially, all of these initiatives have had as one of their prime functions the co-ordination of relevant agencies in an attempt to improve the management of urban resources, without in any way assuming that these resources would increase.

THE NEIGHBOURHOOD SCHEME

In October 1971 the UA programme was allocated £3·8m out of a special, once-only government spending programme for capital developments in the economically depressed areas. As some of this grant was left over, even after demands had been made on it by local authorities, it was decided to set aside £300,000 for two experimental Neighbourhood Schemes (NS). It was hoped that these new initiatives would complement the work then being done by the CDP in that, rather than adopt that project's approach of thinly scattering relatively small resources which were then to be used primarily for community development, the NS would alternatively allocate more substantial sums to one or two small deprived urban areas to be employed more for short-term, socially orientated, capital schemes. Indeed, as details of the project were finalised it was decided that all expenditure would be allocated to such capital schemes, largely because the entire initiative had as one of its aims a reduction in local unemployment. Hence running costs would not be grant aided at all, and as things worked out, the local authorities involved had also to agree to upgrade the physical environment of the selected area out of their own resources. The £300,000 which was to be made available by the government was to be divided between two authorities willing to implement the experiment immediately, and it would be paid out at 75 per cent of capital costs on new social facilities not already confirmed by the authority, in inner city areas of about 10,000 to 20,000 people.

It was originally intended that this sort of initiative would eventually be extended to about 10 projects, similarly organised to co-ordinate and monitor capital and current programmes in areas of multiple deprivation. Because the two initial projects were therefore envisaged very much as pilot schemes, there needed to be a strong evaluative input. This research would primarily examine the effects £150,000 had had in the selected areas; and whether and how greater co-ordination might have been achieved between the various implementary bodies, between environmental and social planning, and between the project and voluntary bodies. What was new about this approach *vis-à-vis* UA, for example, was the determination to create 'multiple schemes' in which concerted attempts would be made to co-ordinate all aspects of social and physical planning, which in reality would mean integrating these additional resources suddenly made available by central government into existing local authority plans in order to provide a comprehensive approach to inner city problems.

The central administration of the scheme was placed firmly within the HO with, in fact, very little inter-departmental co-ordination, despite the fact that this had always been seen as a vital objective of the experiment. The two local authorities were selected through this HO structure. In one case, Liverpool, it had always been known that the authority was very keen on experimental projects likely to bring additional funds to run-down inner city localities. In the case of the other authority, there seems at the time to have been a general assumption that the North-East had not received sufficient attention in the UA programme, despite its high known social and economic malaise. Subsequent informal contacts suggested that Teesside might be receptive to this sort of initiative; and so it proved.

In the case of Liverpool, an Action Area Plan had already been prepared for the Brunswick area of the city, and in discussions towards the end of 1971 the HO began to outline its ideas as to how this new action-research project might fit into existing physical and participatory plans for the area. In this half of the NS experiment there remained a commitment towards involving and consulting the public, quite possibly because the central administration was carried out in the same HO section as were the CDPs, with their heavy community involvement. Discussions in the North-East took on a different tack, partly because no area immediately and obviously emerged as the priority candidate, and partly because there was consistently less emphasis on public involvement. In the event the Newport area of Middlesborough was selected; a large part of this was programmed for rehabilitation, and some for redevelopment. Both this latter scheme and that at Liverpool were to be evaluated by a research team under Professor Greve. The findings of this team, on what admittedly was a rapid, one-off, very concise project, are certainly the most detailed and searching results ever produced on any one aspect of the British urban programme. This section is heavily indebted to the publications of that research.[1, 2] Anyone interested in examining the details of a project, and in particular how lack of carefully devised structures and objectives can bedevil any initiative, would do well to read it.

In Liverpool a Working Party was established in early 1972; this eventually was to consist of representatives from the main local authority departments, the HO, the research team and from local voluntary bodies. Initially the Working Party suggested that some assessment of community needs should be made, based upon census data, the opinions of relevant public and private bodies and through a limited local opinion survey. Although very little time was given to this aspect of the project, a list of five or six pressing needs was produced, including such aspects as poor preschool services, youth facilities and outdoor play provision. Subsequently projects which might alleviate these problems were devised and evaluated according to criteria such as whether proposals satisfied the needs of Brunswick, how much demand there was for the scheme, what community involvement, improved co-ordination or multiple use of facilities the project would entail, and what cost benefits were involved. In the event this evaluation, together with political and departmental preferences, moulded the final list of approved projects, which included a day care centre and a community minibus. Environmental improvements amounting to over £100,000 were made at the same time, including a traffic management scheme and the provision of a play complex. Within the development of both the social and infrastructural additions and the environmental improvements, public consultation was undertaken, although this tended to be of the 'informing after the event' type, rather than the 'asking for ideas before decisions are made' kind.

Organisationally the position was different in Teesside. Here the scheme was very much under the aegis of the Social Services Department, and although the HO had always imagined that implementary co-ordination assumed interdepartmental co-operation, this to a very large extent did not happen. And perhaps because of this rather centralised structure, discussion as to what would happen with the capital was not undertaken on a broad, informative, research based approach. Instead, quite early on, partly in response to more rigid deadlines than apparently operated at Liverpool, the decision was taken to build a neighbourhood centre, and subsequent discussion largely related to issues such as what facilities should be included or run from there. There seems in this instance to have been little debate as to possible alternative uses for the money.

In the later evaluation of the project, under the general aegis of Professor Greve but written by Batley, certain very pertinent comments are made about the experiment as a whole. There was, for example, a distinct lack of defined and concise objectives or of common organisational structures. It had been assumed that one of the objectives for the NS would be to help relieve local unemployment, but this was not apparently made at all clear to the authorities involved. Organisational arrangements over issues such as the existence and composition of Steering Committees were so loose as virtually to prohibit any sort of evaluation of the two very different approaches adopted. The entire initiative, clearly, had too much of the 'hit and run' feeling to it. Deadlines became important, thus inhibiting a wider discussion of potential options and encouraging instead an *ad hoc* approach, which tended to mean that these additional funds were in some way plastered on to existing authority commitments. Tight time limits also did little to enhance the very unclear status of research or public involvement. And it may anyway have been just as valuable to have allowed the development of some non-capital expenditure, rather than to have insisted on capital projects. A small scattering of funds on current expenditure might, for instance, have led to unforeseen side benefits.

Despite these severe problems, Batley did perceive certain advantages in the methodology adopted in the NS approach: some improved interdepartmental co-ordination was achieved, especially in Liverpool; the schemes allowed attempts at policy co-ordination to be evaluated; they helped to develop better relations between the public and the authority; they encouraged more open local government; and for the two areas in question, they provided considerable additional resources. But in the light of later developments within the field of urban deprivation, they must now be interpreted as essentially irrelevant. Even locally, they are now seen as part of the history and not of the continued practice of urban governance. The Liverpool scheme, for example, is seen by the authority as having made an impact within the Brunswick area 'by making specific improvements in the physical provision in the area and also by giving some impetus to the local community groups; it is difficult to identify any other significant continuing benefits'.[3] Nationally, too, they must even more so be seen as redundant. Originally it had been intended that these pilot schemes would be the forerunners of up to 10 similar projects involved with concentrating additional resources in a co-ordinated fashion to counteract what were seen as the interactive forces of deprivation in smaller urban areas. But in the event no more NS were ever commissioned; and although CCPs with their original concern for small-scale integration can be seen as natural successors, they too were ultimately to reject this approach. NS were clearly a reflection of central government thinking in the early 70s. Inadequacies in the definition of objectives and administrative structures, however, militated against their becoming pathfinders in the short term, and as it turned out anyway, changing theoretical frameworks with regard to deprivation and declining national economic performance prevented any widespread diffusion of these small-area, capital-intensive, urban experiments.

QUALITY OF LIFE STUDIES

In 1973 it was decided to set up two-year experiments to see what could be achieved in four different urban areas by locally led campaigns to develop and increase a full range of leisure activities.[4] Four central government departments combined to sponsor the projects: the D of E, which was responsible for co-ordinating the research; the DES; the Welsh Office; and the Scottish Education Department, collectively working in association with the Arts and Sports Councils.

Each of these departments contributed financially towards overall global expenditure of about £1m, of which approximately a quarter was provided by the local authorities involved.

The projects were always envisaged as part of the wider central government programme of initiatives designed to improve the quality of urban living.[5] To evaluate how successfully the Experiments were in achieving this goal, a central Advisory Group on Research Methods was established, which recommended that research should concentrate on establishing how effective the local projects were in improving leisure awareness and participation, how local management structures operated in practice, and how individual action schemes worked within local programmes. To help evaluate the various local management structures created, independent Assessors were appointed to each local team; and to obtain more impartial assessments of the validity of individual action schemes, a Project Evaluator was commissioned, one for each of the four areas.

But it was always anticipated that the main administrative and organisational impetus would come not from centrally devised structures, but from local initiatives. The four areas chosen were Sunderland, Stoke on Trent, Clwyd, and Dumbarton in Scotland. All four areas were thus mainly dependent on industrial employment, and were selected partly because they were seen to be independent communities, not overshadowed by larger regional centres.

In each of the areas the local authorities, sports and arts organisations and other interested bodies[6] were invited to take part in Experiments which were aimed at developing the optimum, co-ordinated use of existing, and some new, facilities. The various agencies involved were encouraged to create their own integrated administrative structures, which in the event varied from the establishment of virtually an independent group in Sunderland through to the position in Clwyd, where it was decided to use the initiative largely to extend and complement existing local authority resources. But whatever type of structure was eventually created, considerable decentralised powers were granted to the various executive bodies to direct the scheme and to administer available resources. As far as possible these aims were to be achieved by tapping the inherent abilities of existing and potential community organisations. From the point of view of this study, of course, these themes of improved co-ordination and community involvement—central to the Experiment as a whole—clearly parallel similar objectives apparent throughout the urban programme.

The various locally devised organisational structures which emerged usually began the action side of the projects by identifying needs and defining objectives. With regard to the former process, efforts were made to establish what local demands existed by assessing the lobbying of relevant groups, by contacting organisations and by expanding on generally held beliefs as to local deficiencies in leisure provision. At the same time general objectives and more detailed project criteria were defined to help generate overall directives and to create a checklist by which to evaluate submissions for action projects.

And there were plenty of these. In all over 400 projects were developed under the auspices of the Experiments. In Dumbarton, for instance, under a decentralised implementary structure,[7] projects which provided new activities or extended the scope of existing ones, and which offered wider activity participation that seemed viable over the longer term, were on the whole preferred. These criteria allowed as appropriate support or approval of projects[8] such as a sports equipment pool, community newspapers, an arts bus, community festivals and so on.

The other three projects adopted similar criteria for approving potential schemes, and in general a great deal of available finance was allocated to information services, transporting participants to activities, mobile community and arts facilities, community festivals and equipment pools. On the whole attempts were made to achieve a financial balance between projects relating to the arts, to sports and to schemes generally beneficial to the community. And to a large extent, too, costs for individual schemes were relatively low, averaging out at about £2,000 per scheme, although 30 projects cost in excess of £9,000. The latter included the development of new theatre groups and the provision of larger-scale infrastructure such as community buses. Whatever the costs of individual schemes, however, efforts were made to balance out available resources spatially in such a way that all districts within each selected locality gained something, and where existing groups and volunteers were unable to develop existing schemes or create new initiatives, professional catalysts were employed to stimulate local involvement in sports, the arts or community development generally.

The Experiment had a strong evaluative flavour to it. The central Advisory Group on Research Methods devised a monitoring programme to investigate the impact of management structures, of local attempts at agency co-ordination and of a number of specific action projects. Some of the results of this research were later published in Volume 2 of the final report. The research design that was adopted, the progression of a number of detailed initiatives, and more generalised conclusions relating to the development of the Experiment generally are outlined here, and those interested in such detailed conclusions would do well to read this.

But here it would be worth indicating a few of the more important policy lessons. The potential for community self-help is seen as considerable, provided that access to some small funding facilities and some detailed technical information are available. Greater co-ordination between the various sports and arts associations, however, is not seen as especially important. On the other hand more encouragement from, and access to, the main agencies concerned, notably local authorities and regional arts and sports bodies, might do much to stimulate greater interest in, and use of, leisure facilities. In general, then, the Experiment concluded that relatively minor improvements in financing, counselling and public relations could provide spin-offs out of all proportion to the sums involved in the development of new and expanding leisure facilities.

But is this a particularly important conclusion? In fact is the initiative at all relevant in debates on urban deprivation? In affluent times, no doubt, improving the standard of leisure provision has local importance and is likely to bring benefits to some residents. But in times of economic depression, and in this context severe urban economic depression, attempting to improve the quality and standard of urban life by improving the co-ordination of leisure associations lacks the immediacy one might expect from a central government ostensibly committed to reversing inner city decay.

Of course, there have been some advantages in establishing such an in-depth analysis of leisure provision. Very many small-scale schemes have been initiated, a substantial number of which are likely to prove viable in the long term. The possibilities of using existing voluntary structures to expand on the implementation of projects has been examined, and the problems of lack of co-ordination within and between relevant agencies highlighted. The administration of the scheme had considerable virtues too. Central government advice was relatively clear-cut and allowed considerable scope for innovatory local level action. Even more effective was the evaluation side of the Experiment. The pitfalls of action-research as a methodological process were evidently understood, partly because of an appreciation of the experience of this approach in other urban initiatives. In practice the creation of Management Assessors and Project Evaluators working within the action teams, or at least seconded temporarily to them, led to the accumulation of a substantial data base relating to the operation of different management structures in general, and the validity of certain schemes in particular, which both helped to disseminate ideas nationally and improved the performance of some projects locally.

But these were administrative innovations which could surely have been used to better effect elsewhere. Even before the accentuation of the slump in the mid-seventies it would have been quite possible to perceive the improved delivery of leisure facilities as probably being of relatively minor significance in the totality of factors implicit in any understanding of urban decline. But after the slump it is hard to see the Experiment as anything other than a rather embarrassing appendage, especially once the other urban initiatives, notably the IAS and the CDP, began to link urban decay to changing structural conditions in the British economy. And it was a relatively expensive appendage too. True, £1m over three years, the length of the Experiment as a whole, might not seem overgenerous, but relative to, say, the £2m spent on a major and innovatory initiative such as the IAS, it is. Fortunately the conclusions of that latter project, together with the similar and more radical conclusions of the CDP, make it improbable now that central government could again commission a project so divorced from what are now seen as issues central to the realities of urban decline. No doubt improved agency co-ordination, together with attempts to engender greater community involvement in the development and implementation of schemes, might have seemed likely avenues of advance in the early seventies, now they seem largely unimportant. And as a result the Quality of Life Experiment has strong claims to be the most irrelevant initiative ever devised by central government in its long search to eradicate urban deprivation on the cheap. For those caught in the syndrome of urban deprivation, better leisure facilities are very low on the list of priorities.

THE COMPREHENSIVE COMMUNITY PROGRAMME

The CCPs emerged from the UDU in late 1974. They were envisaged by Roy Jenkins, the Home Secretary of the time, as administrative arrangements through which more effective action could be taken to alleviate the problems of those suffering from both social deprivation and poor physical and environmental conditions, essentially by concentrating on improving the allocation of resources to them.[9] The real question, as Alex Lyon, Minister of State in the HO under Jenkins, indicated, 'is to find within existing programmes the right order of priority so that money is spent in urban areas of acute need rather than in other areas'.[10] Immediately, therefore, the initiative became embroiled in certain controversial issues: for instance that deprivation occurred in identifiable urban areas, about 90 within the UK according to Lyon; or that an emphasis within the programme should be placed largely on improving the management of existing policy rather than more introspective examination of that policy itself. These have proved difficult assumptions to live with.

But to the HO of 1974, an appraisal of urban deprivation as being areally identifiable and capable of being ameliorated through improved co-ordination evidently seemed quite an acceptable working premise. It was anticipated that CCPs would be evaluated through a number of trial runs in areas of about 10,000 people identified by indicators available from the 1971 Census. Each programme was to take about five years and would aim to generate information about deprivation, to facilitate improved co-ordination and co-operation between central government, local authorities and other bodies and to introduce monitoring procedures on a regular basis to examine the effectiveness of policy at all administrative levels. To implement a programme such as this, it was anticipated that the total costs of each trial run would be about £0·5m.

It is important to place CCPs within the intellectual and administrative context of the time, because they were both a reflection and a development of official thinking about urban deprivation.

1. The exercise was essentially one of improving management and not really policy as such, although clearly the latter might happen if especially grave and amendable deficiencies emerged. Improving the co-ordination of policy would, it was hoped, be achieved through an active partnership set up 'between central government, regional health and water authorities, local authorities, voluntary bodies and residents',[11] which would ensure that the needs of communities would be seen as a whole and not through the specific requirements of a multitude of various independent agencies. In creating this integrated approach, it was clear that techniques such as corporate planning would be useful in setting down objectives for areas, indicating how these might be achieved, by whom, when and how.

And systems such as these operative within local authorities would need to incorporate into their decision making cycles the plans of other agencies, and take into account the interrelatedness of problems and policies. Not surprisingly, with such a heavy emphasis on improved management, CCPs have been seen by at least one more radical commentator as attempts by central government to impose corporate planning on local authorities.[12]

2. In adopting an approach such as this, it was clearly hoped that local authorities, together with other relevant public bodies, would develop the 'one door mini town hall' decentralised structure, where local residents could obtain information and advice, and would be able to make representations on any matters likely to affect them. Corporateness at this local level would, it was optimistically hoped, be mirrored in central government too,[13] where the UDU, then recently established, was expected to provide a single focus, initially for queries concerning the CCP, and later for a wide range of central government activities likely to impinge on urban deprivation in some way or another.

3. The entire initiative was based on the growing concern that at the local authority level political pressures were making it extremely difficult for there to be any substantial reallocation of resources to smaller areas in most acute need.[14] CCPs on the other hand, with their more technocratic organisation providing a bridge between central government—and therefore possibly additional funds—and locally deprived areas, would be able to focus not on the needs of admittedly poorer local authorities as a whole, but on the requirements of acutely deprived smaller areas within them.

4. Although the prime reason for setting up the CCPs was to improve the co-ordination of policies at the local level, it was evident that there would have to be, even if only by implication, some analysis of the intrinsic merits of policy, and possibly therefore changes within its implementation. It was anticipated that some alterations in urban governance might be forthcoming as a result of lessons from existing urban experiments such as the CDP and the IAS[15] and from ongoing refinements in central government policy. But where, too, the CCP indicated particular deficiencies in policy within its analyses, some modifications in approach, possibly with additional direct financing from the central CCP budget itself, might be contemplated.

In order to see how CCPs would work in practice, the HO, with the co-operation of various local authorities, elected to establish a number of trial runs. In the event it was decided to instigate these in Wandsworth, Bradford, Gateshead, the Wirral and at Motherwell in Scotland, where pilot studies would concentrate on small, multiply deprived areas of about 10,000 people. But at this point organisational and methodological problems began to arise in earnest. Apparently some of the local authorities did not accept all of the initial premises of the programme:[16] that urban deprivation was, for instance, limited to certain specific small areas, or that effective policy in eradicating deprivation could be initiated at that scale. This reluctance to commence operations on a smaller scale may well have been justified in retrospect, even within the terms of the programme itself: the Motherwell CCP at Craigneuk did proceed at this smaller scale, dealing with an area of about 6,000 people, but it concluded in a later review of progress[17] that this scale of activity was too small to deal effectively with nationally prevalent problems such as, say, income maintenance—a defect which had been anticipated—but also too small in practice to deal with sub-regional services such as education, and even district services such as housing.

But there were other reasons why the CCP scheme did not operate as originally had been envisaged. For a start, attempts to create greater co-ordination at central government level, which had always been one of the main points in the programme, ran into difficulties, especially apparently over the issue of greater flexibility on loan sanctions, spending quotas and grants.[18] And there is evidence too that the previously held model of deprivation within which acute areas of multiply deprived people figured prominently was being slowly undermined, partly as a result of developments within the urban programme itself, notably within the CDP. Certainly a year after the CCP approach had first been announced, the UDU accepted that disadvantage could not be totally eradicated through special compensatory programmes, self-help projects, experimental schemes within UA or even by pumping relatively large amounts of capital into small areas.[19] Clearly the emphasis within central government was changing away from the idea that deprivation occurred in small, identifiable urban localities, where it was sustained by clearly recognisable forces, towards more nationally orientated structuralist arguments relating to changing forces within employment, housing and education markets.

In the light, then, of these changing attitudes towards urban poverty, how should the CCP operate? The details emerged in a revised HO Note in 1976.[20] CCPs were now to promote appropriate administrative arrangements which would focus on the needs of the deprived through a three-part programme drawn up by the local authority in collaboration with the various tiers of central government and other relevant bodies. Part I of this new arrangement would be a description of deprivation within a local authority, its areal distribution and its changing character. This 'position statement' approach has in fact been adopted in various guises by a number of authorities introducing corporate management structures, and is normally seen as an essential starting-off point, a baseline, by which to judge subsequent policy effectiveness.

Particularly important issues brought out in Part I of the Programme would be examined in Part II and could be raised by the authority, central government or any other body. Consideration of these problems should concentrate on practical policy changes which could be introduced within existing and probable long- and short-term financial constraints. Part III of the CCP cycle would outline in detail the short-term measures which an authority envisaged as being implemented within a year, by itself, central government, outside bodies, or any combination of these. But the essential basis of the approach would be that only those proposals for which funding was available would be confirmed, and vague ideas aiming at generally beneficial results would be avoided. In any case, regular monitoring procedures within the CCP cycle would ensure that only those policies that were effective would be retained from year to year.

An integrated approach such as that envisaged in the CCP would clearly require a willingness within both central and local government to modify existing structures. At the level of the local authority, HO advice was that each CCP should be tied into an authority's corporate internal organisation through a team of independent officers, supported initially perhaps by the HO, undertaking required analyses and reporting these back to, say, the Chief Executive, an administrative arrangement common to many forms of corporate planning. The difference between the CCP and this standard corporate model would be that in the former all tiers of government, together with other interested parties, would be involved. This would clearly require considerable ability on the part of the relevant local authorities to establish what spatial plans were programmed within the very many public and private agencies involved, and in some cases presumably lobbying bodies to identify a spatial dimension, a process which might not have occurred before. But the end result would, it was hoped, create a programme at local level aimed at distributing all resources in as socially just a manner as possible.[21]

This reorganisation at the local level, difficult as it clearly would be to achieve, would be nothing compared with the modifications envisaged at the centre by the HO in their 1976 Advice Note. The HO would retain overall responsibility for the development of a CCP, but central government in general would act jointly in discussions leading up to its adoption. Once this had happened, central government departments would use it as 'a framework for action and will refer to it in drawing up their priorities. In particular it will serve as a guide to central government when considering applications by the local authority for statutory approval, loan sanction and central government specific grant'.[22] This would, apparently, represent a radical new approach to relationships between central and local government, in that CCPs would act as action frameworks outlining an authority's deprivation programme, within which central government would allocate funds according to the viability and potential effectiveness of the plan. In practice of course, this approach would not have been quite as radical as it might appear, since central government would not at all be bound by the recommendations in a CCP, and the sorts of centrally allocated funds that might more automatically be dovetailed into a CCP would include programmes such as UA, generally minute in terms of total government expenditure.

This sort of administrative structure outlined by the HO in 1976 seems to have broadly retained in the recent inner city policy upheavals within the HO, the D of E and indeed in central government as a whole. Wandsworth, for example, which had been selected as a possible site for one of the trial runs of the original 1974 CCP approach, received ongoing documentation from central government as to how CCPs might operate and concluded that the new methodology was very similar to that which it itself wished to introduce in its own community corporate planning. In essence the difference between the latter and the new CCP was threefold:[23] the adoption of any CCP by central government seemed to imply some general commitment on its part to any proposals for loan sanction contained there; formal managerial arrangements were to be set up between Wandsworth and other public bodies in the CCP; and there needed to be a built-in commitment within an approved CCP for the

Council to agree to reallocate resources to more deprived areas within its administration. In essence, then, CCPs were to become forms of extended corporate planning.

These general principles laid down by the HO to Wandsworth, and more generally in advice notes, are to a large extent reiterated in the recent White Paper on the Inner City which sees CCPs as 'district level, authority-wide approaches involving the main policies and programmes of local and central government',[24] which will consist of a description of the local state of deprivation, an appraisal as to the effectiveness of existing policy, and, taking into account the operation of all relevant bodies, an annual, updated programme of action. A new CCP methodology seems therefore to have emerged at last: authority-wide initiatives, not local as had originally been imagined, within a much vaguer definition as to what deprivation is and what causes it, although clearly the emphasis is moving towards structuralist processes operative within much broader spatial frameworks. And in one other obvious aspect, arrangements are to change: the trials themselves are to go on trial and the CCP at Gateshead, funded in part by the D of E, together with some evaluative work at the Institute of Local Government Studies, are to go ahead alone in order to investigate the validity of the approach. Evidence emerging from the Gateshead project suggests that the development team of four, working through a Members' Group of local, county and central government politicians, has attempted to involve the wide variety of public authorities in annual rolling programmes aimed at redirecting resources, public, private and community, to those most in need.[25]

Clearly more substantive research conclusions will be forthcoming. But even before these emerge, it is evident that the CCP methodology has been subject to widespread criticism on at least two accounts: the scope for community involvement in the process, and the emphasis which CCP places on the management rather than the examination of policy. HO advice with regard to the former issue is that the views of the public, and especially voluntary organisations, should be sought out, since many of the recommendations put forward within a CCP should be the subject of general debate. Part III of the CCP was always considered an appropriate document within which to outline the ways in which public participation might be arranged. This essentially paternalistic vision towards 'the community' has predictably been condemned by more radical activists,[26] who see the CCP as a strengthening of internalised central bureaucracy at the expense of local residents. But there is no reason why this must be so. Indeed evidence from the Craigneuk scheme suggests that the central core of the community problem is rather the conflict between 'the community development aspects of the project and the requirement for quick solutions to highly technical problems'.[27]

Complex as the relationships between the community and an authority can be, they nevertheless do not raise the same sorts of fundamental difficulties as does the essential emphasis within the experiment on the management rather than the evaluation of policy. HO has been quite frank on this question and has consistently argued that 'the CCP approach is based on the redirection of existing policies and programmes rather than on new programmes. In the present economic climate when new resources are unlikely to be available, such redirection will involve difficult decisions about priorities and it is these which the CCP is intended to inform.'[28] But what evidence is there to support such an act of faith in the effectiveness of existing policy?

THE GREATER LONDON COUNCIL DEPRIVED AREAS STUDY

By the early 1970s the GLC had become interested in the idea of creating some action-research projects aimed essentially at co-ordinating existing services and providing a priority allocation of funds to certain especially deprived areas within London, identified by indicators from the 1966 and 1971 Censuses. In the event the UDU at the HO was approached, and agreed to fund in part these experimental schemes, provided that some additional expenditure was forthcoming from a combination of the GLC, the relevant local authority and the ILEA. Eventually two areas were selected, Spitalfields in LB Tower Hamlets and Hanley Road in LB Islington, the former consisting of over 9,000 people, the latter of only about a third of that figure. The experiments were to begin in 1975 and to last five years.

It is evident to some extent that the UDU and the London authorities involved were uncertain as to what the projects would actually do and how they should be organised. This general indecision was reflected in the lack of agreed objectives or operational guidelines from any of the interested parties, and has meant that policy and management of the two schemes has not always coincided. With regard to organisational structures for example, although it was

D

always considered advisable to create broad governing bodies to reflect the numbers of interested parties, public and private, the administrative details do differ. In the Spitalfields project[29] executive control is held by a Steering Group of ward councillors, local GLC and ILEA members and five representatives from the community. This structure is supported in turn by a Consultative Committee consisting of representatives of the major community and trade union groups in the area, and an Officers' Support Group of officials from the main relevant GLC and Borough Directorates. Policy formulated through official political structures is implemented by a Project Co-ordinator and other officers under the general control of the Borough's Directorate of Social Services.

Formal arrangements in the Islington scheme are not totally dissimilar. Here there is a Steering Group of Officers, members and representatives from other agencies. Meetings are in public under the guidance of the Chief Executive, and voting rights are given to members and, to a lesser extent, to representatives from the local population. As with the Spitalfields scheme, there is an Officers' Support Group with representatives from Islington, the GLC, the ILEA and sometimes from other agencies too, which meets once a Committee cycle and prepares first drafts of reports to be considered by the Steering Group. The latter, in considering recommendations, can develop interagency or interdepartmental views, and can ask the HO for the funding of specific projects, but cannot make decisions— merely requests—over other local authority resources.

But what are these complex political structures actually supposed to do? Originally the detailed aims of the projects were fourfold: to co-ordinate and bring forward plans and policies from two tiers of local government; to carry out action programmes within the areas; to involve the public; and to carry out research in order to present more general conclusions about deprived areas in London as a whole.

Co-ordination was always seen as a vital aim, partly because of the multitude of public bodies involved in the administration of small areas in London. The formal administrative arrangements encouraging co-operation between different departments and agencies have, of course, brought together officers from a variety of institutions, and this has led to some concrete advances. In Spitalfields,[30] for instance, volunteer interpreters were sought out for the Housing Department about to embark on a rehousing programme, and attempts were made to bring together officers of the GLC, the Borough, the Project, the ILEA, and Spitalfields Market to prepare proposals for environmental improvements and experimental road traffic management schemes. Doubts have however, been expressed[31] about the ability of the middle-ranging officers running the projects, and those on Officers' Support Groups, being able to co-ordinate the very many independently devised and often politically contentious programmes affecting areas such as these in a way which would bring meaningful advantages to local residents. This is a particularly acute problem in the Hanley Road scheme, since the selected area is not markedly any more deprived than other localities in the area, which has created genuine political problems in that some councillors have been reluctant to grant the area priority status for the allocation of additional funds.

Not that, surprisingly enough, funding has been a major problem until recently. Originally the HO, and with the recent transfer of the urban programme now the D of E, set a global limit for the overall programme within which central government will finance 75 per cent of costs, provided that the relevant London borough, the GLC and the ILEA in combination contribute 25 per cent. In practice almost all this latter proportion has come from the GLC, and clearly any reduced commitment on their part will in turn automatically reduce central government's expenditure and hence total global funds.

Finance that has been available—and in recent years this has amounted to more than £200,000 p.a.—has been used for a variety of social and economic facilities. In Spitalfields, to aid in the selection of projects, criteria were drawn up in 1975[32] for the sorts of schemes which might be helped. On the basis of these principles it was clear that innovatory, rapidly implementable, community supported schemes were to be preferred, especially if they could satisfy a known demand, could not be financed elsewhere, and could be easily monitored. In the event a wide range of capital and current projects was approved[33] including community centres, playgrounds, a community bus, and the salaries for a community lawyer and community drama workers. Although decisions on major projects needed to go through the administrative structure and eventually to the HO, smaller grants could be made out of a Contingency Fund at the more immediate discretion of the Chairman of the Steering Group.[34] In Islington, the grant has been spent in a slightly different way, in that a greater emphasis has been placed on the possibilities of using funds to generate local employment through supporting craft and adult education centres and the leasing of local redundant factories. The problem, however, which this widening of the capital support programme seems certain to bring is that of inadequate grant since, although demand for community services could to a large extent be met out of the existing budget, this would not be the case if more expensive industrial investment came to dominate the project.

Nevertheless, until recently much of the latent demand for social investment could be met, an advantage which probably did much to stimulate public involvement in the running of the experiment, always anyway a primary aim. Certainly for one commentator the existence of a substantial budget was vital, since 'without it the community might never have permitted itself to get involved with such an authority-inspired experiment'.[35] This involvement has taken various forms,[36] including the establishment of administrative structures encouraging the election of community representatives, the creation of community newspapers, open meetings between agency officials and local residents, and the development of advice centres.

And it is this sort of development which will form the main focus of research for the GLC monitoring team which has undertaken social baseline surveys of the areas, and is intending to investigate how local groups administer their grant, how it is spent and whether it meets any defined objectives.

Of course a research programme such as this implicitly presupposes that experiments of this sort can provide insights into the generation and eradication of urban deprivation. But is this so? There is very little evidence, for example, that the projects have acted as 'pump-priming' agents stimulating long-term multiplier benefits, and at the end of their five-year life, self-sustained schemes are likely to be very thin on the ground—unless, of course, far greater attention is paid to the possibilities of industrial investment. But whereas substantial and immediate community facilities can be provided out of an annual budget of about £250,000, far greater sums, and hence political commitment, would be required to make much of an impact in the employment market.

THE AREA MANAGEMENT TRIALS

In September 1974 the D of E invited metropolitan district councils to report area management experiences and to indicate any potential interest in taking part in other monitored experiments into decentralised administration.[37] To the D of E at the time it seemed possible that this system of governance might do much to reduce urban deprivation, whilst at the same time stimulating local initiative and political concern. There were, it was admitted, real problems over definition. What did 'area management' actually mean? Who would be involved in its operation? What powers would decentralised administrations actually have? But these were difficulties to be overcome, and the D of E was prepared to allocate some limited funds to do this.

By 1976 six authorities were, to varying extents, being supported. Liverpool and Stockport initiated area management schemes as early as 1974, the former in line with recommendations of the IAS team. By 1976 additional experiments were also being funded at Dudley, Haringey, Kirklees and Newcastle upon Tyne. The project as a whole is also being evaluated in a four-year monitoring programme, to be completed by 1980, by the Institute of Local Government Studies at Birmingham.[38]

The approaches adopted in the six areas differ considerably in terms of administrative structure, the types of powers which have been devolved, the degree of public involvement and so on. In Kirklees, for example,[39] the decision was made to retain a local presence in each of the eleven authorities subsumed by the new administration in the 1974 reorganisation of local government. Initially this decentralised structure was to be effected by using District Officers of the Finance Division, both as local collection points for monetary receipts and also to provide an additional information source for local residents. Later, too, the area management system, here called 'area care', was strengthened by the establishment of five Area Care Officers who were commissioned to oversee the workings of Area Centres and to co-ordinate professional, political and public discussion in an attempt to improve service delivery and public information flows.

The approach evolving at Stockport is very different. Here the idea of area management went back to the recommendations from management consultants in 1971[40] that three area subcommittees of the Housing and Community Services Committee should be established. One of the functions of these subcommittees was to encourage community development, and this happened to such an encouraging extent that they were granted powers to enable them to report to any committee of the Council on matters affecting the area under question. Later fears, too, that the larger post-reorganisation authorities would prove even more remote from local residents[41] stimulated a more thoroughgoing decentralised structure based on eight area committees. In practice the latter have tended to concentrate on planning applications, service co-ordination, providing information and advice, generating community development and providing an areal input to the authority's corporate management system.[42] As at Kirklees, however, no management responsibilities involving the use or allocation of services, nor any authority in respect of the priorities of service committees and service divisions are granted to the area committees.

A spatially more limited experiment was initiated at Liverpool in its administrative District 'D', where an Area Management Unit reporting direct to the Chief Executive and charged with the basic administration of the project has been established.[43] Essentially this Unit has attempted to cut across traditional line structures in the authority by introducing a decentralised approach.[44] Within this overall strategy efforts are made to ensure that priority is given to the area within such generalised programmes as, say, economic development. In this admittedly broad category specific priority policies are expanded, dealing with issues such as making land available for industrial development, or improving training facilities. Similar attempts are made to emphasise the particularly deprived status of the District and its need for priority treatment within housing, community care and environmental development programmes.

Newcastle's strategy is part of an authority-wide attack on stress areas.[45] The application of social indicators suggested that about half of the city's wards were in need of intensive action programmes. In each of the eleven wards eventually selected, Priority Area Teams of local politicians and officers from the relevant departments operate in developing area programmes in consultation with local residents. Considerable emphasis has been placed within these programmes on providing new social and community infrastructure from the budget specifically allocated to each of the stress areas. In 1976/77 this amounted to £500,000, of which about two-thirds was allocated centrally by the Policy and Resources Committee to proposals for the priority areas submitted by departments, and one-third spent locally by the individual Priority Teams. In 1977/78 the budget is to be doubled and a greater focus placed on encouraging new inner city employment. At the same time considerable opportunities will be available for the local priority teams of politicians and residents to spend their locally allocated finance as they see fit, and as any ongoing local financial commitments may eventually be taken over by the relevant service committees, the Newcastle approach does allow the possibility that, in time, there will be a considerable re-distribution of financial resources within the city.

Dudley, unlike Newcastle, has selected just one area for a decentralised experiment, an area which by national standards would not be considered especially deprived. It was hoped that this approach would provide an additional areal input into the authority's corporate planning system, besides helping to involve ward members more in local affairs and helping to use existing resources more efficiently.[46] Both political and administrative area teams have been created, seconded from existing committees and departments, although there is a full-time research assistant too. The intention was always to produce an experimental outlook, and hence considerable latitude was allowed in the spending of the initial £8,000 budget. Later, too, more money may be available, and the project is likely to expand into more general fields of community need and involvement, the potential for areal perspectives within service departments, and better member involvement in the affairs of their wards.

Haringey similarly selected one particular area of its administration for an experimental programme.[47] The project here revolves around an Advisory Committee and a small Area Management Unit, the latter having close links with the relevant district Planning Team. The emphasis has been placed on attempting to generate and co-ordinate community development, through local area forums, and through a policy of actively encouraging public discussion at Advisory Committee meetings. On the other hand no funds or powers are delegated to the Committee, which has to proceed by recommendation and informal persuasion.

Clearly even these brief cameos of the six projects indicate the variety and scope of administrative and political structures which can be subsumed under the general catch-all of 'area management'. The size of unit administered, the size and characteristics of populations involved, and the type of area all vary tremendously. Matters within the jurisdiction of decentralised structures differ, too, from one experiment to another: Newcastle's scheme, for instance, aims to generate and promote policies directly implementable through a local budget; but other projects can consider, though not decide upon, a wide range of locally relevant issues. On the whole, in fact, the evidence from the six case studies suggests that the power of local area political structures to make decisions and to administer any substantial budget its likely to remain very limited, and even where area co-ordinators or departmental working parties have been established, there are few indications of a parallel delegation of executive authority. Certainly, too, there are few suggestions that the various forms of structured public involvement have carried with them any danger of creating a position in which residents might out-vote members.

More clear-cut assessments as to how effective the Trials might be is constrained by the very loose definition of objectives on the part of authorities involved, and indeed also on the part of the D of E. Defined aims for area management include responding more sensitively to local demands, more efficient service delivery, better policy co-ordination, enhancing democratic vitality, reducing political alienation and providing a local dimension to central corporate management schemes.[48] This by no means exhaustive list of objectives implicit even within these few area experiments raises two immediate issues: how can these very different objectives contained within very different administrative structures be evaluated in the research programme? And what has all this to do with urban deprivation?

A member of the evaluation team has pointed out the difficulties inherent in monitoring a programme in which permanent objectives may not be set, and where the degree of similarity between different elements within the overall programme might be so limited as to make comparisons meaningless.[49] At the same time evidence from D of E representatives suggests that central government itself is by no means clear as to the 'best' form of area decentralisation,[50] although it seems to be regarded as 'a neutral technique post Bains'.

Now this comment might be particularly relevant, since it becomes increasingly apparent that the scope for area management exercises to redistribute resources in favour of more deprived localities is extremely limited. Some of the six authorities being evaluated in this exercise do not, in fact, even identify allocating additional resources to poorer areas as one of their objectives, and despite the original D of E position that a moderation in the intensity of urban deprivation might happen through area management exercises,[51] the official view later seemed to be that there may be little scope for areal re-distribution in such experiments.[52] And certainly additional resources granted to the Trials themselves are very limited: some of the authorities involved have granted no project funds at all, and only one, Newcastle, has a discretionary budget of six figures. The D of E has contributed some funds, for example £18,000 in the first year at Haringey, £10,000 to Newcastle and £13,000 to Dudley, but relative to the totality of problems encountered in some of these areas at least, these figures can only be regarded as a form of tokenism. At the same time it might be unwise to assume that improved management at the area level has the innate capacity, whatever funds are allocated to it, to make any substantial amelioration of urban poverty. These Trials, and other urban initiatives too, have assumed that it can, but there are good reasons to imagine that the whole process will have minimal impact and might best be regarded as irrelevant, even diversionary. These arguments will be expanded later.

NOTES TO CHAPTER 5

1 The Liverpool Neighbourhood Scheme, *Evaluation of Projects*, undated.
2 R. Batley, 1975.
3 City of Liverpool, Community Development Section, *Programmes for Increasing Community Involvement in the Planning of Local Authority Services*.
4 D of E, *Leisure and the Quality of Life*, Vols. I and II, 1977.
5 D of E, *Quality of Life*, Interim note, 1975.
6 D of E, Press Notice 490, 'Leisure and the Quality of Life', Report published 27.9.1977.
7 Dumbarton District Community Development Advisory Board, Final Report to Local Sponsors.
8 P. Stott, 1975.
9 *Hansard*, Vol. 877, 18.7.1974.
10 *Hansard*, Vol. 878, 29.7.1974.
11 HO, Official Report on CCPs, 1974.
12 C. Cockburn, 1977.
13 See G. Wasserman, 'Urban Deprivation', in J. Brand and M. Cox (eds.), 1974.
14 G. Wasserman (as 13).
15 HO (as 11).
16 CDP, *Gilding the Ghetto*, 1977, p. 15.
17 Craigneuk, CCP, *Background and Progress*, 5. 1977.
18 LB Wandsworth, Policy and Resources Committee, *The Community Planning Process and the CCP*, Paper No. 7557, par. 8.
19 UDU Note, 4.9.1975.
20 HO, Note on the CCPs, CCP (76) I, 5.11.1976.
21 A point expanded by K. Spencer, 1975.
22 HO (as 20), par. 15.
23 LB Wandsworth (as 18), par. 7.
24 HMSO, *Policy for the Inner Cities*, 1977, par. 65.
25 R. Hambleton, 1977B.
26 See, for example, Community Action, 1975/6.
27 Craigneuk CCP (as 17), par. 6.
28 HO (as 20), par. 18.

29 For details, see M. Myers, 1975.
30 Spitalfields Project Steering Group, Item 10, 1977.
31 See, for instance, C. Huggins, 1977, p. 68.
32 *Spitalfields Project*, Summer 1975.
33 See, for instance, Spitalfields Project Steering Group, Item 6, 1977.
34 *Spitalfields Project*, a Report by the Co-ordinator of the Spitalfields Project, 1977.
35 C. Huggins (as 31), p. 67.
36 See, for instance, Spitalfields Project Steering Group, Item 9, 1977.
37 D of E, Area Management Note, 1974.
38 In March 1977 Inlogov published its first interim report, which has substantially aided the presentation of this section: C. Horn *et al.*, 1977.
39 Kirklees MC, *Area Care in Kirklees.*
40 Booz, Allen and Hamilton, 1971.
41 Stockport MB, 1974.
42 Stockport MB, 1977.
43 C. Horn *et al.* (as 38).
44 City of Liverpool, 1975.
45 City of Newcastle, *Newcastle's Approach to Priority Areas.*
46 Dudley MB, 1977.
47 LB Haringey, 1975 and 1976.
48 Potential objectives within area management exercises are expounded by R. Hambleton, 1976.
49 B. Webster, 1974.
50 S. Garrish, 1974.
51 D of E (as 37).
52 S. Garrish (as 50).

Chapter 6

THE COMMUNITY DEVELOPMENT PROJECT

James Callaghan could hardly have anticipated the hornets' nest he let loose in 1969 in setting up the CDP, for certainly no British urban experiment has come up with so many radical and politically unacceptable proposals. And yet paradoxically, despite its at times chaotic functioning and official neglect, there can be no doubt that this initiative has been a most influential factor in changing attitudes towards the causes and amelioration of urban deprivation.

Not that the original press release suggested such great things.[1] It was certainly seen then essentially as a neighbourhood based experiment lasting from three to five years, aimed at exploring new ways of meeting the needs of people living in areas of high social deprivation, largely by improving the co-ordination and delivery of services and through the tapping of community and individual self-help. To a considerable extent, in fact, the individual figured prominently in official thought, since it was widely felt that, although on the whole social services were quite adequate to deal with most people, it was their less effective, or even totally ineffective, treatment of a minority which was the root problem. CDPs were thus envisaged as complementing the government's existing poverty programme by providing comprehensive and co-ordinated services in a few small areas, from which general conclusions were anticipated, rather than spreading aid very extensively and very thinly, the pattern adopted in UA.

The CDP sites selected would, it was hoped, 'reflect a wide variety of types of areas of high social need', and although in retrospect it does seem clear that very different social problems were encountered in the twelve districts selected, they were all to varying extents suffering from industrial decline. At the same time it could not be said that these areas chosen were the worst twelve in the country, nor that there had been a wide and determined lobbying for this sort of initiative, either there or in general. Indeed, to some of those working later on within the programme, it seemed that 'it was never widely canvassed, publicly discussed or pressed for. It was essentially the product of the thinking of a small group of civil servants, professionals and academics . . .'.[2]

The first four projects, some set up as early as 1970, were located in Coventry, soon to feel the draughts of a major industrial slump, Liverpool, Southwark and Glyncorrwg, in West Glamorgan. The remaining eight teams were established within the next two years at Oldham, Batley, Paisley, Cleator Moor in Cumbria, Newcastle, Tynemouth, Saltley in Birmingham and Canning Town in Newham.[3] The population of the study areas varied from over 40,000 in Canning Town and Batley to under 10,000 in Glyncorrwg; and clearly the social and economic difficulties varied as well, from the semi-rural poverty accentuated by a declining mining industry in Cleator Moor to the problems of a diminishing dockside industry and substantial residential and road redevelopment proposals in the Vauxhall area of Liverpool.

The detailed selection of the sites was undertaken by a central co-ordinating team at the HO, originally in fact within the Children's, later the Community Programmes, Department in co-operation with the relevant local authorities. The latter needed to be receptive to the ideas and initiatives envisaged by the HO, and not all of those approached were. Normally any resultant project was placed within the Social Services or Town Clerk's Department of the local authority, although managerial structures varied in detail. In Coventry, for instance,[4] a Community Development Project Committee was established consisting of the Chairman or Vice-Chairman from the main committees, ward councillors and representatives from central government and voluntary agencies. In Paisley[5] a Management Committee has been created as a subcommittee of the General Purposes Committee of Strathclyde Regional Council and in Southwark[6] a small working party of Chief Officers was given veto powers. Although it might well be argued that flexibility of management structure was a desirable aim to adopt, it does in retrospect seem clear that the HO was storing up problems for itself by not defining at an early stage the relative functions and powers of the various interests: its own, the authority's and the team's.

But in the late sixties it is unlikely that the HO itself had much of an idea as to what would actually happen in practice. The one clear decision which had been made was that the projects would be action-research initiatives, with central government paying 100 per cent of research and social action costs, and 75 per cent of staff salaries and overheads within the action teams. The latter normally consisted of about three full-time workers who were accountable both to the authority and to the HO, and up to 20 or so seconded staff, including teachers and social workers. The research teams affiliated to the projects were to be recruited, as originally intended, from local polytechnics and universities, and from 1971 a Central Research Team was established under Professor Greve at the University of Southampton to co-ordinate research at the national level—although this arrangement was not to last long, and later Greve was to become Research Consultant and not Director of Research, partly because of conflicts between research and action.

Attempts at the central co-ordination of research were paralleled by efforts to integrate action at the national scale too. Until 1970 a Central Steering Group met and attempted both to direct the various approaches of the four pilot schemes and to disseminate their findings to central and local government and to other interested bodies. But by 1971 this attempt at central co-ordination had been largely abandoned, because it was widely believed the project teams were, even at that stage, extending their brief to examine not simply social services but planning, housing and other policy fields within an increasingly radical and theoretical framework, and no civil service supported committee could be seen organising politically volatile initiatives. Nor could the Home Secretary either, and in April of 1972 Maudling announced that greater devolution was to be introduced into the scheme 'in order to encourage local initiative';[7] a more cynical interpretation would be that he was trying to localise its impact. But the local teams were not prepared to be disaggregated so easily, and in May 1972, in response to local field requests, a Consultative Council was established as a focus for discussion within which central government and the local teams could air their views, an experiment which later had the backing of the newly created CDP Information and Intelligence Unit funded by the HO and sponsored by the Centre for Environmental Studies. This new administrative structure was to produce two general position statements in the succeeding three years. In the summer of 1973 the government asked for project progress reports, and these were collated and issued as the 1973 Inter-Project Report.[8] Later, too, in 1974, when the HO asked for a statement from each of the teams indicating key issues, objectives and expectations, the opportunity was used to publish a generalised statement in the Forward Plan of 1975.[9]

But in retrospect it seems evident that discussions as to the best organisational framework for the experiment were by the early 1970s diverting attention from the far more basic issue of the widening gap between the HO and the teams over the direction and scope of the programme. A management review of 1974 suggested that the projects should be subject to stronger central control, and by 1975 it seemed clear that the HO wanted to close or at least curtail the field projects. A letter was sent to the parent local authorities indicating that the HO would continue to fund the CDPs but that the authority itself had the power, if it so wished, to close down the experiment; and in some instances this did happen. Within the succeeding year, too, Home Secretary Jenkins announced the ending of HO finance to the Central Information and Intelligence Unit, originally timed to take place in spring 1976 and eventually implemented later in that year,[10] and, in a heavy hint, that closure would not unduly worry the HO. Alex Lyon announced in Parliament that the HO would pay its proportion of the costs of local projects to authorities 'willing and able to meet their share of the cost of the remainder of the period originally envisaged as the life of each project'.[11] Clearly the HO had by this time lost interest in the scheme as one likely to provide a coherent and acceptable vision of deprivation, and had become much more concerned with quietly forgetting it. There was to be no final government approved report, no government response, but instead a steady drying-up of remaining projects, together with some collective work encompassing the findings of a number of the teams. And yet the project at its peak was employing more than 100 action and research staff,[12] and costs for central and local administration and research were by the mid-seventies amounting to considerably more than £500,000 p.a.[13] What went wrong?

Most critically, the project teams became increasingly sceptical of the methodological framework within which they were originally placed. This was outlined in an *Objectives and Strategy* note issued early in the development of the programme,[14] which highlighted the assumptions inherent within the approved approach. Families suffering from chronic poverty or dependent on social services were for instance seen to exist in large numbers in particular areas, for which additional allocations of social welfare would not be enough. On the other hand, although methods of improving welfare to poorer residents were not at all fully explored, it did seem that individuals and the community as a whole contained enormous 'self-help' and 'self-determination' capacities which should be stimulated and mobilised in, amongst other directions, simply communicating fully their needs to the relevant social service departments.

Within these broad assumptions the CDP team were initially to describe their study area and to improve communications between residents and servicing agencies, for, as the HO saw it, 'one of the prime tasks of the project teams will be to improve networks of communication and co-operation, both between services and the community they exist to serve, the initial aim being to make every effort to see that everyone makes full use of the services which are already available'.[15] But changes were anticipated in services delivery too, sometimes through making them more accessible and relevant to recipients, and sometimes through seeking to 'involve the people living in the area in community schemes flowing from their own perceptions of need, and translated into action with their participation'.[16] Not that such 'action', it was anticipated, would result in the creation of large new schemes, but rather that the project as a whole would depend for its success 'on the cumulative effects of a large number of individually small but carefully co-ordinated initiatives, few of which will be wholly new'.[17] And whether new or not, it was essential, so the HO believed, that the effects of projects should be evaluated by the research teams locally, and co-ordinated nationally, to see how effective they were. To ensure that some degree of national objectivity was achieved, indicators relating to, say, improved personal care, such as reductions in deficiency diseases, or to improved family functioning, such as increased marriage rates and cohabitation stability, were to be employed to assess how successful or otherwise particular action programmes had been in reducing community and individual shortcomings.

In many ways the assumptions and methodologies framed by the HO were the root cause of the growing antagonism between central (and local) government and the project teams, for even as an exploratory statement of aims and directions, the philosophy expounded by the HO had been largely rejected elsewhere by the mid- to late 1960s. As Greve has pointed out,[18] the approach envisaged in *Objectives and Strategy* was heavily influenced by notions of social pathology which tended to put the 'blame' for deprivation on the individual and his community. The Seebohm call for improved service co-ordination, especially in areas of acute social need, had been imbued with the same spirit; and as those involved within discussions surrounding the implementation of that report were also involved in setting up the CDP, it was not at all surprising to see the overlap in assumptions. In detail these included: that deprivation occurred in small, areally discrete localities; that cycles and cultures of deprivation existed which would transmit disadvantage from one generation to the next, affecting people most acutely at certain times, such as when very young or old; that intrinsic capacities for self-help and self-organisation existed within communities which should be tapped to encourage voluntary work and the implementation of small-scale community works; and that the sheer lack of communication between services, and between service agents and clients, accentuated deprivation. There were distinct advantages in assuming deprivation to have this sort of structure. From the point of view of the HO, relatively small amounts of resource input might have cumulative effects through stimulating self- and community help projects out of all proportion to total capital expenditure. And for local authorities there were advantages too: the programme initially envisaged few radical changes, and yet provided opportunities to improve service delivery and some, admittedly small, additional resources from central government. And from everyone's point ot view, politicians, civil servants, local authorities, something was being done.

It is important to stress that this encompassing vision of deprivation which governed the early development of the programme has not been rejected to the same extent, nor in the same way, by the different teams in the field. Virtually all the projects at different times and in different ways worked within this social pathology methodology, during which time attempts were made to improve the relationship between the local authority and residents, to co-ordinate existing services, to provide advice and information centres, and to initiate low-key, often community run, projects. Thus, for instance, in the Coventry CDP an initial phase presumed that solutions might be found to the problems of deprivation within Hillfields, the selected area of research, through, amongst other strategies, improved communication between residents and the local authority, and continued dialogue with officials.[19] In the Paisley CDP, too, attempts were made to improve the co-ordination and effectiveness of services through increased linkages between preschool and community facilities.[20] Almost all the projects, too, created information services which were seen as a means both of providing information to the community and through which the community itself could make known its views and needs to the team and to the local authority. Most teams, anyway, in their initial activities wanted to understand as far as possible the working mechanisms of selected areas and their key problems, normally widely perceived to relate to housing and employment issues. At the same time information and advice centres were envisaged as useful catalysts for initiating and organising the myriad of small social projects which emerged.

This, then, was the initial direction of the CDP: deprivation was seen to relate to, and probably to be caused in part by, inefficient local authority service provision, lack of communications between residents and the authority and the lack of a 'seeding' agent capable of generating community self-help projects. Answers, therefore, should be sought out through better communications within the authority, between the authority and its clients and through the culturally beneficial effects of induced, and later, it was hoped, self-perpetuating, projects. And it was this sort of approach, with variations between projects, that typified the early direction of the programme. But really quite early on, because of the response locally from authorities and nationally as results from the different projects were collated and disseminated, a whole new methodology came to characterise the CDP. Most pertinently, this change occurred because it became increasingly clear that, irrespective of the philosophical shortcomings in social theories relating to personal and community inadequacies, the CDP initiatives based on this approach simply did not work, or were not really relevant to the causes and generation of deprivation anyway.

It had always been imagined, for instance, that local authority inefficiencies were one cause of the perpetuation of deprivation. But CDP teams in investigating this line of attack soon came to perceive this as a false line of argument. For a start some authorities simply were not prepared to make any, or any substantial, changes within their organisation, even though in private CDP recommendations might be favourably received. In effect there was frequently an inbuilt organisational conservatism which simply rejected outside suggestions, for experiment, and ensured that 'dialogues' between the authority and residents remained one-sided and peripheral. But more fundamentally, it was becoming increasingly apparent that even if authorities were prepared to innovate, there was no certainty whatsoever that they had the power to undertake changes which would reduce deprivation in any real sense. As the Coventry team state in their analysis of this issue, 'during the course of our work . . .

we had become increasingly aware of the extent to which the fortunes
of an area like Hillfields are influenced by forces operating largely
outside local democratic control'.[21] What, then, is the point of co-
ordinating local policies which in the long term have very little
relevance to the problem?

Nor, the CDP teams suggested, should the roots of deprivation be
ascribed to community or personal inadequacies. The entire focus of
social research in general was clearly moving away from seeking out
causes of deprivation at the level of the individual to an examination
of the economic and power structures within which individuals
operated, and this was as apparent in the CDP as elsewhere. In part
this was due to the increasing realisation that deprivation was not
limited to small, abnormal areas which had somehow missed out on
affluence, but had a huge and not especially areally concentrated
distribution and a growing awareness that, as Meacher pointed out,
'experience in several fields has shown that "topping up" or supple-
menting an otherwise unchanged structure of inequality cannot more
than marginally alter the contours'.[22] Certainly within the CDP it
seems clear that these sentiments were becoming widely discussed
and accepted at a very early stage, and with this transformation also
came growing eagerness to redirect the focus of action and research
strategy. The Batley team, for instance, suggested that 'while cultural
deprivation and institutional dysfunctioning co-exist with poverty
and may be contributory causes of poverty they cannot be separated
from the more fundamental external factors of economic structure
and national and local government policies'.[23] This comes over more
baldly from Hatch, commenting on the 1974 Inter-Project Report and
seeing in it deprivation defined as 'a product of structural factors—of
the decisions by large companies affecting employment opportunities, of the functioning of the housing market, or of the distribution
of political power'.[24] Perhaps not surprisingly, parallel American
experience encountered a similar discrepancy between what policy
makers have been doing and what they actually believe are root
causes of deprivation. In Cleveland, for instance, a recent planning
policy report concludes that the problems of the city have less to do
with questions such as land uses and zoning—the traditional domain
of planners—and more to do with 'personal and municipal poverty,
unemployment, neighbourhood deterioration, abandonment, crime,
inadequate mobility and so on'.[25] And the CDP within the British
context, freed from the immediate constraints of government, expanded
this structuralist line of reasoning in a quite radical and unique manner.

This has occurred through the voluminous publications emanating from the CDP teams at both local and central levels, covering an enormous range of analytical and prescriptive issues. Any attempt to categorise these findings will inevitably merely scratch the surface. But nevertheless some trends are apparent. Initially a considerable emphasis was placed on the development of information and advice centres. Probably it was always intended that these would offer more than simply advice, and in the event some of them rapidly adopted more radical stances. Residents themselves, for instance began to run some,[26] and advocacy, rather than simply the dissemination of information was widely accepted as an acceptable operational model.[27] This inevitably generated conflicts between the CDP organised centres and the local authority in a manner not anticipated by earlier co-operative models of interaction. But, of course, to some extent conflicts at this local scale were being perceived anyway as irrelevant to the central issue of deprivation. As Greve commented in 1972 in an analysis of some early reports from local CDPs, there was an 'early identification of the origins of many social and economic problems as lying outside the deprived areas, and the corollary that the solutions to these problems can only be obtained by influencing the sources is one of the early conclusions reached by the projects'.[28]

And indeed from that time the focus of examination moved away from activating social experiments at the local level towards collating and expanding locally determined findings into national programmes. In housing, for instance, a report into inadequacies in the government's improvement policy within eight local projects concludes that additional new centrally implemented financial and legal powers are needed to improve working-class housing.[29] Other reports on housing suggest, too, that reforms are needed in finance structure to ensure that more centrally allocated funds go on constructing houses and are not spent on subsidising tax relief or the profits of the many professional groups involved in the housing market.[30] A number of other studies, such as that at Coventry,[31] conclude that the details of local housing programmes are often too ambitious and lead to blighting and delay, and that a much greater emphasis should be placed on longer-term financial planning aimed at rehabilitating existing properties, which in turn will require more efficient central government financial planning. Similarly, an analysis of the leasehold problems in the Birmingham CDP sees the necessity for centrally administered legal reforms to overcome this locally perceived, but in fact very widespread, problem.[32] In the field of income maintenance and benefits, too, there has been a growing awareness that the extent of locally perceived problems will need national reforms if advances are to be made. Evidence from Coventry suggests, for instance, that better national advertising and administration of substantially higher benefits will be needed to reduce local poverty,[33] and a report on the Batley CDP concludes that there is a need for a new political initiative at central government level 'to override departmental interests and direct a rapid integration of the principal means-tested benefits and the production of a single claim form'.[34]

Interestingly enough, anyway, the teams have not interpreted income maintenance solely in terms of improved benefit delivery but have expanded the definition to include all forms of social welfare and community resources, many of which are seen as having maldistributions which militate against the residents of poorer areas. Local authority resources are one aspect of this wider question, for instance. Existing patterns of central government allocation are seen as unsatisfactory in that they are unstable from year to year and do not compensate poor authorities adequately. Instead, the CDP would want to see a system of local taxation, equalisation schemes to balance out variations between authorities and an Urban Needs Pool.[35] The latter might be used to help certain sectors of the population seen as particularly deprived. In Coventry, for instance, facilities for the old are seen as quite inadequate and a new concerted policy from authorities, central government, and trade unions is mooted.[36] Elsewhere similar problems occur with a marked local impact: poor transport in Cumbria,[37] the need for better playground facilities in North Tyneside; and helping immigrants in Oldham,[38] for example.

But in no field is the interaction between local, national and international scales of operation seen as so marked as in the employment market. From all the teams there is evidence that acute employment problems have occurred within older urban areas through rationalisation and reorganisation of industry as a result of financial, technical and market changes which in spatial terms have encouraged the migration or closure of considerable amounts of older industry. In Cleator Moor it is the iron ore industry,[39] in Saltley the gas and railways,[40] in Canning Town the port industries;[41] in all the CDP areas in fact the older primary and secondary industries have been declining and not been replaced, and the process has left behind substantial numbers of poor, unemployed, often unskilled people.[42]

And increasingly it is clear that for a number of the CDP teams industrial shrinkage is not one aspect of urban deprivation, it is the main cause of it. The decline in jobs correlates directly with reduced family and community incomes, and ultimately with poverty. To some extent, the teams believe, declining incomes should be compensated by increased benefits; but the main prong of attack should be directed towards the financial and spatial control of private industry. Thus Flynn, in commenting on the output of the Saltley team, points out that job decline was seen as massive and that 'the one solution the team sees in this area is radical change in the ownership and structure of industry in the long term, and in the short term, resistance to the effects of change by the local labour force'.[43] This sort of positive policy would clearly require action at both local and national levels. In the case of the former, information would need to be collected about land, ownership and production patterns; consultative committees of trade unions, trade councils and small firms would need to be established, and political initiatives instituted to create alliances between the neighbourhood, the factory floor and sympathetic political parties.[44] At the same time local authorities should be much more prepared to support inner city initiatives and to redirect their interests inwards and not outwards, as has tended to be the case. In adopting such an attitude, authorities are therefore envisaged by the CDP as helping to implement an avowedly interventionist approach by, say, monitoring changes in local industrial structures, by allowing facilities for information gathering to be used by trade unionists, and through powers of land acquisition.

But if radical changes were to be introduced to counteract national and indeed international economic trends, the main focus of action would need to be at the central level through better working-class political organisation and through modifications in central government policy. In the case of the former, labour organisation is seen as fundamental to the entire programme. It will be required specifically to ensure that sufficient political thrust is achieved 'so that measures can be formulated and implemented which will begin to control investment in the social interest, to produce a socially rational distribution of industry, and to ensure that the costs and benefits of industrial change are shared evenly by all sections of the community'.[45] And once political organisation has been attained it should be used to lobby for specific modifications in central government policy: a more refined regional policy to help inner city areas; greater intervention by central government through acquisition and planning agreements, in the organisation and operation of industry; the decentralisation of D of I grant administration to the local authority level to allow the local community itself to decide which industries, under what agreements should be supported; greater worker participation; more sensitive use of government contracts.

This concern for greater intervention in the employment market essentially to benefit a sector of society is then one, and perhaps the most important, cornerstone in an increasingly radical framework which came to characterise the output from many, although by no means all of the local projects. As an approach, through its emphasis on differing sectoral goals and powers, it clearly rejects traditional consensus models of social interaction, which certainly were assumed when setting up the initiative. In 1969 it was, for instance, anticipated that one of the aims of the project teams would be that of 'securing the co-operation of the providing services (both statutory and voluntary) in developing a strategy of support which is both comprehensive and relevant to the particular needs of each area'.[46] This methodology represents a sort of rational, pluralistic approach in which everyone acts sensibly in reorganising the provision of services, and the allocation of resources generally, to iron out malfunctioning within the system. But this simply did not work, according to the CDP, partly because local authorities were often not at all enthusiastic in supporting the aims of the projects, and partly because more disadvantaged sectors of society just did not receive enough in the way of compensatory resources through existing power structures.

So instead of labouring fruitlessly under existing political formulas, an increasing proportion of the CDP teams adopted, explicitly or otherwise, new operative methodologies based on theories of conflict, often within an avowedly Marxist framework.[47] In this view of social interaction different groups are envisaged as having widely different goals and manipulatory powers. Traditionally what has happened is that working-class groups have simply not been adequately organised nor had a sufficient level of political consciousness to appreciate, and if necessary oppose, changing structural conditions which have directly militated against their interests. But agencies such as the CDP, active at both local and national levels, freed from the immediate constraints of government, might be in an ideal position to stimulate and direct this necessary political organisation.

The genesis of this more radical framework can be seen most

acutely in the evolving approach of local teams such as that at Coventry, which has recorded its changing strategies as steadily more structurally orientated theories of deprivation became accepted.[48] Initially attempts were made to improve co-ordination and communication between residents and public agencies, an approach modified later to an apparently futile phase in which efforts were made to alter local authority attitudes and policy from within, and finally through to a much more radical and overtly political third phase, in which the emphasis was placed on improving the organisational ability and the political relevance of working-class groups—both geographical, within the neighbourhood, and sectoral, at the factory floor level. And certainly this transition at the local level was paralleled in turn by increasingly radical, nationally orientated positions on the part of the CDP. Sectoral biases within public spending cuts were pointed out, for instance,[49] calls made for greater political organisation on the part of public sector employees,[50] and efforts heightened in general to increase public ownership of national wealth and to generate greater political awareness on the part of working-class groups.

Yet this should not be taken to mean that the CDP developed a uniformly radical position, because strategies differed remarkably between some teams eager to retain close contacts with parent local authorities, and others which adopted more antagonistic positions. Indeed what makes the CDP quite the most interesting of the urban experiments is exactly this variegated pattern of operation. Whilst this might make general evaluation difficult, it allowed different strategies to be explored, it highlighted the sorts of problems action-research projects are prone to, and it illustrated the sorts of contradictions a relatively undefined experiment such as the CDP will accentuate. And these contradictions are worth exploring, not simply because of the light they throw on the history of the CDP, but because they tell us a great deal about central government's attitude to deprivation, the problems inherent in local projects operating within structuralist frameworks, and the almost inevitable conflict between action and allied research.

CONTRADICTIONS BETWEEN THE TEAMS AND CENTRAL AND LOCAL GOVERNMENT

Close and consistent co-operation between government and the teams had initially been regarded as an important, perhaps unique, characteristic of the programme. But after almost ten years of operation it seems clear that really from quite an early stage disillusionment set in in both camps which, well before the end of the programme, erupted into outright conflict. Why?

At the local level is seems that one of the main reasons for dissension was because relationships between the project, its community and the authority were not adequately defined before the programme began in earnest. The CDPs were, an early commentary suggested, 'to act as catalysts, critics and innovators; to stimulate, teach, question, propose and implement, but to do so in a constructive manner',[51] which, it was envisaged, would help to make existing services more effective and to promote more unorthodox arrangements, with the agreement of the authority. This sort of catalytic influence should take place through policy critiques which, if found valid, would help to modify existing procedures. To some extent this process might be refined, as happened in Coventry and Oldham for instance, through the team actually becoming part of the governing system, sitting on area committees and the like, where it would have a more direct influence on policy but would come face to face with the day-to-day constraints encountered in local authority decision making.

Now this sort of model of interaction had considerable advantages from the point of view of elected members. Relatively minor changes in policy, if any, would be implemented at little cost, quite possibly with actual cost benefits; power remained with the authority itself, and any dissension from either the community or the CDP could be channelled into semi-official forums where local officials could outline the sorts of constraints operative within authorities, and on the basis of these 'bargain' with the community over what often were minimal modifications anyway. And at the same time the authority, of course, received central government resources. It was too good to miss.

And not all CDP teams rejected this approach either since, depending very much on the composition of the council, changes in policy and resource allocation might be altered to the benefit of the more deprived. Better then, one argument went, to achieve immediate, relatively minor improvements than cut off discussions and wait for the revolution. One CDP publication, for instance, indicated how community groups might achieve more from authorities as a result of appreciating the mechanics of decision making and the personalities of politicians.[52] And indeed some teams did discern a welcome change in attitude, such as the Oldham CDP, who saw 'some small evidence of shifts in attitude and response'.[53]

But for most of the teams this was not enough. Local authorities were seen increasingly as monolithic, bureaucratic institutions unwilling to countenance major changes, quick to blame other public bodies for deficiencies, and most importantly weak in relation to many problems, particularly the control of employment markets. Sitting down and working out minor changes in their administration did nothing to alleviate the root causes of deprivation, and might in fact be counterproductive, since it used up the team's and the community's time and effort to no effect. What needed to be done was to organise working-class communities at the local level through advice and advocacy centres and to secure strong community and trade union collective commitment to the making of meaningful changes.[54] This was conflict theory in practice, and clearly, because it bypassed traditional local authority institutions and generated far greater demands, many overtly political, it was unlikely to find favour in council chambers. In the event the CDPs at Cumbria, Newham and Batley closed before completing their five-year programmes, and the last case especially saw an open conflict between the new Kirklees authority, created in 1974, and the local teams, whose advisory centre had advocated measures unpopular with local politicians.[55]

Not that relations with central government have on the whole been much better either. Originally, it seems that the projects were to examine the effects of central and local government activities on the ground. As Greve saw it in 1972, 'the evolution of the projects, the social and administrative situations in which they operate, their strategies and the results are recorded with a view to providing a rich source of material, for local authorities and central government in particular, about social problems and the effectiveness or ineffectiveness of various policies and administrative forms.'[56] This is the 'up, along and down' model of policy evaluation: policies are monitored at the local level and any recommendations for change sent to the central agency, which responds by altering its programme. As an approach it had considerable benefits for central government: something was being done at minimal costs, changes proposed within this model would normally be well within the compass of political reality, and nothing basic was being questioned.

However, the model assumed a subservient CDP. But by the early 1970s the teams were perceiving deprivation as a result of structural changes, especially in housing and employment markets, and not because of personal inadequacies or institutional malfunctioning. In this later vision of things the 'up, along and down' model was at the very least irrelevant, since it would not accommodate the sort of basic policy modifications at the centre being increasingly advocated locally by the teams. These tended away from 'tinkering' with official, and largely discredited, policies, and towards a framework of strong local and national working-class organisation, campaigning for much greater public control and accountability. In this model the CDPs can be seen as a loose federation of projects involved with both local and national aspects of deprivation and their interconnecting mechanisms, in which local findings would be diffused through a national co-ordinating framework and locally through 'ripple' effects as allied sectoral and neighbourhood groups become associated with the parent CDP.[57] In this approach the projects and the HO set off on very divergent and ultimately irreconcilable paths: the one towards radical 'democratic' and interventionist policies, the other eventually towards administrative arrangements devised to quieten, even eliminate this Pandora's Box. Certainly as the teams moved ever further away from the low-key, 'pump-priming' projects the HO had in mind back in the late 1960s, more and more hints were given to local authorities as to the possibilities of a premature demise and less and less encouragement given to the teams to co-ordinate and disseminate their findings nationally.

CONTRADICTIONS BETWEEN THE TEAMS AND THE LOCAL COMMUNITY

One of the original and seemingly unique features of the programme was the emphasis on the participation of residents in identifying deprivations, proposing solutions and sharing in their implementation. This side of the project was seen as enormously important by early commentators. To Holman, for instance, the prospect of the granting 'of public money without sanctions and with every prospect of angering local authorities would be a major policy breakthrough'.[58] And for the *New Society* of the time, if 'the community teams manage to energise neighbourhood populations, convince them that they are in a position to make local government serve their needs, we may be witnessing a major new departure in both British politics and British social reform'.[59]

Many of the early teams did in fact take their starting-off point to be 'the community'. Liverpool, Southwark and Coventry, for instance, all placed a strong emphasis on working with local people on their needs as they perceived them within the study neighbourhood.

This approach was very much in line with early HO advice, which advocated a number of smaller local initiatives improving whatever could be remedied without large-scale redevelopment 'in a way which progressively builds up the capacity of the neighbourhood to express its needs and feelings'.[60] And indeed the impressive number of playgroups, recreational projects, youth and old people's schemes, local newspapers and so on highlight the continuing relevance of the low-key, community initiated and run development. It had also been anticipated that the accent on community development would be important because of the fear that the impending reorganisation of local authorities would create larger and more anonymous institutions, hence making it even more necessary to strengthen community resources and skills, and to forge closer, more sensitive and responsive links between citizens and the enlarged authorities. The development of local community schemes would therefore, it was believed, highlight the possibilities of this sort of action, its optimal relationship with official delivery agencies and quick rectification of shortcomings in normal provision.

But of course, early on in the development of the CDP programme, the shift in emphasis moved from local to national government scales of operation as basic structural factors were seen to have a profound and primary relationship with deprivation. This was perceived officially, and attempts were made to integrate this new methodology within the programme. Specifically, the close causative links between national, structural factors and deprivation were acknowledged, but the teams were asked to develop a dual strategy which included a substantial local element aimed at expanding 'the community's participation in supplying data about needs and aspirations, about the effects of policies and in controlling resources'.[61] It was anyway felt that the dichotomy between central and local policies was something of a false one; centrally devised policies would always need to be evaluated in terms of their local effects.

But in practice changing spatial emphases within the programme have created difficulties. The inevitable criticism which can be directed at locally stimulated projects within a theoretical framework stressing national and international structural changes is their irrelevance. No matter how well playgroups, nurseries, summer schools, advice centres and the like are organised, if the basic cause of deprivation is ascribed primarily to changing economic forces, there is a limit to the effectiveness of the small-scale effort. Of course, to some extent self-generated and -maintained schemes can help to stimulate political awareness and organisational capabilities, but then the transition between local grievances and national, coherent, permanent and powerful lobbies is notoriously wide.

It is interesting too in this context to see the similarities between such problems and similar ones encountered in the States. Marris and Rein[62] have pointed out the strong community action element within deprivation programmes there in the 1960s which, although apparently granting enormous implementary powers to residents, in fact created substantial difficulties. One obvious shortcoming was that as the community achieved its organisational awareness through the project team, power still tended to remain with the latter, since it created the administrative structure through which power was vested. There was also the allied point that even when organisational arrangements had been decided, the sorts of problems being inflicted on poorer neighbourhoods, notably poor housing and unemployment, remained beyond the political scope of resident committees anyway. Similar British experience raised questions within the CDP programme. If the teams themselves increasingly perceived problems to lie at national scales of operation, what reason was there to imagine that as local residents organised and implemented projects, this realisation would not occur to them too? And how powerful then, especially once the catalytic influence of the team diminished, would forces need to be to forge local groups into national and viable agencies? Is not the ultimate conclusion to the CDPs' prognosis that, although rigid central/local dichotomies are too simple, basic improvements in the generation and distribution of deprivation will never occur at the local level, no matter how much organisational expertise is assimilated, but ultimately only through changes in national policy working their way through to the local level?

CONTRADICTIONS WITHIN AND BETWEEN PROJECTS

It is not at all easy to summarise the 'CDP position', since although its lasting impact has undoubtedly been through the diffusion of structuralist arguments, that should not be taken to mean that all projects have moved in the same direction, or at the same rate, nor indeed that conflicts have not arisen within individual teams. One obvious example of the latter occurred within the Coventry team, where some members of the project, in a dissenting note,[63] expressed their unwillingness to go along entirely with the rapid transition in methodology towards a neo-Marxist third phase of operation, which stressed very heavily a causative link between fluctuations in the car market and the position of many unskilled workers within Hillfields. For two members of the team this was not a totally acceptable position: statistics could not confirm the basic premise, nor was there any action to back this hypothesis, even down to a neglect to discuss the approach with local trade unions. Moreover those dissenting from the main report felt that the second phase, within which attention had been focused on attempting to understand and modify policies within relevant public bodies, had not been evaluated to a satisfactory degree.

But on the whole dissensions within projects have not been as acute as those between different teams. The drift to a more radical programme has not been carried out to anything like the same extent within different teams; attitudes within, say, the Newcastle, North Tyneside, Birmingham and Canning Town projects being that much more radical than the Paisley, West Glamorgan or Oldham experiments for instance. These divisions should certainly not be over-stressed, partly because, ostensibly at least, a considerable emphasis within all the projects has remained on local-scale activities.[64] In Birmingham, for instance, considerable aid has been given to the local immigrant community; in Cumbria research has been under-taken into the direct local effects of a regional growth pole economic strategy; in West Glamorgan promotional work has been done into the problems of industrial retraining; in Newcastle there has been a steady emphasis on information provision and advocacy, and so on. But what does tend to differ between teams is the extent to which they have been prepared to expand local findings and initiatives into nationally orientated structuralist positions. Contrast, for instance, the Coventry team, which by the end of its period of action-research was explaining the problems of its study area in terms of fluctuations in local industry, local finance and the economy in general, and hence seeking solutions to urban deprivation through greater public ownership and control, with the attitude of the West Glamorgan or Oldham teams. Commenting on detractors of the former for example, one member suggested that 'critics of CDP consider that it can only be effective on marginal issues but they have not yet realised how important such effects might be'.[65] This apology for a more incre-mental, perhaps realistic, outlook would clearly be in sympathy with the position of the Oldham team too. Here one member, in discussing the structure of a council estate, expanded on the operative constraints within the project as a whole and admitted that whereas the team rejected notions of personal and community pathology, it was prepared to work within an environment which accepted the existence of the local authority and the constraints this brought with it, and within a methodological framework which allowed, albeit unwillingly, structural inequalities in society; the 'Oldham CDP has not tried to "sloganise" away reality by issuing its personal quasi-sociological/political/philosophical treatise on how the world ought to be'[66] is his conclusion. Similarly for the Southwark team, one possible line of advance is seen to be with improved area management techniques which should help to provide increased access to, and power over, local authority resources on the part of both residents and relevant ward members without impugning basic administrative and political organisation.[67] Clearly radical and unprecedented change is not for everyone.

CONTRADICTIONS BETWEEN ACTION AND RESEARCH

It had always been intended that the CDP would be an action-research project in that each local action team would work in association with a research unit set up, preferably, in a local institution. In fact administrative arrangements were not always as simple as might be imagined, and at times there was a considerable geographical split between the two sides of certain initiatives. The Social Administration Department at York, for instance, linked up with the action team in Cumbria. But whatever the spatial divisions between the two sides, formal working arrangements, it was anticipated, would operate according to a strategy laid down early on in the development of the experiment.[68] This outlined the functions of the research team as being description of the area, evaluation of the action programme and the communication of information.

Description was seen as an essential and early prerequisite for any effective research programme. A long list of social and physical criteria was presented, which central government considered should be provided as a baseline against which to compare subsequent changes, if any, in the structure of the study neighbourhood. Social action projects themselves should be described too: why they were undertaken, by whom, at what costs, with what anticipated and actual results. These results could in turn form the basis for examining underlying social and cultural hypotheses which underpinned the entire experiment, and for the delimitation of more viable definition of concepts such as 'deprivation'. The conclusions emerging from these evaluation processes should finally be disseminated to politicians and others involved in social policy decision making. The results were thus not to remain introverted, but rather individuals and groups were to co-ordinate findings and publish these nationally under the general aegis of the central research team. That was the theory.

But in practice relations between the two sides, action and research, have been notably unhappy. There were acute practical problems to start with. Fruitless negotiations with academic establishments, delays in appointing staff both at central and local level, and poor phasing between the commencement of work by action and research teams led to basic working constraints early on in the development of the project. But later more fundamental issues began to emerge. From the point of view of the action team, research could take on the appearance of Big Brother, examining activities without contributing in a direct way to alleviating deprivation.[69] But for some of the research teams this missed the point entirely. CDP was not to be seen as an attempt to provide additional resources specifically or primarily to the twelve lucky areas, but an experiment in setting up and evaluating projects at the local level, the results from which should be collated nationally to direct and modify central policy effective throughout the country. Research was therefore in this analysis not a question of fact finding subservient to the direct local efforts of the action teams, but a process of in-depth evaluation of hypotheses and assumptions through, amongst other parameters, the findings of the action teams.

Tensions of this sort became increasingly acute within some of the projects. In Southwark, for instance, there was a gradual disengagement of the research teams over the question of the creation or otherwise of even a broad strategic framework of action, which the research team saw as essential. This dispute in turn highlighted the general and more basic problem that the research team here saw a distinct difference between evaluation, which was their concern, and collaboration, which need not be. Conflict such as was apparent at Southwark was apparently accentuated by inadequate servicing from the central research team which, so some local teams considered, did not produce the necessary framework for the analysis and continued development of the local projects.[70] Certainly the central team seemed uncertain whether its role was to direct, co-ordinate or monitor local projects adopting ever more divergent paths.

Perhaps the problems between action and research within the CDP should not be divorced from difficulties possibly intrinsically inherent in such a partnership. In the States, for instance, the same sort of problems apparently emerged. To Marris and Rein, examining these phenomena in experiment in the 1960s, it seemed that 'research cannot interpret the present until it knows the answers to its ultimate questions. Action cannot foresee what questions to ask until it has interpreted the present.'[71] And really they are different intellectual processes wherever the conflict between them arises. Action may work better in ignorance, without clearly defined paths, redirecting its attentions in a somewhat *ad hoc* fashion according to the changing perceptions its own efforts produce. But research needs aims, is better at abstracting a few variables for analysis and may be totally undermined and made virtually incomparable with other action-research projects elsewhere if the action it is attempting to evaluate moves off in an unpredictable fashion.

CONCLUSION

Attempts to summarise the influence and activity of the CDP present problems totally different to similar exercises elsewhere, because of the sheer quantity and variety of its descriptive, analytical and prescriptive findings. Early on in the development of the project, it is interesting to see criticisms of it in terms of its assumedly too close relationship with local authorities, too divorced partnership from activists and its working premise that change ought to be engineered through consensus dialogue.[72] One test of its relevance was also then seen to be 'whether it can pull together its experience, identify successful strategies and set out a framework for policy development in poverty areas'.[73] How markedly inappropriate these misgivings seem now. It has not worked entirely within the compass and approval of local or central government, activists have been involved, consensus has been rejected and claims for its 'success' could be made, although no coherent viable overall strategy for future development has been presented.

'Success' is a very relative concept. Certainly the government has not welcomed its findings as wholeheartedly as those from the IAS, although, considering the sorts of analysis being presented by the

CDP in the mid-1970s, that is hardly surprising. Yet there have been real successes. At the local level the teams have been able to create community support groups, law and advice centres, neighbourhood councils, decentralised administrations and a whole host of small-scale projects. Many of these were community run and certainly the CDP did much to highlight the innate abilities of residents to originate and implement community schemes. So much so, in fact, that the HO announced in 1977 that a Community Projects Foundation was to be set up to help communities to stand up and compete with officialdom over the development of their areas. The CDP might reject the ultimate validity of the scale of operation inherent in these essentially localised experiments, but its own stimulatory activities in certain communities were undoubtedly locally successful and nationally influential.

There is evidence, too, that some CDP teams enjoyed success within their parent authority. In Coventry, for instance, as a result of CDP initiatives certain administrative changes were introduced, including free legal and welfare surgeries.[74] In Oldham as well, possibly because of the more pragmatic, reformist position of the team, there were advances. According to the team, it seemed that its activities had induced a more sensitive appreciation on the part of the authority of the consequences of its actions.[75] Analyses were more socially orientated, officers showed a wider social perspective in their activities, improved contacts between the authority and residents were achieved, member and community participation in local affairs was heightened, the constraints of government diffused to residents and community awareness accentuated. To some extent these advances might be temporary, and the essential political and administrative support which this team obtained for community development be diluted after its demise. But nevertheless, within the favourable environment that Oldham offered, a constructive, reformist action team, divorced from the day-to-day realities of administration, but very much integrated into wider policy making bodies, undoubtedly considered that it had altered authority attitudes. The authority thought so too. 'A more ready response is available and more careful consideration is given to cases presented by the groups within the CDP area', is its evaluation of the long-term consequences.[76]

Whether that is a particularly important conclusion is, however, a different matter. The teams themselves pointed out the necessity to examine processes operative at wider scales if urban deprivation was to be understood, still less ameliorated. And anyway the CDP was

E

not devised primarily to improve local authority attitudes within the selected areas, but rather to undertake local initiatives which could form the basis of a national poverty programme. Ostensibly it has not. Attempts have been made to close it. Politicians ignore it, teams are disbanded. Largely this is because so many commentators consider that the strong emphasis on 'dramatic conflict and sweeping social and economic upheaval is absurd',[77] containing as it does assumptions about structural causes of deprivation which call for more radical policies 'than either of the main political parties is going to take up under present conditions'.[78] The whole exercise can be validly perceived in one way as a political con-trick to show politicians 'cared',[79] but quite evidently, in terms of the cash and commitment paid to it, it was foredoomed to be a blustering but not a biting effort.

And yet the real impact of the CDP may be far more deep-rooted than is normally admitted, enough for instance to allow one analyst to consider it '*the* British attempt to tackle the deprivation of inner city and declining industrial areas, not excluding the D. of E's IAS'.[80] This sort of evaluation can be justified on a number of counts.

First, because of the sheer volume of analytical and prescriptive publications emerging from the teams, covering a whole range of social policies and administration, some of them of immediate and practical relevance.

Second, because the teams have highlighted how bureaucratic and inappropriate many local authority decision making structures can be. Many would certainly see parallels with the Southwark team's evaluation of that local authority's administrative structure as hierarchical, 'with procedures which are increasingly bureaucratic in the sense that as departments have become larger and more complex in their organisations and specialisation has meant officers performing narrower, less comprehensive roles, the departments have become more immune to outside pressures and the potential division between the interests of the organisation and the needs of the public has widened'.[81] Efficiency, corporateness, specialisation may be widely divorced from equity, welfare or administrative justice.

Third, because the CDP has shown just how closely interactive are local and central economies,[82] and just how problems in the latter can elicit acute deterioration in the former. The logical progression in this sort of thinking has been to move the focus of attention away from attempting to alleviate urban deprivation at the local level towards national policy modifications. The decision to allow CCPs to embrace entire authorities, and not small areas within them, has been credited to the influence of CDPs and their concern for linking larger administrative areas to the localised effects of their policy decisions.[83]

Fourth, because the CDP has encouraged the drift away from consensus and pluralistic models of social interaction and decision making. Cosy notions that different sectoral groups have similar goals, or if different goals at least equal powers of political influence and manipulation, needed firm handling, and the CDP has done much to undermine them. Working-class sectors have interests very different from those of other groups, and are not normally in a position to apply political influence commensurate with their numbers.

Fifth, and the most important reason, the teams have stimulated the diffusion of structuralist arguments of deprivation. Batley and Edwards have pointed out how the CDP took up lines of thinking which were totally divorced from, say, the social pathology arguments inherent in the propping up mechanisms of UA.[84] It has been this line of reasoning, blaming deprivation on changes within economic, educational and housing markets, allied to weak working-class bargaining positions, that has come to characterise an increasing proportion of the CDP output. And it is a message which has not all been lost on politicians and civil servants. Recent government acceptance, for instance, that changing employment structures have much to do with urban deprivation, and the heavy and quite late emphasis within the IAS on the regeneration of manufacturing industry and better income maintenance policies, are clear indications of that. Of course some of the later CDP publications, with heavily political, largely destructive and descriptive analyses of problems, are likely to fall on very deaf ears all round. But not all analyses working within structuralist constraints need assume nothing can happen short of huge and unprecedented changes. Corina, for instance, in discussing housing allocation in Oldham, points out that 'there are gaps in the monolithic fabric of structuralism which permit the belief, albeit hypothetical, that certain interventions are possible within the structural constraints and these interventions carry the possibility of ameliorating some of the conditions which exist . . .'.[85] Structuralist arguments can certainly be invoked without necessarily assuming the futility of all change at the margins.

Urban programmes need the maverick and the unorthodox. There could be little confidence in a programme entirely acceptable to central government, for after all, its policies have done little to improve or even to hold steady the decline of urban areas. The CDP was never going to be popular in official circles once it moved from playgrounds to politics. But social reform requires a few committed individuals to pave the way. The CDP has done this for the British urban programme. Not all of its recommendations will ever be achieved, nor will some of its assumptions be widely held outside a small political circle. But it has done more than any other initiative to promote and examine a completely new vision of deprivation which, despite the disturbing nature of its profound implications, central government has found hard to ignore.

NOTES TO CHAPTER 6

1 For details of early assumptions behind CDPs, see CDP Press Release, HO, 'A Major Experiment in Improving the Social Services for Those Most in Need', 16.7.1969; and *Hansard*, Vol. 787, 25.7.1969.
2 S. Hatch, E. Fox and C. Legg, 1977.
3 For details of selected areas, see NCDP Inter-Project Report, 1974.
4 J. Bennington, 1970.
5 Paisley CDP, 1976.
6 S. Hatch, E. Fox and C. Legg (as 2).
7 *Hansard*, Vol. 835, 28.4.1972.
8 NCDP (as 3).
9 NCDP Forward Plan, 1975.
10 *Hansard*, Vol. 905, 9.2.1976.
11 *Hansard*, Vol. 905, 12.2.1976.
12 *Hansard*, Vol. 878, 31.7.1974, when about 110 staff were employed in either action projects or research.
13 *Hansard*, Vol. 899, 10.11.75, when Lyon indicated that the costs of the central administration and research element of the CDP, but excluding specific social action projects, was running at about £450,000 p.a.
14 HO, *CDP Objectives and Strategy*, 1970.
15 HO (as 14), par. 8.
16 HO (as 14), par. 13.
17 HO (as 14), par. 15.
18 J. Greve, 1973, pars. 5–10.
19 Coventry CDP Final Report, Part I, 1975, Ch. 5.
20 Paisley CDP, 1974.
21 Coventry CDP (as 19), par. 6.23.
22 M. Meacher, 'The Politics of Positive Discrimination', in H. Glennerster and S. Hatch (eds.), 1974.
23 M. McGrath, 1976, p. 61.
24 S. Hatch, 1974, p. 97.
25 M. Krumholz, J. Cogger and J. Linner, 1975, p. 298.
26 See, for instance, N. Bond, Coventry CDP Occasional Paper No. 2.

27 See, for instance, H. Butcher, I. Cole and A. Glen, 1976.
28 J. Greve, 1972B, p. 4.
29 NCDP, *The Poverty of the Improvement Programme*, 1975.
30 NCDP, *Profits Against Houses*, 1976.
31 P. Skelton and N. Ginsburg, 'Planning and the Decline of Hillfields', Working Paper No. 2 in Coventry CDP Final Report, Part II, 1975.
32 See, for instance, Birmingham CDP, *The Cost of Buying Your Freehold*, 1975.
33 See, for instance, N. Bond, Coventry CDP Occasional Paper No. 4, 1972; and N. Bond, 'Income Support and Citizens' Rights', Working Paper No. 3 in Coventry CDP (as 31).
34 J. Bradshaw, P. Taylor Gooby and R. Lees, 1976, p. 2.
35 C. Tyrrell, 1975.
36 See, for instance, G. Sharp, 'Support Services for the Elderly', Working Paper No. 4 in Coventry CDP (as 31).
37 R. Sugden, 1975.
38 See NCDP (as 9).
39 R. Barber, Cleator Moor Local Studies Group.
40 Birmingham CDP, *Workers on the Scrap Heap*, 1975.
41 Canning Town CDP, 1975.
42 N. Moor, 1975, outlines industrial experiences in four CDPs.
43 N. Flynn, 1977.
44 Many of these recommendations are from Southwark Trades Council and J. C. Roberts (Southwark CDP), 1976.
45 NCDP, *The Costs of Industrial Change*, 1977.
46 HO (as 14), par. 10.
47 For one example of this transition, see J. Bennington, 'The Flaw in the Pluralist Heaven. Changing Strategies in the Coventry CDP', in R. Lees and G. Smith, (eds.), 1975.
48 Coventry CDP (as 19).
49 NCDP and Counter-Information Services.
50 NCDP, *Gilding the Ghetto*, 1977.
51 J. Greve, 1972A, p. 6.
52 L. Corina, 1975.
53 NCDP (as 9), p. 55.
54 See A. Mackay, 'Expectations of a Local Project', in R. Lees and G. Smith (as 47), for differing expectations on the part of the authority and the team as to how a project should evolve.
55 J. Edginton, 1974.
56 J. Greve, 1972A, p. 5.
57 For an expansion of this process, see G. Green, 'Community Power', in H. Glennerster and S. Hatch (as 22).
58 R. Holman, 1969.
59 *New Society* Editorial, 1969.
60 HO (as 14), par. 16.
61 J. Greve, 1972B, p. 5.
62 P. Marris and M. Rein, 1974, p. 24.
63 G. Sharp and B. Rowley.
64 See details in NCDP (as 9).

65 M. Howell, 'The Glyncorrwg Community', in M. Broady (ed.), 1973, p. 66.
66 N. Shenton, 1976, p. 17.
67 A. Davis, N. McIntosh and J. Williams, 1977.
68 J. Greve, *CDP Research Strategy.*
69 For a detailed exposition of conflicts between action and research in Southwark CDP, see S. Hatch, E. Fox and C. Legg (as 2).
70 For details of this shortcoming see M. Mayo, 'History of CDP' in R. Lees and G. Smith (as 47).
71 P. Marris and M. Rein (as 62), p. 258.
72 See, for instance, J. Bennington, 'The CDP', in E. Butterworth and R. Holman (eds.), 1975; and R. Holman, 'Combating Social Deprivation', in R. Holman (ed.), 1970.
73 G. Smith, 1974, p. 382.
74 Coventry City Council, 1975.
75 L. Corina, 1977.
76 Oldham MB, 1976.
77 J. Pratt, 1975, p. 789.
78 S. Hatch, E. Fox and C. Legg (as 2), p. 289.
79 So interpreted by J. Higgins, 1974.
80 G. Weightman, 1976, p. 608.
81 A. Davis, I. McIntosh and J. Williams (as 67).
82 A. Rowe, 1975.
83 Suggested by *New Society* Editorial, 1975.
84 R. Batley and J. Edwards, 'CDP and the Urban Programme' in R. Lees and G. Smith (as 47).
85 L. Corina, 1976.

Chapter 7

POSITIVE DISCRIMINATION AND ITS DEMISE

One basic traditional assumption of the urban programme has been that deprivation occurs in areally discrete and identifiable pockets, usually in older urban districts, and hence that its eradication will most readily be achieved through the creation of projects operating at local levels and not, on the other hand, through city-wide or national programmes aimed at more deprived people as opposed to areas. There are clear advantages in presupposing that deprivation has a markedly concentrated distribution, for, as Sinfield has pointed out, 'an all-out attack on a number of specific areas is much more administratively attractive—certainly cheaper and potentially quicker—than the careful re-examination of the basic fabric of society'.[1]

And precisely because it represents a simple and attractive proposition, it has been widely advocated by politicians and policy makers, and the whole history of policy innovation within the last decade is littered with assertions to the effect that deprivations of most types occur within small areas and can be eradicated through the funnelling of additional resources to these localities. Milner Holland, for instance, talks of the need for concerted action to improve housing conditions in London in certain 'areas of special control',[2] the Plowden report talks of a vicious circle of deprivation operating in certain, usually urban, areas, which ought to be removed through area based discrimination,[3] and the Seebohm Report suggests that 'social distress and dependence is significantly high in some identifiable places and this in our view warrants priority treatment.'[4] Similar suggestions have been made in recent formal housing legislation: the call for local authorities to 'direct their main efforts to the improvement of whole areas' in Circular 65/69,[5] and the suggestion in Circulars 13 and 14/75[6] that areas of housing stress exist where the stock is old and in poor condition and where a combination of acute

133

physical and social problems makes remedial action most difficult, are clear examples of discriminatory thinking which heralded the arrival of General Improvement Areas and Housing Action Areas.

With specific relevance to this study, it is clear that many of the urban experiments were initiated on the assumption that deprivation occurred within small areas in older urban communities, and potentially ameliorative action could be undertaken and assessed at this scale. An HO Press Release in 1969, for example, explained that the CDP would be a neighbourhood based experiment aimed at finding new ways of meeting the needs of people 'in areas of high social deprivation'.[7] Similarly the IAS consultants were appointed in 1972 'to provide a base for general conclusions on policies and action, within the sphere of the D of E appropriate to such inner city areas as present a combination of poor or declining housing, bad environment and a concentration of social problems'.[8] And it is this methodology, which supposes such areas exist, can be identified and aided through spatial forms of positive discrimination, which is under discussion here. Of course, not all forms of social discrimination are either positive or spatial. As Pinker points out, discrimination may not at all favour the most needy: tax relief on mortgages, for example, tends to favour the better off.[9] And similarly, not all the positive discrimination which does exist in Britain is of a spatial kind: supplementary benefits, for instance, whilst aimed at poorer people, have no specific areal distribution. No, what is at issue here is the assumption heavily implicit in the urban programme: that deprivation has a specifically identifiable distribution, and ameliorative action can be undertaken at the local level.

Clearly, one vital constraining factor in this debate is the issue of scale: regional, urban and intra-urban. At the regional scale within Britain, policies have been in operation for more than 50 years to alleviate perceived inequalities between the North and West of the United Kingdom and the South and East, and there would be little dispute that until recently these discrepancies were very real and persistent.[10] At the intra-regional scale, too, deprivation is not usually perceived as having a uniform distribution. Jackson, for instance, in examining various published plans in the early 1970s, points out that typically these studies express concern at the 'contrasts between areas of opportunity around the edges of major cities and areas where the geography of need predominates'.[11] But it is at the smaller scale, at the intra-city level, that the debate sharpens. Politically and administratively, especially within the urban programme, deprivation has been seen to have an areally discrete and identifiable distribution. And not all academic commentators have disagreed. Holman, writing in 1970, for example, accepts that socially deprived families can be found everywhere, 'but generally there is a tendency for such families to be concentrated in particular and definable areas which come to be called deprived areas or communities. Although one result is that the families are embroiled in a circle of poverty, at least their location, if identified, should allow local and central government to allocate extra resources to them on an area basis.'[12] And it is this idea which has become a major keystone in the continued operation of the urban programme in at least three ways: first, the projects, notably the IAS, the CDP and UA, have concentrated on small 'pockets' of deprivation, which they themselves may have identified; second, it was normally intended that these experiments would be a prelude to wider-based national programmes attacking the localised incidence of poverty which, it was felt, occurred almost exclusively within urban areas; and third, the urban initiatives were virtually all developed on the basic premise that deprivation would be found in small urban areas because of the influence of cultures of poverty operating in such localities.

Perhaps the single most important trend in thinking on the distribution and generation of disadvantage is that these assumptions, widely held in official circles, practised within the urban programme and collectively encompassing what has become the 'theory of positive discrimination' have been conclusively undermined in recent years, ironically enough as much by the findings of the urban experiments established to try out positive discrimination in action as by anything else. Positive discrimination as it has been understood in Britain was based on three premises: small deprived areas could be identified; they clearly therefore existed; and they existed because of the localised, cyclical effects of cultures of poverty. On all three fronts a substantial body of theoretical and empirical evidence has built up to suggest that these assumptions are, at the very least, debatable.

HOW ARE DEPRIVED AREAS TO BE IDENTIFIED?

Indicators can be used for a variety of purposes: to monitor policy, to inform, to test social hypotheses and, as is especially important here, to highlight areal differentiation. Three sorts of indicators have been used by central and local government to fulfil this last function. Some indicators, such as unemployment, are regarded as direct, in that there is presumed to be a straightforward causative link between the indicator and assumed disadvantage. Others which have been used, for instance large families, are defined as indirect, and others, such as age groups, are termed demographic. In the case of both the indirect and demographic factors, there is an assumed, but not necessarily proven, relationship between the indicator selected and the areal distribution of deprivation. But whichever sort of indicator is selected, and frequently in practice criteria from all three categories are used, often in combination, the general assumption remains that the chosen criteria will highlight more deprived areas. But will they?

1. Comprehensive lists of indicators will almost always be available only from the 1971 Census. Clearly, these data are already years out of date, and with the cancellation of the mid-decade census, a new baseline will not be available until the mid-1980s, when the 1981 census will be available in full. But some social and economic trends have been so acute over the last few years, notably the decentralisation of population and employment from older city centres, that a hiatus of this order could substantially bias results.

2. Not all information is available at the ED (Enumeration District) level. Indicators which might normally be required as evidence of deprivation, and which are not available at this scale, include sources of income, health standards, the provision of infrastructure such as shops, parks and schools, the level and quality of local services, proximity to work and so on. Similarly, data such as educational attainment or journey-to-work patterns, which are collected on a 10 per cent sample basis in the 1971 census, need to be treated with great care, and obviously not given the same significance as the 100 per cent material.

3. Sometimes attempts are made to introduce greater operational rigour into the process by weighting information. For example an appraisal of potential Housing Action Areas in London[13] weights data by factors of 1, 2 or 3 according to whether there is overcrowding or whether two standard physical amenities are absent. But is this valid? It might well be argued that dwellings lacking two amenities and subject to overcrowding are in a substantially different category to those deficient in say, one amenity, and this distinction would not be reflected in simple arithmetical progression. Other difficulties can emerge when inadequate attempts are made to weight data. Over-

crowding, for instance, is normally taken to occur at and above 1·5 persons per room. But if absolute and arbitrary cut-off points such as this are employed, the implication is that EDs with 1·49 persons per room would not be recorded at all. Graduated scales would help.

4. Normally indicators are evaluated at the ED scale, which is generally small enough not to conceal major internal variations. But that need not be so. It could be possible that within a particular ED a small amount of say, particularly poor housing might create an ED ranking not justified in terms of overall conditions. In effect the apparent intensity of deprivation is directly related to the scale chosen: the larger the areal units examined, the more likely it is that acute areas of stress will be overlooked; and the smaller the units involved, the more likely it is that overall rankings will be biased by a few maverick statistics.

5. Some indicators have been employed which need not necessarily be related to deprivation at all. These are the so-called indirect indicators, and include criteria such as large families or low economic activity rates. But there is in fact no inevitable correlation between deprivation, however defined, and either of these indicators. Holtermann and Silkin, for instance, examined the possible use of low economic activity as an indicator of deprivation,[14] as indeed many official bodies have done. But, as they point out, social trends such as early retirement, unearned incomes and the existence of large numbers of students can mean that low economic activity rates amongst males between 50 and 64, and females 15 to 59, can be associated with both high and low levels of other parameters of deprivation. They conclude that 'these results tend to confirm the view that these indicators cannot be reliably used on their own to identify areas of deprivation.' The same might easily be said of other indicators as well.

6. It is clear, too, that at times there has not been a logically thought-out connection between the use of a specific indicator and assumed or actual deprivation. Brand, for instance, in examining the indicators which have been used to identify EPAs, points out that 'system blaming' indicators such as, say, pupil-teacher ratios tend not to be used, but those criteria which relate to personal or community inadequacy, such as unemployment or socio-economic groupings, are, presumably because it is easier to see educational need in terms of

counteracting personal or community shortcomings than in terms of blaming the entire social and economic structure.[15] Edwards has taken up this point too, and suggested that the lack of definition as to what is and causes deprivation has created an end result which has been 'to define (assume) deprivation in terms of the indicators used to identify its areal concentration'.[16] Thus the use of social criteria such as juvenile delinquency or crime rates might clearly lead to the implicit, if not explicit, assumption that in some way deprivation is related to (caused by) personal inadequacies compounded by anti-social community moulding, and hence that attacks on the distribution and generation of deprivation should concentrate on improving social behaviour in certain areas. Apart from obvious problems such as how this might happen, and how irrelevant and diversionary it would be in practice, there emerges too the allied statistical difficulty of deciding whether indicators relating to, say, crime or vandalism should refer to the site of the person or the incident involved. They would clearly produce very different distributional patterns. And one other point: sometimes other criteria relating to community inadequacies are employed, such as for example the percentage of educationally subnormal children. But once children are designated as such there is a very real danger that this status will become self-fulfilling and they will remain ESN throughout their education and hence continue to appear within the relevant statistics. But whether they should or not is a different matter.

7. Sometimes indicators are employed which reflect local authority provision, such as referrals to children's departments or school non-attendance. But these sorts of criteria can cause problems: first because this sort of indicator is not at all universal, but rather varies through space and time according to the attitudes of the local authority involved; and second because an assumption inherent in the use of such indicators is that additional provision of facilities such as children's homes, home visitors and social service infrastructure in general will reduce deprivation. But is this true?

8. Traditionally, policy makers have concentrated on the use of 'objective' indicators culled from the census. But this raises one obvious issue: how does any objective assessment compare with the subjective appraisal of residents involved? Knox has stated the problem: 'in relation to the whole question of measuring well-being we must recognise that there may be a considerable difference between

an individual's own judgement of his or her degree of satisfaction or well-being and that of any outsiders (based on conventional hard data) . . .'.[17] There have in fact been attempts to introduce subjective social indicators,[18] and there would appear to have been some degree of coherence of results in experiments asking people to indicate degrees of 'satisfaction'. But this approach would seem fraught with problems: if, say, indicators are used to differentiate between two or more areas, does that area containing the least satisfied residents receive more in the way of resources? Would not everyone then claim to be dissatisfied? And is dissatisfaction anything to do with deprivation? And of more immediate relevance, what about the reverse problem, where apparently 'objectively' defined social ills such as overcrowding are used to delimit disadvantage? But in London and some other large cities many people actively seek out shared flats and would not at all feel deprived by living there.

9. An additional problem associated with the use of indicators occurs in a sense after the initial assessment has been made as to which are the more deprived areas. The issue is this: should additional resources be allocated to that locality which emerges top (or bottom) of the list as a matter of course? Doing so would eliminate political discussion or dissenson, any weighing up of non-quantifiable evidence and any possibility of residents themselves influencing decisions. It also assumes that such areas ought to have resources, even though it may be that the policy package which emerges with any additional resources, and which clearly constrains them, might not be appropriate for all areas. Housing Action Areas, for instance, are much sought after now and involve the spending in small areas of what might be potentially large sums. But not all areas are suitable for HAA status, being, say, either physically so deficient that they ought to be demolished or not anything like bad enough to justify HAA status. But will those areas top of the list and apparently most in need of priority action be refused HAA status if they do not fall in line with central government criteria, and other, apparently less suitable areas be selected? Coming 'top' of the list should not inevitably imply priority status.

And even if particular areas are say selected for HAA status, or indeed any form of positive discrimination, will improvements in one area simply mean that more fundamental difficulties emerge elsewhere? Housing problems, for instance, might migrate to neighbouring localities where residents anyway will quite reasonably enquire as to why one area is receiving so much more in the way of additional resources, and will demand their fair share. This might not be available, or justified in terms of other areas within an authority according to 'objective' indicators.

10. The whole process of selection clearly assumes that those areas chosen for priority action will in fact benefit. But, of course, this need not at all be true. The example of GIAs is clearly relevant here, especially in London where existing residents, particularly tenants, frequently suffered financial hardship in the early 1970s as landlords improved and rents rose. Batley has expanded on this problem and commented that, in general, 'it can be assumed too readily that concentrating any resources in an area which is underresourced both in private spending power and in the social infrastructure must be in the interests of residents.'[19] Historical evidence shows that this need not at all be so.

11. The use of indicators assumes in some way that those areas which do emerge as most likely candidates for positive discrimination should receive additional resources. But this presupposes that local and central government operate through rational, objective procedures. Clearly they do not, and in practice a sort of pluralistic bureaucracy is at work, with certain communities or members attempting to obtain additional resources from a local authority, and some local authorities trying the same thing with central government, which, strictly speaking, their ranking in the mathematics of poverty would not justify. Lobbying can achieve wonders. But what it means is that most, or more deprived, areas may receive less than their due. One can see this discrepancy at work in the operation of UA which, because of the bidding operation, puts a premium on local authority efficiency and awareness, not on deprivation. Similarly it is interesting to compare research undertaken by one arm of the D of E to establish where HAAs ought to be declared according to criteria such as overcrowding, lack of basic amenities and male unemployment,[20] and practice, where another arm of the Department has approved them as a result of local authority requests.[21] The results, as one might expect, do not suggest that there has been any attempt to balance centrally defined deprivation and centrally approved HAAs. The Northern region of England for instance, with approximately the same number of multiply deprived EDs, has twice as many HAAs declared in the first 130 than Yorkshire and Humberside. And the

South-East, with twice as many deprived EDs, has only slightly more than half the declared HAAs of the North-West. The point is this: using indicators to highlight more deprived areas assumes that these localities will in fact receive additional resources. The permissive nature of the relationship between different levels of government means that in practice this may not happen.

Definitive conclusions as to the technical and methodological validity of selectors are at the moment premature, partly because this whole approach has become a veritable boom industry, with substantial research being undertaken into the functions and implications of indicators. But from the point of view of the urban programme, the essential issue must be that its traditionally strong emphasis on positive discrimination assumes in turn that deprived areas can be selected almost as a matter of course through the use of indicators. But clearly this process and its implications are far more complex than have been imagined. Even allowing for this redefinition of the problem, however, one presumption might still be that, despite the technical difficulties involved in their selection, deprived areas do exist. But do they?

DO DEPRIVED AREAS EXIST?

A number of investigations have been undertaken into the spatial distributions of selected criteria at national, regional and citywide scales. Some analyses conclude that there is, in fact, considerable spatial coincidence in the distributions of indicators of deprivation. For instance, a detailed examination of Glasgow aimed at identifying areas of multiple deprivation states that the most striking feature of the maps showing census and other data 'is the coincidence of the various distribution patterns'.[22] But on the whole, this is not the conclusion reached by most commentators.

Craig and Driver, for example, combine a number of indicators from the 1966 Census for England and Wales into indexes and conclude that their distribution on the face of it 'would seem to indicate a fairly wide dispersion of the "deprived areas" '.[23] Similarly, Holtermann, in examining indicators throughout the country, suggests that in fact many criteria are surprisingly widely distributed, and in particular whereas there are substantial numbers of areas with high levels of both housing deprivation and unemployment, 'the spatial coincidence of these problems is far from complete.'[24]

This sort of empirical, often independently researched, evidence is in turn strongly supported by the D of E through its *Census Indicators of Urban Deprivation* reports, which have examined indicators of deprivation available at the ED scale from the 1971 Census in order to identify and analyse the distributions of deprivation throughout the country, within specific regions and within certain conurbations. Over a dozen reports have been published which provide a fascinating and important evaluation of deprivation, its distribution and hence implicitly the viability of area based policies. And what is especially relevant is that the reports consistently emerge with surprisingly small degrees of overlap between indicators. An examination of the spatial coincidence of indicators of deprivation in conurbations, for instance, concludes that 'the degree of spatial concentration of each kind of deprivation is not very great.'[25] Similarly, an analysis of the concentration of deprivation in urban areas throughout the UK finds that although there are many areas with high levels of two or three kinds of deprivation, 'the spatial coincidence of the highest levels of deprivation is far from complete.'[26] Neither, apparently, is the concentration of some nine indicators of housing deprivation selected in an attempt to highlight areas of acute housing stress,[27] a situation which is seen as potentially serious because of the inequitable treatment between those households covered by area improvement programmes and those which are not. To put figures on this apparent spread of deprivation, an analysis of the North-West region points out that the extent of overlap between the worst 10 per cent of EDs for overcrowding and the worst 10 per cent for lacking a bath, both very common indicators frequently combined to provide a single 'objective' index, is so low that only 191 out of a possible 1225 EDs are in the worst 10 per cent for both criteria.[28] And furthermore, again within the North-West, the effect of concentrating area based policy in the worst 5 per cent of EDs according to the number of households having more than 1·5 persons per room would be that 70 per cent of households beyond this baseline would remain unaffected because they are not located within the 5 per cent of EDs under examination.[29]

National and regional analyses undertaken by the D of E, suggesting a much more complex and widespread distribution of deprivation than that normally assumed under the traditional methodology of positive discrimination, are themselves supported by a number of independent intra-urban analyses. Berthoud, for instance, examining the areal concentration of deprivation in London, points out that any notion of poverty being concentrated in particular districts has been a common sense one based on observation.[30] But in using household income data he concludes that it is not possible to explain inequality or poverty in terms of exactly where people live, and that deprivation needs to be related to other non-spatial factors.

This would be the implicit conclusion of other researchers, notably Barnes who, using an educational cohort in the ILEA, establishes that disadvantaged children, defined according to uptake of free school meals, father's occupation, and if from immigrant or large families, are far less concentrated than might be imagined.[31] Children in EPA schools who might be disadvantaged were outnumbered by those who would not be so defined, and of seven children at risk of being multiply deprived, five were located outside EPAs. This would not surprise Hatch and Sherrott who, in an examination of spatial patterns of disadvantage especially in London, conclude—and many observers would agree—that 'deprivation seems to be widely though universally distributed in the kind of inner city working-class areas which we studied and areas suffering from multiple deprivation do not seem to form a quite separate category easily distinguished from other less deprived areas.'[32]

And finally, in the examination of empirical data relating to intra-urban patterns of disadvantage, mention needs to be made of the more sophisticated approach adopted by Webber who, in looking at Liverpool and its deprivation, uses cluster analysis to regroup individual aspects of disadvantage and suggests that there are different distributions of apparent deprivation depending upon indicators selected, and that no such thing as unambiguous areas of deprivation exist since, in particular, overcrowding, sharing of amenities and lack of an inside WC or fixed bath have very different distributions. Hence, 'clearly the definition of areas of housing stress is highly sensitive to the relative weight attached to each of these three dimensions.'[33]

This very variegated pattern of disadvantage identified by Webber is in itself important because a number of research contributions have suggested that, although deprivation may not have a simple uniform distribution with close spatial coincidence of indicators, a binary pattern seems quite possible. The Lambeth IAS, for instance, distinguishes between residual areas of deprivation and transient ones. The former would consist of older, working-class housing where, although physical conditions might be acceptable, economic structures have declined so much with the reduction in local manufacturing industry that there are substantial numbers of unemployed or poorly paid workers. Transient areas, on the other hand, would tend to consist of areas of poorer housing standards but with a resident population of young, single or newly married people who might have reasonable, even good, jobs and who might expect to move onwards and upwards in the foreseeable future. The evidence from Webber's more rigorous analysis indicates, however, that this twofold pattern might be a too simple explanation as well. In a sense this particular debate is anyway a little sterile, because it would be difficult to argue that central government policy with regard to inner city deprivation has been geared towards a dual distribution of disadvantage, let alone anything more complex. The overwhelming impression must remain that, until very recently at least, the 'pockets' argument ruled supreme and deprivation was perceived, officially at any rate, to have a limited and identifiable spatial distribution. But clearly, severe methodological constraints have emerged in that, first, the identification of these pockets is fraught with technical and procedural difficulties, and, secondly, they may not exist anyway.

WHY SHOULD SMALL DEPRIVED AREAS EXIST?

It seems quite clear that widespread acceptance of the idea that deprivation has a limited and spatially definable distribution is related to theses advocating cycles or cultures of poverty. It is important here to distinguish between the two. The former refers to particular types of poverty likely to be encountered at certain stages in the life cycle, notably when people are very young, old or at child rearing age. But more acute manifestations of this process are sometimes seen as acting most obviously in certain working-class communities, where deviant subcultures are operative at variance to generally held beliefs and standards of society as a whole.[34] And it is this culture of poverty, accentuated by the specific problems encountered during the life cycle, which has been widely advocated as the prime causative agent in the development and generation of urban poverty.

In part the thesis clearly drifted over from the States, where ideas relating to cultures of poverty had been widely aired and incorporated into the sixties urban poverty programme.[35] This perceived a vicious cycle transmitting poverty from generation to generation, accentuated by an evolved culture of poverty that inhibited people from achieving their optimum opportunities because of poor community and family socialisation. But not all the impetus for this sort of thinking was imported. In Britain it has been argued that since at least the thirties the emphasis within social work has focused on the individual and his or her deficiencies or social pathologies rather than on say society as a whole and its shortcomings. Partly this bias seems to have been caused by the early domination of psychoanalysis with its concern for individual neuroses or maladjustments—and its corollary that the client should be helped to accept and adjust to the 'real world'.[36] But on the other hand it is also possible to trace a general concern for conformity, and a reluctance to blame structures rather than individuals, back at least to the Poor Law. And certainly it is not too difficult to see why, until very recently, attitudes within the government's social administration, including the urban programme, have assumed that the key to improvement lies in examining and ameliorating the problems, pathologies, almost illnesses, that occur in those individuals and small communities imbued with deviant subcultures of poverty.

Although doubts had been expressed about the validity of this approach by the mid-1960s the greatest stimulant to this sort of thinking, ironically, came in the early seventies when Sir Keith Joseph became Secretary of State for Social Services. In a number of key speeches at the time[37] he pondered aloud on the fundamental problem he faced: why so many children were still being born into family and cultural environments which he, at least, saw as inadequate, precisely because they were likely to envelop these children in a sort of preordained pattern of failure. This process operated through, for instance, poor community and family imprinting, which reduced the opportunities available for self-advancement, minimised self-help capacities and encouraged instead tendencies towards early school leaving, early marriage and early child rearing. And of course, any new generation of children would in turn become encapsulated within the same subculture of apathy and poverty. So for Sir Keith Joseph there were two essential aspects to this issue: the problem was continuous in that disadvantages inherent in one generation appeared to reproduce themselves in the next, and these forms of social instability were being transmitted by the community and especially the family. And because, as he saw it, the family was the central focus to the problem, then the emphasis within his department should be on programmes which operated at this level and which could reach parents within poorer areas. Hence the concentration in his term of office on policies such as family planning, home visiting by health visitors and social workers and, especially, the Preparation for Parenthood Programme. This last initiative, whilst accepting that there might be no single solution to the problems of transmitted deprivation, nevertheless saw the way families functioned as vital to the health of society.[38] In particular, if a greater awareness and understanding of the processes of child development and parental roles could be promoted, there was every chance that inherent cycles of disadvantage could be broken by improving the socialising performance of parents.[39] And to see how effective this and other policies would be, and to examine in general the extent of transmitted deprivation, a research programme[40] was initiated in 1974 by the DHSS, working in conjunction with the Social Science Research Council.

But it should not be imagined that sentiments favourable to culture of poverty arguments were confined to the DHSS, for clearly several aspects of the urban programme were devised to expand on, or to examine, its spatial mechanics. EPAs, for example, can be interpreted as attempts to break cycles of deprivation apparent in poorer areas at their weakest point: during early education before 'antisocial' behaviour had been inculcated into children. Similarly, UA can be seen as a programme aimed at providing additional support to families in need[41] through its funding of family advice centres, health visiting, the development of preschool infrastructure, and most pertinently, family planning services aimed at reducing the very numbers of children entering supposed subcultures of deprivation. Many of the management studies too, were clearly designed to improve service delivery to families in need of care—improved servicing which, it was anticipated, would reduce intrinsically antisocial family pathologies or inadequacies. And nowhere is the suggestion made more clearly that the urban experiments might reduce these social inadequacies than in the early development of the CDP programme. In guidelines laid down in 1970, for instance, the success or otherwise of CDP teams was to be evaluated according to indicators relating to improved family functioning, such as reductions in home desertions, improved personal care, for example increases in those being vaccinated or immunised, or improved physical conditions in the community, such as reductions in infectious diseases.[42] This is culture of poverty thinking with a vengeance, where improvements in eradicating deprivation are tied in almost exclusively to supposedly better personal and community functioning.

And in this context too, it is certainly relevant to see that the later CDP interpreted its role, and that of the urban programme in general, as one in which cultures of poverty were always intended to figure prominently.[43] To the CDP of the mid-seventies it remained trans-

parently clear that it and most, if not all, aspects of the urban programme were created on the assumption that deprivation was limited
to a minority whose influence was out of proportion to their numbers, and who encouraged others to adopt antisocial behaviour, such
as delinquency and crime at one extreme and, more generally,
stimulated social attitudes sympathetic towards early school leaving,
early marriage and early child rearing which trapped successive
generations in a quagmire of poverty. Hence deprivation was to be
seen as spatially limited and family generated, and capable of intrinsic amelioration at this scale. It is the demise of this argument, and
the corresponding rise of structuralist arguments, that have undoubtedly been the most important factors in undermining the very
raison d'être for an urban programme.

But why has this intellectual metamorphosis happened? Partly,
and somewhat embarrassingly, because the research initiated by Sir
Keith Joseph into transmitted deprivation emerged with some rather
startling conclusions in its review of existing empirical information.
Rutter and Madge examined work done on the extent of inter-
generational continuities in a wide range of psychological, social and
economic phenomena.[44] Their conclusions indicated that present-day
Britain is characterised by considerable social movement and inter-
generational change; that even when forms of disadvantage are
strong, discontinuities are striking; that at least half the children
born into a disadvantaged home do not repeat the pattern of disadvantage in the next generation; that even where continuities are
strongest, many individuals break out of the cycle whilst, on the other
hand, many people become disadvantaged without having been born
to disadvantaged parents; and that in general the causes of deprivation are multifactorial and interactive, and that different sorts of
deprivation will have different causative factors. Other more detailed
empirical work by Paterson and Inglis[45] and by Jordan[46] on the
extent of generated disadvantage tends to support Rutter and Madge's
general prognosis. The former conclude, for instance, that although
there is an element of interoperational transmission in the records
they examined, 'this pattern is neither as extensive, nor as regular as
is generally assumed.'

It would, however, be unwise to imagine that deprivation is in no
way related to parental or neighbourhood characteristics. Berthoud,
examining the disadvantages of inequality, suggests that there is an
observed correlation between the material circumstances and socio-
economic characteristics of parents, the preliminary development and

school performance of children and their subsequent social status.[47] But as he sees it, this pattern can be attributed either to the socio-cultural characteristics of the parents involved, which is of course one of the main strands of thought in culture of poverty theories, or—and this opens many doors—to their income. The implication behind this latter assertion is that deprivation cannot be explained solely in terms of social imprinting or personal and community pathologies, but that basic inequalities in economic circumstances might be at least as important. Donnison has expanded on this point, and contrasts movements towards priority area policies within the general methodology of positive discrimination, with another, to him more substantive theory.[48] According to this view, deprivation may be causatively linked to at least two other processes: cycles of poverty related to specific periods of reduced income, and inequalities in social and economic structures. In the case of this latter argument, disadvantage is perceived to occur when inadequate education and training make it inevitable that individuals remain incapable of entering anything other than unskilled or semi-skilled, poorly paid and insecure occupations, which in turn inhibits them from dwelling anywhere but in public housing. In this position it is political, economic and educational inequalities within society as a whole which largely define deprivation.[49] Structural and inbuilt dysfunctions militate against poorer, working-class residents acquiring generally better educational and training standards, better paid and permanent occupation, easier access to, and within, certain housing markets and greater openings to, and power over, politically disposable resources.

This more radical position has been expanded by a number of analysts. Holtermann, for instance, defines deprivation in terms of deficiencies of consumption or income in relation to needs which eventually causes personal or family welfare to fall below that normally accepted as a reasonable minimum.[50] Then, significantly, she ties in this definition to concepts of political power, and hence sees one characteristic of deprivation as a lack of political control over resources. And it is this redefinition of deprivation, in particular its linking to inequitable political structures, that lies at the root of one important branch of CDP thinking which defines disadvantage not simply as inadequate consumption or income, but as a lack of political control over public and private resources too, and a general inability on the part of working-class residents to compete within housing, educational and employment markets. To the CDP then, and indeed to the later IAS as well, the way to attack poverty must be through improvement of the economic, educational and political status of poorer inner city residents. Of course, one essential debate then must consider how this might happen. Whereas reformist IAS and radical CDP might agree on programmes such as increased benefits and pensions, higher wages and a more secure pool of permanent jobs, there would be substantial disagreement over the latter's more interventionist approach implicit in, say, greater public control and direction over private employment. The CDP would also clearly be in sympathy with Holman's suggestion that improving the lot of the poorest cannot be divorced from 'a direct reduction in the power and resources of the privileged minority'.[51]

So what does this new line of structuralist thinking mean for the urban programme in general? At the very least it undermines its early and dominant assumption that deprivation is generationally transmitted in small and definable localities, through social pathologies relating to inadequate personal and community behaviour. As long as this model of action persisted it was quite possible to argue that the welfare state, although generally satisfactory, was not capable of dealing with the long-standing and inbred problems of certain areas. Consequently, these areas needed experimental policies, such as urban poverty programmes, to boost social infrastructure, to involve residents in self-help and self-sustaining schemes, and generally to redirect aberrant individuals and communities into acceptable modes of behaviour. As long as this position was held, the causes of deprivation could be seen to rest with individuals and their inadequacies, and not with the economic system. Hence, as Meacher points out, an urban programme could be devised which could claim to be helping the poor 'without in any way impugning the structure of rewards in society or demanding any significant sacrifices from the privileged'.[52]

Now it would be far too sweeping a statement to suggest that the concept of subcultures of poverty has sunk without trace, because it has not. Nor would it be correct to assume that cultures of poverty and structuralist arguments are mutually exclusive, because one can envisage them working in tandem. Nor would it be right to assume that these are the only factors which have been invoked to explain deprivation and its generation: life cycles of poverty, regional inequalities and poor local authority service delivery are amongst the more obvious alternative candidates. But in terms of the urban programme, it cannot be denied that the continued welter of criticisms levelled at social pathological arguments have weakened the previously held tenets until now they are clearly quite inadequate to explain exclusively the distribution of disadvantage. The implications for the programme are profound. Deprivation cannot be seen now to occur in small, definable localities; policy operative at this level may make minimal difference to poverty because it is divorced from national and international operative forces which so clearly define and accentuate deprivation; advances in coping with the problem may need to focus on national campaigns aimed at improving wages, benefits, political organisation of poorer working-class residents and reducing the power, wealth and privilege of the few. Ultimately such a programme would find urban experiments irrelevant, since their limited powers and limited spatial scales would inevitably question 'their utility in achieving the fundamental shifts in the distribution of real income and the means of its production that are clearly necessary'.[53]

Whilst central government has not at all been prepared to accept as yet the total irrelevance of its urban programme, it is clear that structuralist arguments have seeped through even the thickest of Whitehall walls. The Inner City White Paper, for instance, indicates an increasing acceptance that economic decline might have as much to do with urban deprivation as inadequate community imprinting. The IAS too, with their late, but very marked, switch to an examination of industrial decay and community poverty—and this under the general aegis of the D of E—clearly too reflect changing attitudes. But this realignment should not be taken too far. Resources to be invested in inner city areas under the expanded UA programme will still be trivial, and powers available to regenerate economic activity minimal. But, of course, structuralist arguments bring their own problems too, and are not going to be embraced enthusiastically by any government, for once system blaming factors are invoked to explain deprivation, where will it all end? And how much will it all cost?

Positive discrimination as it was understood in the early urban programme has been intellectually destroyed. Small deprived areas are not easy to identify, they may not even exist, and certainly the theoretical framework originally used to explain them has been largely discredited. Deprivation is a far more complex phenomenon, having a far wider spatial distribution than early official apologists would have us believe. No doubt cultures of poverty do operate in certain localities, but other factors, especially structural dysfunctions, must be invoked if the totality of disadvantage is to be understood.

Yet policy makers need to be realistic. Deprivation does not have a totally random spatial distribution. As Flynn has pointed out, at the intra-regional scale distributional issues should not be ignored since 'there are important questions about uneven development within metropolitan counties which could be obscured by a too general set of explanations which ignore the spatial dimension.'[54] And at this sort of scale the Rate Support Grant may be the most effective and sensitive agent of discrimination. Even then, however, as the Liverpool IAS team suggest, resources provided by central government to individual local authorities need to be used for 'the benefit of the inner areas and not either subsumed in general local authority expenditure or used to release resources for other parts of the city'.[55] But it must be remembered that the sort of 'inner areas' assumed in these intra-regional and intra-urban discussions are likely to consist of tens, or even hundreds, of thousands of residents, not thousands or hundreds as many of the urban experiments did. Even then, however, it is possible that some sorts of programmes might best be introduced at a more localised scale for, as the Birmingham IAS team suggest, 'the size of areas selected for programmes would depend on the sort of programme—smallest for physical programmes such as housing, larger for social programmes and much larger for employment.'[56] And to complete the argument full circle, if certain areas are to be highlighted for a range of compensatory programmes how should they be identified? If the programme is specifically concerned with, say, housing improvement, then housing indicators should be employed, not an inchoate mish-mash of apparently randomly selected social and physical criteria. And if more general compensatory policies are to be introduced over larger, but still perhaps identifiable areas, then the chosen indicators need to relate to the assumed model of deprivation.[57] And if this model, as seems very likely, has to incorporate some structural component, then disadvantage must be seen as an inability to compete in housing, educational and employment markets, and the selected indicators need to reflect this.

NOTES TO CHAPTER 7

1 A. Sinfield, 'Poverty Rediscovered', in J. Cullingworth (ed.), 1973, p. 134.
2 HMSO, Report of the Committee on Housing in Greater London, 1965, p. 122.
3 HMSO, *Children and Their Primary Schools*, 1967, pars. 131–6.

4   HMSO, Report of the Committee on Local Authority and Allied Personal Social Services, 1968, par. 453.
5   MHLG Circular 65/69, 1969, par. 3.
6   D of E Circular 13/75, 1975, par. 5; and D of E Circular 14/75, 1975, pars. 9–15.
7   HO Press Release 16.7.1969, quoted in CDP, *Gilding the Ghetto*, 1977.
8   IAS/LA/I, par. 1.1.
9   R. Pinker, 1971, p. 190.
10 See for instance M. Rutter and N. Madge, 1976, p. 303: '. . . regional continuities in disadvantage . . . are very striking.'
11 N. Jackson, 1972, p. 68.
12 R. Holman, 'Combating Social Deprivation', in R. Holman (ed.), 1970, p. 157.
13 London Boroughs Association, 1975.
14 S. Holtermann and F. Silkin, 1976, p. 345.
15 J. Brand, 1975.
16 J. Edwards, 1975B, p. 284.
17 P. Knox, 1975, p. 55.
18 See, for instance, M. Abrams, 1973.
19 R. Batley, 1975, p. 89.
20 S. Holtermann, 1975A, Appendix F.
21 D of E Housing Improvement Group, 1976.
22 Scottish Development Dept Central Planning Research Unit, 1973, par. 20.
23 J. Craig and A. Driver, 1972, p. 34.
24 S. Holtermann, 1975B, p. 44.
25 F. Silkin, 1975, par. 39.
26 S. Holtermann (as 20), p. 14.
27 J. Fawcett, 1976, par. 30.
28 S. Holtermann, 1974, par. 7.
29 T. Knight, 1974, par. 10.
30 R. Berthoud, 1976A.
31 J. Barnes, 'A Solution to Whose Problems?', in H. Glennerster and S. Hatch (eds.), 1974.
32 S. Hatch and P. Sherrott, 1973.
33 R. Webber, 1975, p. 92.
34 As defined by P. Townsend, 1974.
35 See P. Marris and M. Rein, 1974, p. 24.
36 See, for instance, J. Greve, 1973.
37 See, for instance, Sir Keith Joseph, 'The Cycle of Disadvantage', in E. Butterworth and R. Holman (eds.), 1975.
38 DHSS, *The Family in Society*, 1973.
39 DHSS, *The Family in Society*, 1974.
40 For research framework for this programme, see SSRC/DHSS, 1974.
41 As admitted by B. Castle, 1974.
42 HO, *CDP Objectives and Strategy*, 1970, Annex A.
43 CDP (as 7).
44 M. Rutter and N. Madge (as 10).
45 A. Paterson and J. Inglis, 1976.

46 B. Jordan, 1974.
47 R. Berthoud, 1976B.
48 D. Donnison, 1974.
49 For an expansion of how educational disadvantage can cement inequalities, see F. Field, 1973.
50 S. Holtermann, 1975B.
51 R. Holman, 1973B, p. 443.
52 M. Meacher, 'The Politics of Positive Discrimination', in H. Glennerster and S. Hatch (as 31).
53 B. Coates, R. Johnston and P. Knox, 1977, p. 236.
54 N. Flynn, 1977, p. 16.
55 IAS, Liverpool IAS, Summary of the Final Report, 1977, par. 40.
56 IAS, Birmingham IAS, Summary of the Final Report, 1977, par. 56.
57 An argument expanded by J. Edwards, 1975A.

Chapter 8

THE POTENTIAL FOR URBAN ECONOMIC REJUVENATION

Many urban commentators have become increasingly concerned at the extent of economic decline and how, and if, it might be reversed or at least moderated.[1] It is a decline that has been quite startling, especially in the larger cities of the North and in London, particularly in the last decade or so; 20 per cent of Manchester's manufacturing base in 1966 had disappeared by 1971,[2] 20 per cent of Islington's jobs in 1961 had gone by 1971,[3] Wandsworth lost about half of its manufacturing labour force between 1951 and 1971;[4] London's employment base was reduced by half a million jobs between 1961 and 1974, mainly in the manufacturing sector. But in fact, almost everywhere decentralisation of economic activity became a characteristic of the British city, although the process was most accentuated in the larger, older cities.[5]

In fact industrial decentralisation postdated a similar demographic process, and it is curious to see that until relatively recently it was the decentralisation of people, and not jobs, which was seen as the pressing problem because of the spatial mismatch this was creating.[6] As late too, as 1970, a discussion of London's planning problems[7] could talk blandly about the sorts of industries which ought to be retained in London, as if there might be a choice in the matter. And not all more recent commentators have considered that the centrifugal forces at work necessarily create a problem. The D of E's officially commissioned Study of the Inner Areas of Conurbations, for instance, concludes that 'while it cannot be denied that employment in inner areas is declining at a faster rate than in the outer areas . . . this trend does not seem to be accompanied by any large-scale adverse effects.'[8] Not many would agree with that opinion. Not, ironically, the Secretary of State for Environment himself, who suggested in 1976 that the causes for the decline in inner city areas 'lies primarily in their relative economic decline, in a major migration of people,

154

often the most skilled, and in a massive reduction in the number of jobs which are left',[9] and that the future of such areas was inextricably bound up with the fortunes of manufacturing industry.

The urban experiments which he and other central government politicians commissioned have been equally concerned. To the IAS[10] and CDP,[11] for instance, it seems unavoidably true that the prime cause of urban decay is the rapid destruction of economic bases, and unless these forces are reversed the problems of inner cities are not likely to be overcome. As these initiatives have seen it, industrial decentralisation inevitably leads to unemployment, to poverty, to a reduced rate base, to declining public and private investment, to the migration of better-off and more skilled residents and eventually to the creation of a pool of unskilled, unemployed inner city workers making steadily greater proportional demands on social services of all kinds. By the late 1960s and early 1970s there was plenty of evidence to indicate that unemployment rates were rising substantially in inner urban areas, at a proportionally greater rate than for conurbations as a whole.[12] In 1975 in Liverpool for example, there were 70 per cent more unemployed males than in 1971, and in certain pockets of the city unemployment rates were rising to over 30 per cent. At the same time, throughout the country, economic activity rates remained substantially lower in the inner parts of conurbations than in other areas within conurbations or within entire regions. It seems very likely, too, that this discrepancy has continued and possibly been accentuated within recent years.

Because so much attention has been paid to this process in the major urban experiments, this chapter will critically examine the sorts of policies put forward by central and local government and other urban exponents too, in an attempt to evaluate the potential viability of these programmes in the light of current administrative, financial and legal constraints. But as the effectiveness of these policies must clearly relate to processes underlying decentralising forces in the first place, the causes of urban economic decline ought to be outlined.

WHY HAS INDUSTRY LEFT OLDER, INNER AREAS?

Presenting definitive and conclusive indications as to why urban economic activity has declined may not be possible other than in certain regions over certain periods of time. But more general suggestions can be presented as to the relative importance of different forces at work.[13]

1. Decentralisation is not a new process, nor is it one limited to Britain. It seems rather to be one generally apparent in industrialised societies where technical and distributional processes increasingly favour the peripheral site. Originally, by minimising costs, inner city sites offered optimal locations. But shifts in industrial and communication technology,[14] and the ever increasing importance of internalised scale effects, have placed a premium on high land-to-output ratios, extensive, cheap and expandable sites and access to motorway infrastructure, all of which have clearly militated against inner city locations. In addition to the pull factors which have encouraged firms to migrate to suburban and ex-urban locations, there are obviously push factors involved which have stimulated the movement of industry outwards, or alternatively restricted their potential *in situ* expansion. Older inner city sites tend to have to pay for poorer internal layouts, poorer access arrangements, diminished opportunities for expansion, especially because of higher land costs, higher rates and rents, higher wage rates, unionised labour and shortage of skilled workers. This decentralisation process has been further accentuated in certain cities because of the particular problems of dockside industries, in that containerisation has encouraged the migration downstream of many port and allied industries, a process especially prevalent in London. And as with so many other manufacturing declines, this trend has been encouraged on the one hand by the ability of other land users, especially commercial ones, to outbid other potential manufacturers, particularly near the city centre, and on the other hand, because redundancy payments involved in the decentralisation of manufacturing firms are tiny in comparison to the cost of the social disruption involved. It still remains a cheap option for many companies. It is not surprising, then, to find that in the light of advantages in moving out and disadvantages in remaining that so many firms have migrated, that so few have been started in inner areas,[15] that so few existing establishments are prepared to invest in expansion[16] and that the perceived diseconomies of older urban areas are seen to be ever more centrally important.

2. But not all economic decentralisation can be ascribed to the relative advantages and disadvantages of inner urban locations. Enormous changes have also occurred in the organisation and production of British industry, reflecting the growing desire on the part of central government for British industry to become competitive in European

and world terms. This has meant the tacit and even explicit encouragement of reorganisation and rationalisations which have on the whole encouraged the creation of larger companies, seeking ever greater proportional profits. As these profits are clearly more likely to be achieved through more modern physical infrastructures concentrating on more buoyant sectors of the economy, the inner city has lost out on two accounts: its infrastructure tends to be redundant, and its remaining industrial base tends to concentrate on older, often stagnant, sectors. It is this process of company amalgamation and rationalisation, a policy at times actively supported by central government[17] as, for example, during the existence of the Industrial Reorganisation Corporation, which has been as powerful a factor as any in the reduction of urban industrial bases. As one London commentator points out, 'company takeovers and mergers often result in "rationalisation" which means redundancies. Often the productive capacity of firms taken over is not required by the parent company and so the works are reduced in size or closed.'[18]

3. Although initiatives such as the Industrial Reorganisation Corporation have had the, probably unintentional, effect of reducing the viability of inner city industrial establishments, other central and local government policies have also been influential. At the local level, planning policy has traditionally regarded non-conforming industrial users as unsuitable for residential areas, and through processes of compulsory purchase done much to reduce the local economic base since, although sometimes alternative sites might be made available, this did not always happen; and even when it did, rents might be prohibitively expensive for the smaller, low-profit concern. Wandsworth, in an analysis of its redevelopment policies, admits that in the ten years before 1972, 250 firms had been displaced by housing programmes, only 13 of which had been re-located.[19] But nevertheless this factor of local authority redevelopment can be overstressed. Certainly some analyses suggest that global figures, within London at least, indicate that closure of firms rather than decentralisation is largely to blame for industrial decline.[20] And more detailed borough-wide figures from Lewisham, for instance,[21] suggest that few remaining firms have encountered problems which might widely be defined as 'planning problems', and of those firms which had either moved or died, reorganisation or liquidation factors were far more relevant than, say, the effect of council redevelopment.

Besides the putative influence of local government policies, central government has clearly been involved in encouraging both intra- and inter-regional migration, from older cities to their hinterlands and from the supposedly more prosperous South and Midlands of Britain to the North and West. At the intra-regional scale, policies have encouraged the migration of expanding firms to suburban, ex-urban and new and expanded town sites, by inhibiting the development of firms in older urban areas through the control of Industrial Development Certificates (IDCs) and by the complementary increase in decentralised industrial estates and the like. Some analyses, such as one for Glasgow,[22] suggest that a policy of intra-regional industrial migration has failed to fulfil demands placed upon it, in that anticipated industrial growth rates in new towns have not been met. But alternatively, there is substantial evidence that, although in, say, London, most industrial decline is due to closure, the effects of decentralisation cannot be ignored. Almost all industrial moves here are outwards, and it is possible that because of this process a 'London factor' has set in. This occurs because of 'the operation of negative multiplier effects resulting from reduced inter-industry demands, falling incomes and incomes per head,'[23] costs and diseconomies which ultimately tilt 'the scales in favour of a London closure'.[24]

Inter-regional migrations must be explored too. For almost 50 years central government policy has been to encourage the movement of industry away from the prosperous areas to the depressed regions of the North and West. A variety of tools have been used of an increasingly powerful nature, with the effect that in the period from 1966 to 1971 the movement of manufacturing firms from the South-East led to the creation of 50,000 jobs in other regions. But relative to other factors, regional decentralisation is not of primary significance in explaining urban economic decline. Normally most analyses credit about 10 per cent of London's industrial decline to it, for instance. Certainly it seems that many IDCs, intended to control the growth of established industrial firms in the South-East and Midlands, are in fact granted on request and hence *in situ* expansion allowed. Of course, not all are, and many firms may never apply for an IDC, assuming, often incorrectly, that it would be refused.

4. Much of the current debate on inner city employment equates jobs with manufacturing jobs. This might seem surprising, since one model which attempts to explain the evolving economic structure of cities suggests that manufacturing industry ought to be allowed, even encouraged, to move to new outer locations, and that in its place

healthy and expanding commercial sectors should be developed. That might be the theory, but in practice it has not happened like this at all. First, there has been a consistent policy to decentralise office jobs as well as industrial employment. The Location of Offices Bureau, for instance, has moved well over 100,000 jobs from London in that period from 1965 to 1976. Very little of this office employment, however, has relocated in the inner city districts of the depressed regions but rather has tended to locate in the suburbs of larger cities or in the older free-standing towns of the South and East. Not surprisingly, the lack of sectoral and spatial refinement in regional office policy has come in for criticism.[25]

But even then, this discrepancy might not have been so disturbing, since there are indications that central London, for example, still has considerable unused office accommodation and office workers still seem able to acquire and retain jobs.[26] The problem remains, however, that although office jobs might be relatively plentiful— much more so than manufacturing jobs—they have nevertheless been declining at a very rapid rate, certainly from some parts of London. Even when there are still opportunities within this sector, it remains apparent that the skills and aptitudes of unemployed manufacturing workers may not at all be appropriate for vacancies which occur. Increasingly it seems that there is a mismatch between the sorts of jobs available and the growing pool of largely unskilled and semi-skilled ex-industrial and service workers. On the one hand, some posts will require professional and managerial skills and experience unlikely to be encountered by the average manufacturing employee, and on the other hand, the growing demand for unskilled workers in the catering and some service industries would not normally attract many ex-industrial workers because of the unsocial hours, poor pay, and non-unionised nature of the employment.

Clearly then it is not hard to see why many urban authorities consider themselves to be in a critical predicament. Economic trends have forced out many manufacturing firms, a process often, ironically, accentuated by previous policies adopted by both local and central government. Office employment, too, seems to have declined, or at least not increased at the rate previously anticipated, and may not anyway be especially suitable to accommodate the industrially unemployed. Public service industries, the transport sector and particularly the construction industry have suffered severe recessions as well. The net result is the growing polarisation of city regions with the poorer, unskilled or semi-skilled increasingly concentrated in older urban cores, unable because of rigidities in the housing market to move out, often unable because of diminishing economic bases to obtain a job, and hence unable to contribute greatly to public and private consumption. Additionally too, many of the unemployed are young, unskilled and black,[27] perhaps with unreasonably optimistic appraisals of their potential economic status or alternatively, becoming far less concerned with integrating into, and operating within, orthodox social and economic structures. Hence for many urban authorities, diminishing industrial performance is *the* problem they face. Other analysts concur, and collectively there has been a quite unprecedented interest in the possibilities of economic planning by local and central government and through the private sector. But what sort of economic planning is envisaged? How would it operate? And would it succeed? Three basic strategies can be defined: local authority activity, the potential of independent entrepreneurs and centrally devised policies.

LOCAL AUTHORITY PROMOTION

Until recently, local authorities adopted a generally passive attitude towards employment.[28] Likely sites might have been zoned for industrial development and some basic infrastructure provided in any new industrial estates, which were generally located in suburban sites, close to motorways. A largely neutral position was, of course, perfectly understandable in the sixties, since the basic problem to solve seemed to be one of where to locate new employment bases. But as relative affluence gave way to relative poverty, a far more interventionist outlook has come to characterise some authorities, generally those in older urban areas where the continued decentralisation of employment, combined with both a reduction in the amount of footloose industry generally and virtually no expansion of the remaining inner city firms give grounds for grave concern.[29] The response from authorities can be seen as twofold: an expansion of what might be called 'orthodox' promotional policies, and also a continued search by a number of councils for more effective, innovatory programmes.

The 'orthodox' approach towards more intensive economic planning is based on a wider use of existing powers.[30] Larger areas of land might be allocated for industrial use, and would be strategically located with regard to public transport services, housing markets and intra-regional communication routes.[31] Although some of this newly allocated land might be created on the edges of older cities, there seems to be no reason either why some could not be sited on vacant sites nearer city centres of which, in some cities at least, there is no shortage. By creating industrial zones such as these it may then be possible to ensure that existing firms blighted by proposed council redevelopments would have ample opportunities, rent levels permitting, to relocate, and hence not to die out.

Generally, however, the mere provision of land is not regarded as adequate. Authorities have powers, which are being exercised to an increasing extent, to acquire land and build factories on it, especially under the 1963 Local Authority (Land) Act which allows either councils themselves or, through the provision of loans, other agencies, to acquire land and develop it industrially. This measure may be particularly useful in developing small, 'seedbed' factories of under 5,000 sq ft, for which there is considerable demand. Equally so, of course, wider implementary powers within the Community Land Act might allow, subject to adequate financial and political commitment, a greater intervention by authorities in the purchasing, leasing and developing of land for particular uses.

More direct financial aid might also be forthcoming, for instance through schemes such as industrial mortgages and purchase and leaseback arrangements which can be introduced by local authorities. The previously mentioned Local Authorities (Land) Act, for example, gives councils powers to provide 75 per cent mortgages for the erection of premises on land owned or leased by themselves, at rates slightly higher than those they pay on capital loaned from the Public Works Loan Board. Some other private Acts allow 90 per cent loans, and sometimes grants may be provided by authorities for the improvement of sites or services. Equally the financial outlay faced by companies in their initial development can be eased by allowing firms to buy land on an instalment basis. Rents, too, can be reduced for specific periods for factories made available by the council.

Other improvements can be made at the local level through better promotion and co-ordination of available industrial agencies. In London, for instance, it has been thought necessary to create an Inner London Consultative Employment Group consisting of representatives of authorities and interested parties who, collectively, are interested in the amelioration of unemployment and the general economic regeneration of inner London. Bodies such as this and, within individual authorities, Industrial Development Departments, can provide services generally beneficial to manufacturing industry. Inventories of vacant land and relevant local expertise can be built up; established firms given long-term guarantees about the stability of their sites, even if these may be in largely residential areas; or if removal proposals are contemplated, adequate relocation sites provided at rents smaller firms can afford. Statutory undertakers, too, can be encouraged to release land for industry, and this resource, together with the council's own land, and any it might want to acquire compulsorily, should provide a sensible and balanced supply to meet anticipated demands at the price and quantity required by local industry. To establish exactly what sort of demands exist, trade associations representing local firms could be created, which would remain in close contact with the authority concerned. On a more directly entrepreneurial level, authorities might try to create more industrial estates, either new ones or developed out of existing factories, where the council could operate surgeries, crèches, trade fairs, exhibitions, contact registers and so on. Larger advertising budgets and a more promotional attitude generally towards industry can also clearly help to generate local and national interest in the employment potential of the older urban areas.

Sometimes it is evident that benefits would accrue to the employment sector simply through a more sympathetic approach towards the allied policies of housing, education, retraining, transport and planning. With regard to housing, for instance, it may be necessary to provide accommodation for key workers and others as new firms move in or older established ones wish to expand. Increased labour forces will in turn require additional community and health services, and this may necessitate a more overtly favourable approach on the part of some central government departments. This applies equally to education and retraining services, which are sometimes perceived as quite inadequate to fulfil the tasks intended.[32] Certainly a more integrative philosophy which attempted to match skills and education to job shortages could be one line of advance. Transport policies could also be made more responsive to the demands of industry by providing better public transport between major residential and industrial centres, by improving road infrastructure around major industrial areas or by creating localised traffic management schemes. Clearly planning policies, too, need to be more refined, to provide a faster and more flexible approach to industrial expansion proposals and, where these remain unacceptable, sensible relocation procedures applied or adequate compensation paid.

The wide-ranging powers available to most local authorities, and which have been outlined above, are intended either to subsidise firms directly, or to assist their allied development factors such as land, labour and transport. But in some authorities these powers have been supplemented in various experimental and innovatory manners. In particular these include policies designed to introduce industrial improvement areas (IIAs) and of greater relevance, more direct financial intervention by authorities.

IIAs were developed initially in Rochdale[33] in an attempt to overcome the problems there of industrial obsolescence, in this particular case of an area of about 60 acres. Local industrialists, residents, union representatives and the D of E have all been involved in its eventual implementation through an Environmental Improvement Committee, with its own (original 1975) budget of £400,000 made available through Section 137 of the 1972 Local Government Act.

The policies undertaken through this administrative and political structure have, however, to a large extent been physically orientated. Some unfit housing has been removed, thus facilitating more sensible land use planning and vehicular access. Area landscaping and other environmental improvements have also been programmed, such as clearing the local canal, implemented in part through labour available in the Job Creation Programme, physical improvements to existing factories, sometimes financed by owners, the revival of recreational facilities and better pedestrian circulation. These sorts of improvements, combined with a more thoroughgoing promotion of available UK and EEC regional economic grants, have apparently done much to instil long-term confidence in the area by ameliorating infrastructural constraints operating on existing firms, and indeed by attracting new companies.[34] Certainly other public authorities, such as Tyne and Wear, have adopted the approach, and central government itself has welcomed the new strategy. For the latter, IIAs evidently provide the right sort of inner city initiative and local authorities, according to the Inner City White Paper, will be able to establish IIAs where they can 'carry out, or assist owners to carry out, the conversion of buildings to create new employment, improvements of access and improvements to amenities'.

For some local authorities the sorts of policies which might be introduced through largely environmentally orientated packages such as the IIAs are, however, inadequate and they have sought out more direct financial intervention. There has also been a growing academic interest in the potential for local authorities to become directly involved in the financing, structure and profitability of their economic bases. Policies have been suggested[35] such as greater discrimination in local authority purchasing requirements and the establishment of Development Laboratories by councils, both to encourage local innovation and to help the subsidisation of new industrial investment, but as yet these programmes have had limited impact.

Recently, however, there are indications that a few authorities worried about lack of investment and profitability, especially in smaller local firms, have been attempting to provide risk or equity capital.[36] Normally such financing would probably be of a temporary nature, and may be intended very largely to prop up ailing firms until they achieve economic stability. Nevertheless this more overtly interventionist approach to local economic planning which the widening use of equity finance allows admits eventually the possibility that councils will expand away from the provision simply of physical infrastructure, away even from loan financing, to a position where investment of risk capital became commonplace. For some urban commentators, at least, this would be welcome. To one it seems evident that 'strategic planning authorities could have their own budgets from Parliament to enable them to acquire a proportionate share in the ownership of firms in return for providing investment in the form of loans and grants.'[37]

But just how prevalent is this trend? In practice not very. South Yorkshire has elected to invest a proportion of its superannuation fund in small, viable firms.[38] And some private Acts of Parliament, such as the Tyne and Wear Act of 1976, have attempted to provide local authorities with greater economic powers over the provision of long-term loans covering a wide range of facilities, grants towards the financing of local authority loan interest and rent and removal costs, and the powers to invest in company shares. However, whereas powers sought with regard to grants and loans were approved in the case of the Tyne and Wear Act, those sought for wider equity financing were, interestingly enough, disallowed in Parliament.[39] Nevertheless, this authority has set up a Small Companies Finance Board to provide venture capital for smaller, local firms.

With this veritable panoply of local economic planning powers ranging from the totally permissive to the directly interventionist, it might seem that the goal of economic regeneration, widely advocated by urban commentators in general and by major urban experiments in particular, could readily be achieved. But will it?

1. Local authorities are under no obligation to introduce more comprehensive economic planning powers. Indeed many still adopt largely permissive policies, and remain reluctant to expand into more extended forms of economic planning. And yet Stone is surely right to see the former sorts of powers, even when combined with more sympathetic local authority policies towards housing, education and transport, as unlikely to 'provide sufficient stimulus to secure the revival of the badly run-down industrial areas'.[40] Although he was discussing London and its problems, it still remains a generally valid evaluation.

2. But where authorities are prepared to become more interventionist in outlook, they enter a minefield of legal, and financial difficulties. Much industrial development would need to be financed out of the small and competitive Locally Determined Sector budget, a constraint which would largely inhibit more intensive experimentation. Besides generally deficient financing, lack of specific funding for, say, industrial renovation grants is seen also as a shortcoming in the existing administrative structure.[41] So, too, is the generally inadequate position over land costs,[42] which are seen as too high, allowing little possibility for local authorities to acquire land and subsequently and hence dispose of it at more realistic and attractive prices. Furthermore, for those councils which are eager to acquire and develop land for industrial uses, there remain nagging problems of disparate and often very specific legislation. In Southwark, for instance, it has been pointed out that seven Acts allow the authority to acquire land and build factories on it, but none of them encourages the building of factories on land not owned by the authority.[43] A wider and more comprehensive legal framework would clearly help. It is of course anticipated that this constraint will be moderated in any Inner City Act, but under what conditions and for exactly which authorities remains to be seen.

3. For those authorities prepared to declare IIAs in an attempt to alleviate industrial obsolescence, progress is by no means plain sailing either. As yet IIAs are not statutory instruments; they depend rather on existing grants for residential improvement and redevelopment, the clearance of derelict land and regional economic development. Certainly in the Rochdale case there seems to be a perceived need for larger renovation grants to improve industrial buildings, works and machinery, and a general grant to ameliorate the local environment.

Some of these constraints may be removed in an Inner City Act, but if the White Paper is to provide the framework for the subsequent legislation, then IIAs will eventually only allow local authorities opportunities to convert buildings for new employment and improve access and amenities. Even then these powers are likely to be spatially limited to authorities with 'serious inner area problems'. Clearly as matters stand now, IIAs are unlikely to provide a framework encouraging greater intervention within the financial and organisational structures of firms involved. It is certainly true that even relatively modest physical improvements can considerably improve the profitability of smaller firms, but whether they are likely to have a significant effect through increasing investment by local firms, or attracting new companies, seems very debatable. IIAs are a sensible step forward in combining physical and—to a limited extent—financial powers, but whether this advance is far enough is an altogether different proposition.

4. For the most interventionist inclined authorities, constraints remain correspondingly acute. To councils like Tyne and Wear, wider economic powers such as investing in shares and hence acquiring voting rights in companies, even potentially guiding control, seems one way to increase economic resources, to fill any gaps left by central government and to test new approaches. But there are tremendous problems.

Schemes intended to provide equity capital for small local firms normally run into the problems of finance. Central government is still clearly reluctant to encourage this sort of function within local authorities, and therefore provides no formal financing arrangements. Hence councils have to scrape the barrel to find likely sources of equity funding. And as the very schemes themselves are the object of considerable local and central interest, even concern, there has been a tendency to ensure the absolute viability of any company aided in this way. This has tended to mean that the number of industrial, as opposed to commercial, firms enjoying local authority equity financing remains minute. The extremely close, usually independently undertaken, vetting of prospective companies has ensured that. Whether, of course, such a process undermines the very function the policy was intended to fulfil in the first place is a moot point. And even if more generous regulations were to be introduced, encouraging more companies to apply for available resources, how long would such resources last? Not long, in all probability.

Of course it is not just the financing that remains a problem. There are no legal powers, other than in a few private Acts, allowing authorities to provide risk capital to local firms. Further recent attempts by other authorities to acquire such powers have failed, partly because central government would appear to prefer these to be contained within a general Bill to ensure that all economically distressed areas can benefit.[44] But as the chroniclers of the only partially successful Tyne and Wear Act point out, no such general Bill is likely to emerge in the near future, though some authorities clearly consider that the private market is failing and hence intervention is essential, and on the whole it is those authorities with the gravest economic problems which have done most to introduce innovatory policies. To a large extent they have done this because existing economic policy has done very little to help the older, established inner city firms which tend not to benefit from regional policy and which, although they may be able to obtain loan financing, tend to become too highly 'geared' because of the proportionally limited risk capital in relation to total financing. All this may do is to encourage their closure, and hence to reduce still further existing inner city economic bases.

It is for these reasons that some authorities are eager to acquire greater powers of financial intervention and control. Of course, there will be objections from those who see the process as tending towards corporatism, from those who object to public money being used to subsidise the profits of private industry, and from advocates of *laissez-faire*. But if inner cities are to be regenerated, existing local economic powers will not suffice. They might have a role to play in distributing and directing development in an era of growth, but we are no longer in that happy position. Cities are in a cumulative cycle of decay, and if this is to be reversed far more interventionist policies will be required. IIAs, wider loan powers, more sympathetic policies relating to housing, education, transport and so on will all help, but only powers of positive intervention will directly work towards keeping ailing firms going, allowing profitable ones to expand and new ones to be created, and will at the same time allow authorities to acquire a profit sharing, even controlling, interest in its local economy. Central government might be reluctant to see authorities assume such powers, but then its own policies have largely ignored the position of the existing, older, urban based firm. That local authorities should now wish to usurp, and expand on, such powers as do exist should not come as a surprise.

PRIVATE ENTREPRENEURIAL ACTIVITY

For some commentators[45] the powers of local authorities will never be totally sufficient to regenerate inner city manufacturing bases because the public sector lacks the necessary commitment, entrepreneurial skill and political, financial and legal power. To this school of thought it will be essential to involve other regenerative agencies divorced from, although probably working in association with, local authorities. In particular there has been a growing sentiment that part of the shortfall in employment opportunities apparent with the decline in older manufacturing firms could be made up through the more vigorous activity of small urban industrial establishments cashing in on the latent physical and human resources of cities.

In the last few years, for instance, there has been widespread interest in the possibilities of urban industrial conservation. Sometimes, as at Rotherhithe in east London, administrative structures have been relatively complex. Here a group of nineteenth-century workshops have been converted by the Industrial Buildings Preservation Trust, a registered charity, to provide workshop space for a variety of crafts and related industries. Initially, however, the development required the co-operation of the local authority, Southwark, which acquired the freehold of the property from the Port of London Authority and subsequently leased out the site to the Trust. A similar experiment has occurred in Clerkenwell, where an early twentieth-century storage depot has been converted into small workshops, under the general management of the Clerkenwell Trust, which raised the necessary finance for the conversion, helped negotiate a lease, and initiated general environmental improvements in the area. As with the Rotherhithe project, existing local craftsmen are encouraged to rent the new workshops, through a policy of low rents, in an attempt to create and sustain local industrial linkages.

These sorts of developments and more spontaneous ones, as for instance around Covent Garden after the departure of the market, have been cited as clear indications of the viability of craft industries within the older urban areas. The TCPA, for example, considers them 'particularly appropriate'[46] for inner city regeneration. Clearly too, these sorts of proposals are intimately bound up with the growing interest in the fate of the small firm generally. As early as 1971 the Bolton Committee pointed out the beneficial influence of small firms, especially in providing cheap, specialist components, in stimulating innovatory approaches to management and production, and in acting generally as seedbeds encouraging the development of allied, linked enterprises.[47] Although at that time the Committee saw no particular need to provide especially favourable services to such firms, sentiments have changed, and by 1977 central government had introduced policies[48] such as reduced Corporation Tax levied on such companies, increased counselling services, the provision of grants to undertake feasibility studies into collaboration amongst such enterprises and some additional aid through the provisions of the 1972 Industry Act. Clearly some of these policy initiatives will benefit inner city companies.

So too will the 1976 Industrial Common Ownership Act. Under this provision central government, in the form of the D of I, is to provide a revolving loan fund of £250,000 over five years to co-operative schemes with a reasonable chance of success, a possibility made that much more realistic if the legal and technical experience available from the Industrial Common Ownership Movement are tapped. But even then the regulations covering proposed loans are tough. Loans of £7,500 must be supported by the Industry Secretary, security has to be provided to ensure repayment, and relevant trade unions must be consulted before any loan is granted.

Nevertheless, the whole tendency towards supporting small firms, co-operatives and the like has acquired considerable impetus recently. Central government has provided financial aid and some local authorities, such as Wandsworth, have appointed officers directly involved with promoting small industrial projects and common ownership schemes. Some independent organisations, too, have suggested that advances might be made in this way: the National Council of Social Service, for example, considers that co-operatives and small workshops need urgent support and encouragement, and would welcome the establishment of locally controlled budgets for this purpose.[49] But how realistic is it to imagine that small workshops and co-operatives are likely to make any meaningful improvements to inner city economic structures?

1. The idea of the small renovated industrial workshop has its attractions, especially in those older urban districts where the scope for this sort of policy might be considerable. But typically it depends on the unusual combination of individual and group initiative with a local authority sympathetic to questions such as financing and the waiving of some public health and development control regulations.

Even then, the costs involved in rehabilitation can be prohibitive, and hence the desirable policy of low rentals difficult if not impossible to achieve.

2. With regard to small industries generally, no doubt tremendous possibilities exist for increasing the potential employment capacity of such firms. But several points need to be made. Not all small firms are dynamic, expanding establishments eager to take on new employees. Many are inefficient, dynastic and unable or unwilling to use sources of equity financing which are available. The latter may anyway be very limited in scope. Export arrangements may be poor for small firms too, which generally see far too many bureaucratic pressures without compensatory government inspired benefits such as research grants, lower taxation rates, the ability to offset losses on new ventures against taxation and so on. The D of I has certainly been prepared recently to listen more to the grievances of smaller firms. It has, for example, raised the ceiling for the reduced rate of Corporation Tax, increased retirement relief, simplified the administration of VAT, increased IDC limits, improved counselling and informative services and built some 'nursery', advanced factories, all of which policy modifications are intended to help smaller firms.

But this transformation needs to be put into perspective. The Department's concern for the small firm is still minimal in terms of committed resources and staff. A great deal of the financial aid available, moreover, is not especially suitable for the smaller concern. The minimum limit on grants or loans may for instance, be too high for many companies, and attempts to rationalise certain industries under Section 8 of the 1972 Industry Act may be, in practice, disadvantageous to inner city industry, which is frequently less efficient than that elsewhere. Not all small firms, of course, are in inner city areas anyway, and indeed perhaps those most likely to expand would not be located there. Furthermore, the main focus of interest at both central and local government has traditionally been the larger, footloose, often multinational, company and not the smaller unit. It will take a long time to overcome this bias.

3. The ability of the co-operative movement to alleviate inner city unemployment must remain very doubtful. Available resources are minimal, and even where these might be supplemented through finance from the Job Creation Programme, proposed schemes have to receive the tacit approval of local trade unions and local competi-

tors. Clearly these requirements may not always be met. Neither need the local authority necessarily approve of the activities of co-operative schemes, which can often create crucial conflicts and strains, as for example occurred in projects supported by the Cumbria CDP.[50] Even where authorities such as Wandsworth[51] have shown active support for the approach, problems are likely to occur, especially with the perennial problem of financing. This is so because even those resources specifically available to local authorities are extremely limited, normally to the 2p rate provision in the Local Government Act 1972.

4. Even if workshops, co-operatives and small firms in general were to enjoy a general renaissance, who would benefit? Not unemployed, unskilled or semi-skilled workers, since to a large extent it would be skilled employees who would be provided with additional employment opportunities, exactly those for whom jobs can anyway normally be found in inner city locations. No doubt a limited number of unemployed might be taken on if such firms were to expand. No doubt too, small establishments have a place in inner city economic structures, by acting as the third force in capitalising on local funds and community initiatives, in providing sources of advice and expertise and in developing innovative projects. But surely not in any large-scale regeneration of economic bases.

CENTRAL GOVERNMENT INITIATIVE

Even supporters of increased local economic planning on the part of both public and private sectors usually acknowledge the importance of centrally devised policies. In particular there have been consistent calls for either a refinement of existing economic policies or the development of new ones.

With regard to the former point, regional policy, for instance, has exercised many minds. It seems evident that the approach has benefited a few larger industrial firms and the suburban residents of older cities in the Development Areas, but not existing firms or the inhabitants of older city areas. To Nabarro, for example, it remains one of the most telling criticisms of regional policy that 'most of the money ends up in the pockets of a small number of very large companies introduced from outside the region.'[52] On the other hand some London agencies consider that IDC and ODP policies, designed to control industrial and commercial development, have in practice helped to over-decentralise the capital's economic base.[53] In fact the amount of London's industry which has moved to Development Areas has been small, and generally most IDCs are granted to firms wishing to expand in the South-East and Midlands. Nevertheless, it seems clear that if regional policy is to aid inner city areas it needs to be more site specific, more sectorally specific and more generous in helping existing industrial firms rather than generally concentrating on the small amount of footloose industry. Equally, if national policies to decentralise, say, civil servants from London are to be carried out it must be appreciated that this process will not help inner city economies unless spatial distributions are controlled at the sub-regional scale.

Other central government policies, too, may be inimical to the development of inner city employment. Large parts of inner London, for instance, have been legally prevented from advertising potential industrial sites. Sections 7 and 8 of the 1972 Industry Act under which the D of I administers financial assistance, are also seen as inappropriate for older urban areas[54] in that grant thresholds may be too high, hence eliminating many smaller firms, loans normally granted for too short a period, and the entire procedure dependent upon the Secretary of State believing that such assistance is in the national interest. These administrative regulations are clearly likely to act on the whole to the disbenefit of many inner city firms.

The permanent problem of land costs cannot be ignored here either. Inner city land, often owned by public authorities, remains generally expensive, partly because the District Valuer dictates its price. Small, or negligible, amounts are often available anyway, and since more and cheaper land tends always to be located in suburban areas, quite understandably more industrialists have relocated or started there. The Community Land Act, despite brave promises to begin with, has not at all balanced out this particular equation.

Inner cities are discriminated against in other ways, too. Take the English Industrial Estates Corporation, for instance. Central government provides long-term mortgage lending to finance purchases of factories which it provides through the Corporation, but not for the purchase of other factories owned by the local authority or by private developers. And as most government sponsored industrial estates have, until very recently, been built in suburban locations, this policy has undoubtedly affected inner city economic viability.

Finally, in this discussion of potential changes in existing government policies, mention has to be made of what is often seen as the chaotic field of retraining.[55] A number of national and local organisations are involved, without adequate long-term planning or co-ordination, and without a thorough understanding of which skills are required, where and in what quantity. Local educational authorities, too, are often not sensibly integrated, and there remains a lack of interest and concern within schools as to the sorts of industrial skills and work expertise that children may need. Where, too, specific employment generation schemes are created, such as the Job Creation Programme, too many one-off, *ad hoc* projects may be supported instead of those with prospects of longer-term viability.

But apart from remedying deficiencies in existing central government policy, there have been suggestions by inner city analysts that an entirely new interventionary approach is needed by central government if there is to be any prospect of inner city regeneration. The Birmingham IAS, for instance, has floated the idea that unless central government departments and agencies—and here we are largely talking about the D of E, the D of I and the National Enterprise Board (NEB)—adopt a more favourable attitude towards inner city economic revival, the decline may become irreversible.[56]

In the case of the D of E its regional administration has been seen as a possible agent for directing intra-regional economic development. Also, the generally favourable response on the part of this department towards industrial improvement areas can be interpreted as an indication of growing concern at the problems and potential solutions to industrial decay. But on the other hand, the D of E has limited legal and financial powers when it comes to industry, and its regional structure has typically largely refrained from attempting to intervene in this market.[57]

Not so the D of I. Its regional organisation has been interpreted as a possible development agency using the wide powers available, especially in the 1972 Industry Act, to operate in Assisted Areas and also in inner city areas of the Midlands and South-East. A new attitude towards older urban areas has apparently been assumed by the D of I, for instance in its policies such as the building of more advanced factories in the inner parts of conurbations, and the provision of selective financial aid and advice about inner city sites and premises. In non-assisted districts too, IDCs will be granted more easily to inner city firms to allow them to expand, and for truly mobile projects the government has 'decided that inner London and inner Birmingham will in future take precedence, after the Assisted Areas and in front of the new and expanded towns, in consideration of IDC applications for mobile projects coming forward from the relevant region'.[58]

But it has been the NEB rather than the D of I which has often been seen as the most likely inner city development agency.[59] Established in the 1975 Industry Act, the Board and the Scottish and Welsh Development Agencies were granted wide powers to promote industrial efficiency and competitiveness through planning agreements, the provision of loans or the acquisition of interests in certain firms. Although these operations were as far as possible to 'create employment in areas of high unemployment', this was to occur through 'commercially sound public enterprises and joint ventures with private enterprise'. Certainly for some inner city organisations the powers of the NEB to direct subsidiaries to expand in older urban areas and its power to establish manufacturing companies have been seen as potential saving graces. But are the NEB and other central government agencies likely to, or even to want to, attack the problems of the inner city?

1. The D of I has traditionally had a regional spatial dimension but not especially an intra-regional one. True, some inner city factories have recently been constructed by the Department, which is more prepared now to provide information and advice on the possibilities of locating in older urban areas than ever before. But in terms of total investment and totality of aims, the inner city clearly remains relatively unimportant to the D of I. There would have to be far more in the way of inner city promotion and guidance from its regional branches, and substantially greater legal and financial commitment, for that evaluation to be altered. Moreover even long-term, national industrial strategies outlining the potential for future economic development[60] largely ignore any spatial context, let alone a sub-regional or an intra-urban one, and concentrate instead on sectoral improvements. Planning agreements too, which some inner city authorities, such as Wandsworth, see as one way of ensuring that private industry which expands does so in a socially just manner, and that industry which relocates or contracts pays for the social and economic disruption this might cause, have to a very large extent been eschewed. Not surprisingly, then, more radical suggestions[61] for there to be a decentralisation of central government's industrial grant administration to local authorities, or for such grants to be applied automatically when a certain proportion of local industrial jobs are lost, have been ignored. Such programmes might well satisfy

the 'need for substantial and direct public sector intervention in industrial investment in the inner city'[62] which independent observers have perceived. But then the D of I and the government in general are far more concerned with global industrial productivity than with the localised disbenefits this policy will bring.

2. The NEB has undoubtedly evolved a more spatially sympathetic attitude. Policies discussing the investment potential for the North-East and North-West regions[63] have been produced which outline, for instance, possible expansion of service industries in Liverpool. In that authority too, the NEB has become involved in funding a small scheme which allows some of its capital to be invested in viable local firms identified by Merseyside County Council. But it would be very easy to overemphasise the capacity of the NEB to alleviate inner city unemployment. Much of its finance is allocated to the 'Big Five' companies it supports. It is charged additionally with creating productive employment and hence obtaining a good return on its investment, a constraint likely to inhibit any massive inner city intervention. The small-scale administrative structure of the Board, too, prevents substantial promotional activities, and this tends to limit its interests to a relatively small number of establishments.

Because the NEB is empowered to concentrate its activities in areas of high unemployment, because there are likely to be specific North-East and North-West England regional boards, and because of the possibilities of it being expanded massively as North Sea oil reserves accrue, it has been seen as a saviour of inner cities. But certainly as it stands at the moment its commitments to established companies, its limited promotional activities and its need to obtain a commercial return on investment will prohibit large-scale inner city intervention. Indeed, exactly because central government has based its national economic strategy on industrial regeneration and because conventional wisdom has it, probably correctly, that this is more likely to be achieved on new, virgin sites, inner cities might enjoy very little benefit from the oil bonanza. Blandly invoking the NEB to redeem the fate of older urban areas simply ignores the political and economic realities of national government.

Once industrial decline is identified as a cause rather than a symptom of urban decay policies will inevitably emerge which attempt to reduce, even reverse, this drift. An air of optimism, officially at least, has descended on some central government ministers who evidently feel this Canute-like act can work. To the Environment Secretary it seems that 'the opportunity to attract industry back to the inner areas now exists in a way in which it did not a decade or so ago.'[64] And as indicated above, the private sector and local and central policies have indeed been designed or invoked to attract or reju- venate manufacturing industry.

And yet any thorough analysis of these programmes must remain pessimistic. The private sector has so consistently run down inner city locations, and its recent rush towards industrial rehabilitation is so dependent on the happy coincidence of many factors, that one must remain sceptical of its powers to create large-scale employment for unskilled or semi-skilled workers. Local authorities are certainly becoming far more economic-minded. But their limited powers, especially to invest directly in firms, mean their total impact will remain small. Central government, on the other hand, through part- nership agreements, grant powers in the 1972 Industry Act and the NEB, might have the power, but not really the inclination. It has to think of national recovery, national unemployment and regional, rather than intra-regional, inequalities. And of course, there are not many votes in inner cities, literally and politically. Most of them, from a Labour Government's point of view, will vote Labour anyway.

If that might seem a cynical interpretation, it is not a unique one. To the more radical branch of the CDP, for example, it seems very unlikely that inner cities will be regenerated under existing powers because so little mobile industry is available at present, thus making the entire 'work to workers' policy a 'liberal utopian dream'.[65] Rather than continue to develop the essentially permissive and yet nationally expensive policies of the past, what is needed, according to the CDP, is a much more positive approach based on powerfully enforced planning agreements, and powers of state and local author- ity financial intervention. The private owners of industry have failed to guarantee efficient production, jobs and even decent living con- ditions. 'It is time the workers began to consider the alternatives' is the CDP prognosis.[66]

A radical programme such as that put forward by the CDP might well retain more inner city employment, but at a political and finan- cial cost which no central government is likely to consider. And there would be plenty of academic support too, to suggest that the con- tinued decentralisation of urban industrial bases, especially if its social costs could be reduced, is perhaps the only, even the only desirable, policy. Many would agree with the conclusion that 'the derelict urban areas are in fact caught in an appalling dilemma. They have totally lost the capacity to retain, let alone attract, the jobs and the industry on which their hopes of regeneration depend.'[67] Even a substantial sector of tertiary industry, traditionally seen as the natural successor to urban manufacturing employment, would appear to be entering a cycle of decentralisation.[68]

Faced with these overpowering centrifugal forces, solutions have been posited which would attempt to guide rather than confront the processes of urban industrial decline. Outer parts of conurbations could be developed for manufacturing industry as the inner city declined, a trend which might be implemented in a more socially just manner if transport and housing policies were developed to allow inner city residents to follow their employment bases on either a diurnal or a permanent basis. And for the inner city itself, the so-called quaternary and quinary industries, concentrating on health and education services, administration, research, development and tourism, might prove the most viable policies in the long term.[69]

Many would be reluctant, of course, to accept the eventual demise of urban manufacturing bases, but perhaps it is a decision already made. The urban experiments identified the primacy of economic factors in attempting to explain city decline, and because of the powerful nature of these processes, suggested that correspondingly powerful policies would be required. But they will not be forthcoming. They would require from central government a commitment to sanction new legal, and especially financial, powers over private industry which would be unacceptable to any foreseeable government. Reformist policies attempting to help industrial bases might reduce the rate of decline, or even allow local increases, but unless policies are designed both to intervene financially and to control spatially the structure and performance of British industry, urban economic decline will persist. And as long as central government perceives its policy in essentially aspatial, macro-economic terms, such a policy transformation remains extremely unlikely.

NOTES TO CHAPTER 8

1 See, for instance, London Boroughs Association, 1977; Southwark Trades Council and J. Roberts (Southwark CDP), 1976; and from central government, HMSO, *Policy for the Inner Cities*, 1977.
2 Quoted by P. Shore, Manchester, 1976.
3 LB Islington, 1975.
4 LB Wandsworth, 1972.

5   D of E, *British Cities 1951–71*, 1976.
6   See, for example, D. Smith, 1971: '. . . industrial dispersal has failed to keep pace with the planned relocation of slum dwellers in peripheral "overspill" estates', p. 487.
7   W. Luttrell, 1970.
8   D of E, *Study of the Inner Areas of Conurbations*, Vol. I, p. 6.
9   P. Shore (as 2).
10 See, for example, the stress laid upon economic revival in IAS, Summaries of Consultants, Final Reports, 1977.
11 See for instance NCDP, 1974: 'Employment has become an issue of central importance not merely because of the deteriorating economic conditions of many areas, but because it is clearly a key variable with repercussions across the board', p. 28.
12 P. Gripaios, 1977A.
13 This section is largely based upon P. Gripaios (as 12); *The Economist*, 1977; and B. Smith, 1975 and 1977.
14 G. Cameron, 1977.
15 A trend seen as important in both London and Glasgow: see P. Gripaios, 1976; and R. Henderson, 1974.
16 See, for instance, R. Nabarro, 1976: commenting on Liverpool's industrial structure, he found a 'virtual absence of new investment', p. 285.
17 D. Massey and R. Meegan, 1976.
18 Southwark Trades Council and J. Roberts (Southwark CDP) (as 1).
19 LB Wandsworth, 23.9.1975.
20 *The Economist* (as 13).
21 LB Lewisham.
22 R. Henderson (as 15).
23 P. Gripaios, 1977B.
24 R. Dennis, 1976.
25 See, for example, J. Goddard, 1977.
26 J. Blake, 1977.
27 A. Evans with L. Russell, 1976.
28 For details of local authority powers over, and attitudes towards, industry, see M. Camina, 1974.
29 See N. Flynn and K. Thomas, 1977; and R. Nabarro (as 16) for a more pessimistic appraisal of the potential for expansion in small firms.
30 For more detailed expositions of the 'orthodox' local authority attitude towards economic planning see, for example, Docklands Joint Committee, 1976; LB Wandsworth, 1972, 11.11.1975, 6.4.1976, and 11.1.1977; K. Thomas, 1977; B. Smith, 1976; and P. Stone, 1976.
31 As, for instance, recommended by Docklands Joint Committee, 1975.
32 See, for instance, R. Nabarro and C. Watts, 1977: 'The impact of training and placement services on men currently out of work in inner Liverpool is virtually nil.'
33 For details of IIAs in Rochdale, see R. Hargreave, 1976; and Rochdale MB, 1977.
34 With the creation of some new industrial establishments, one analysis

suggests that council investment of only £15,000 has yielded a return in the way of private investment of £1·3m: M. Franklin and F. Stafford, 1977.

35 R. Nabarro, 1977B.
36 For an expansion of why and how local authorities should become involved in equity financing, see R. Minns and J. Thornley, 1977A and B.
37 R. Minns, 1975, p. 484.
38 South Yorks Council, County Regional Investment Scheme.
39 P. Rogers and C. Smith, 1977.
40 P. Stone (as 30), p. 13.
41 M. Franklin and F. Stafford (as 34), p. 214.
42 See M. Allan, 1977.
43 Southwark Trades Council, 1977.
44 For an expansion of these arguments, see P. Rogers and C. Smith (as 39).
45 See M. Franklin and F. Stafford (as 34), N. Falk, 1975; and M. Franks, 1975.
46 TCPA, 1977.
47 HMSO, Report of the Committee of Inquiry on Small Firms, 1971.
48 *Guardian*, 29.4.1977.
49 National Council of Social Service, 1977.
50 J. Pearce, 1977.
51 LB Wandsworth, 11.1.1977.
52 R. Nabarro (as 35), p. 230; and (as 16).
53 London Boroughs Association (as 1); LB Wandsworth, 4.6.1976.
54 P. Rogers and C. Smith (as 39); and Association of Metropolitan Authorities, 1976.
55 London Boroughs Association (as 1).
56 IAS/B/9, 1976.
57 D of E, *The D of E and Its Work*, 1975.
58 HMSO, *Policy for the Inner Cities*, 1977.
59 See, for instance, Southwark Trades Council (as 43).
60 See, for example, HMSO, *The Regeneration of British Industry*, 1974; and HMSO, *An Approach to Industrial Strategy*, 1975.
61 Canning Town CDP, 1975.
62 Inner City Working Group . . ., 1977, p. 13.
63 NEB, 1977.
64 P. Shore (as 2).
65 For an expansion of the CDP position see CDP, *The Costs of Industrial Change*, 1977; N. Moor, 1974; and Canning Town CDP (as 61).
66 Birmingham CDP, 1975, p. 36.
67 *AJ* Editorial, 1976, p. 814.
68 See J. Goddard, 1975.
69 As suggested by P. Hall, 1977B.

Chapter 9

MANAGING

A cynical view of the urban programme would be that it has never seriously attempted to provide additional resources to deprived people or areas, but has instead placed an emphasis on more effective use of existing facilities and organisations. The CDP for instance, as originally envisaged was, amongst other functions, to examine possible improvements in efficiency of local government services;[1] the UG were commissioned to examine decision making processes and to formulate guidelines to help establish a 'total approach';[2] the IAS placed a heavy emphasis on the better co-ordination of services to ensure that the most deprived received additional resources;[3] and the CCP was charged with evaluating co-operative management schemes between central government and local authorities.[4] Indeed it could be argued that with the possible exception of UA, all the elements within the programme have had as one of their *raisons d'être*—if not the prime one—better agency co-ordination or improved service delivery at either the local area scale or at the level of the overall local authority.

It is not at all surprising that this should be so, for apart from the obvious advantages of cheapness and 'flexibility', this approach has received a great deal of official and academic mileage within the last few years which has done much to influence the policy making environment. On the official front, for instance, it is possible to trace an interest in, and a call for, better co-ordination through the Maud[5] and Mallaby[6] committees of 1967, with their recommendations for better management organisations and improved services, through the Seebohm report,[7] with its concern for the improved co-ordination and delivery of social services, to the Bains report[8] five years later, which aimed at providing 'a system of management which will lead to the most effective service to the community'. Complementing these events, there has also clearly been an interest within central government policy fields in improving management structures at all administrative levels, either as an end in itself or, more usually, to improve policy effectiveness in fields such as housing or planning. The establishment of the Urban Deprivation Unit, and some years later the Cabinet Committee on inner city problems, the calls for local authorities to improve their administration to deal with the interdisciplinary problems of GIAs and HAAs,[9] and the publication by central government of management networks to aid the implementation of structure plans[10] are all indications of this trend.

Academically, too, there has been enormous interest in the problems of local authority administration, and in particular in the potential of management structures, notably corporate planning, to improve the effectiveness of local authority policy. Stewart, for instance, in 1971 saw an increasing emphasis being placed on the management of local authority affairs in relation to their environments[11] and three years later, together with Greenwood, suggested that there had been, and ought to be, a greater shift away from the older local authority approach of departmentalised service committees towards wider federal management structures.[12] These should be supported by corporate planning which would aim to improve the unity of local authority action and adjust activities to changing needs and problems. Other commentators have expanded on this issue,[13] and certain key components seem to be widely accepted as integral to the operation of corporate planning: an attempt to understand the interactions of problems and policies; a clear statement of objectives; a precise indication as to how these objectives are to be attained and in what priority; a thorough evaluation of programmes; a willingness to alter policies; and an operative structure which attempts to combine longer-term objectives with more precise short- and medium-term aims.

There are, it is quite evident, advantages in introducing greater precision in local authority policy making, in clearer definitions of aims and in a willingness to experiment with, and to amend, policy. In particular this is so because local authorities are normally hindered in their administrative capacities by management problems such as, say, a lack of monitoring of policy; poor communications between departments, officers, councillors and resident clients, and poor co-ordination in manpower policies, resources and in the continuity of programmes. These problems may be particularly acute in inner city and deprived areas because, as the Liverpool SNAP project points out, 'the really intractable nature of multiple deprivation is that to solve one problem is but to succumb to another, and since public action is always conceived in a fragmented fashion, resulting pro- grammes have not been relevant to the real circumstances of the inner city.'[14]

Exactly because of this perceived inability on the part of local authorities to tackle urban deprivation through traditional manage- ment and organisational structures, a number of urban experiments and allied initiatives have been devised to improve administration both at the centre—normally through some form of corporate or co-ordinated activity—and at the local level, through various forms of decentralised area management. In this chapter both these trends will be examined within the basic premise that, although traditional management structures and operations have been inadequate, the whole emphasis towards 'better management' has been overstressed, its beneficial effects exaggerated and its overall influence in general, and specifically within the urban programme, been to deflect atten- tion away from a reconsideration of policy and resource allocation. Improved co-ordination is certainly not sufficient, and perhaps not even necessary, to implement an inner city programme.

Attempts at improved co-ordination take various forms. Some local authorities, for instance, have created central Policy and Manage- ment Committees to lay down guideline objectives for overall local authority effort which are passed on to lower committees, who adjust their own, more specific, programmes to conform with this financial and policy planning. The whole system operates by means of a series of plans setting down objectives, alternative and selected programmes, financial distributions and monitoring arrangements. Specialised interdepartmental or areal issues may be dealt with through indivi- dual reports, perhaps prepared by a central co-ordinating or planning team. In fact it is the standard corporate planning system.

Within the urban programme itself there have been similar calls for improved efficiency through, for example, Urban Deprivation Plans[15] to which central government would allocate block grants, and which would examine policies and budgets through a community review reflecting the totality of problems and policies applicable to deprived areas and the potential for improved co-ordination between all rele- vant bodies. This approach is clearly very similar to the 'total ap- proach' advocated by a number of urban commentators, but perhaps most specifically by the Liverpool IAS,[16] with its call for improved co-operation at central and local levels, the allocation of additional resources to people and areas most in need, the involvement of residents, businesses and voluntary organisations in attempting to alleviate deprivation, and its general switch of emphasis from concern for departmentalised efficiency to encouragement of integrated, collective and effective action focusing on the most severe problems. And finally, out of a multitude of examples which might be selected, the UG ought to be mentioned because of their marked and persistent call for improved organisation through community reviews, operational planning and so on, which are obviously methodologically linked to corporate planning, and indeed can be seen as manifestations of it.

Despite the avidity with which many urban analysts have jumped on the 'better management' bandwagon, there has been a steady groundswell of what is, if not opposition to the whole movement, at least healthy scepticism. In particular misgivings have been voiced at two operative levels: technical questions apparent in the workings of corporate planning; and, at a more general level, dissatisfaction with the implications behind a heavy emphasis on improved management as a major tool in the eradication of urban deprivation.

Attempts to introduce more rational management procedures through various forms of corporate planning, as advocated by some of the urban experiments, have been criticised on a number of technical issues.[17]

1. General objectives which are usually stated as an initial procedure in many forms of co-ordinated management may be bland to the point of being completely innocuous. The Oldham Study, for instance, sees desirable objectives as including the development of new housing and shopping facilities and the attraction of new industry. But does this sort of statement really help at all? The development of any of these objectives might be generally regarded as beneficial; it would be hard in fact to disagree with them. But unfortunately they do not even begin to state the problems inherent in such broad statements of intent: what sort of industry, where, who for, how will it be attracted, are really the starting points of any debate on industrial regeneration for instance; bland statements which imply or ensure broad consensus preclude essential political debate into policy and its spatial priority.

2. At the opposite end of the spectrum, general objectives are often fined down to very detailed programmes capable of exact monitoring:

the building of x houses, or the attraction of y jobs. The difficulty here is that there is an inevitable assumption to suppose that if x and y have been achieved within the scheduled period the policy is a success. But in so doing, this detracts from any discussions on policy itself: the sort of housing being built might not be appropriate for needs; the jobs attracted might not be of a suitable nature for the unemployed.

3. The adoption of a 'corporate planning' system can mean a multitude of things, and co-ordination in specific departments might not at all help overall local authority unity of purpose. The Rotherham Study seems to make this mistake by divorcing environmental problems from other pressing issues. In creating stronger departmental co-ordination, it might in practice actually reduce overall authority corporateness. Similarly, some systems advocate a strongly centralised corporate élite of chief officers who might become, to their minds, corporate—but will the authority? Moreover, if a tight central body of officers is mirrored by a similar body of councillors, the inevitable result will be to remove most of the latter from any semblance of real power, which will remain firmly in the hand of older, respected, but probably less experimentally minded politicians.

4. There may be a tendency for some corporate systems to become self-perpetuating, almost frozen in an introverted cycle of certainty. In particular, because of the cyclical nature of the process, it may well militate against residents and other interested parties being able to make their views known other than at specific times over specific issues. The system, rather than its output, becomes the focus of attention.

5. There is a tendency for corporate planning to stress efficiency and not equity. The whole concept, anyway, emerged from business circles, where clearly the former is more important than the latter. But in local authorities an emphasis on efficiency may guarantee an 'adequate' provision of services without considering, say, whether these services are achieving desired aims or whether certain areas or people should be given additional resources not strictly justified in numerical terms. In emphasising efficiency and not personal or areal need there may be a tendency to actually reduce resources to specific areas, whereas previous, less 'efficient' management systems catered for the unusual, particularly deprived, location. Attempts have, of course, been made to introduce greater spatial dimensions into cor-

porate systems through area management, and these will be examined later.

It is, however, not simply that the techniques of improved management, as exemplified by corporate planning, seem to create greater problems than their apparently 'objective' image would suggest, but also that severe doubts have been expressed about the overall implications of stressing improved management, both as a generally desirable aim and, in particular, as a means of alleviating urban deprivation. Much of this disquiet has centred on the extent to which a concern for how policies should be co-ordinated deflects discussion away from policy itself. As Cullingworth has pointed out, the whole trend towards corporate management (and participation) may simply not be enough, since 'they may well be seductive, contradictory and self-defeating mechanisms which will help to keep politicians and administrators frantically busy and ineffective while the problems on the ground continue and increase . . .'.[18] Any discrepancy between policy and its co-ordination may in fact be that much more acute in practice in deprived areas simply because existing policy has clearly proved so ineffective in dealing with inherent problems. It is quite clear, too, that some commentators involved with analysing the sort of management structures applicable to areas of urban deprivation see them as but one aspect of a broader question. Stewart *et al.*, for instance, in examining the possibilities of improved local authority structures, point out that the sort of co-ordinated Urban Deprivation Plan they had in mind for disadvantaged authorities would in effect be meaningless unless it led 'to new policy initiatives and new patterns of resource allocation'.[19]

The above interpretation clearly sees 'better management' as one, and perhaps an overstressed, aspect of government in deprived areas. But it is possible to be far more cynical about the whole trend. It could be suggested in fact that improved management is specifically encouraged because neither central nor local government is prepared to implement radical changes in policy. In this new interpretation, it is not that improved management is seen as a minor and over-emphasised addition to the scene, but rather that it is directly stage-managed to remove the focus of attention from policy a phase beyond: the organisation of that policy. Edison evidently sees how this works in practice, in that 'new departments, new units of administration, new divisions of organisations are the general response of governments to problems.'[20]

Now it is possible to imagine two reasons why central and local government may not be prepared to undertake major policy revisions: because they are incapable of introducing new initiatives, or because they are unwilling to do so.

A number of independent observers of urban deprivation have, for instance, made the point that even if public authorities might agree informally that inadequacies are present in existing policy, or that potentially ameliorative changes to that policy might be made, in practice these changes may never occur. Thus the Coventry CDP suggests that there is no problem with the local authority's planning, management or administration, but rather that potential changes in policy which might improve the circumstances of disadvantaged residents are beyond the scope of any local authority, particularly with regard to the employment market.[21] It is not that the authority has attempted to disguise the inadequacy of its policy through a focus on management, but rather that policy which might have improved the situation is not within the scope of that authority.

Of course in other cases, it may not be that the authority is incapable, but rather that it is unwilling to accommodate major changes in outlook. The SNAP report on the history of its progress in the early 1970s points out that changes in local authority procedures simply did not happen, despite constant lobbying, in particular for some form of decentralised administration.[22] It could be argued that the authority, for very good reasons, did not want to do this; and clearly not all recommendations from pressure groups will, or ought to be, carried out. Yet nevertheless anyone with experience of local authorities is likely to encounter their very limited capacity for undertaking major policy reviews, partly, no doubt, because existing procedures are seen as fair and sensible, but also because of an almost inbuilt reluctance to innovate. Now whereas this inflexibility can be interpreted as being due to legal and financial impotence, other commentators see more sinister motives. Dearlove for instance, examining political administration within a London borough, concludes that it is not weak at all, but 'strong, is closed and unresponsive, able actively to avoid and resist demands for change and innovation'.[23] And if this interpretation has general validity, it is clear that for many authorities major policy changes are unlikely to be countenanced and any emphasis on the eradication of deprivation will continue to be placed largely on the improved management of existing policy, since radical changes are traditionally avoided by all forms of government.

It is interesting to note here that many of the urban experiments were in fact commissioned exactly for the purpose of improving management and, as indeed explicitly stated at the time, they were to experiment into ways of achieving better co-ordination of policy without much prospect of additional resource allocation. But notwithstanding this, the two major experimental schemes, the IAS and the CDP, both reject this thesis and call, in varying ways and to varying extents, for the allocation of additional resources to inner city areas, combined with far greater political commitment towards them. The CDP, for instance—and here many examples could be quoted—in examining the government's area improvement programme, specifically states that additional finance and greater political powers should be made available for housing improvements in older urban areas.[24] Similarly, the IAS considers that existing resources are inadequate to deal with urban deprivation. The Birmingham Study suggests that even with improved co-ordination and better use of existing resources, 'there will have to be a greater share of the rate support grant going to deprived areas',[25] and the Liverpool study, which in many ways is the most active in searching out improved co-ordination through the 'total approach', admits that 'the motivating forces will lie in the strength of political commitment to the aims of inner area policy.'[26] The need to evaluate policy, and to provide resources to implement its intensification, will not disappear. Even those experiments established to examine the possibilities of achieving more with the same resources in fact implicitly reject an initial premise: that urban deprivation can be ameliorated through 'better management'.

But of course, not all the demands for improved local authority management relate to modification at the centre, since there is a school of thought which suggests that, although overall local authority management improvements might have some applicability in the eradication of deprivation, they need to be complemented by a decentralisation of services and, perhaps, to a limited extent, of power.[27] But as with the drift towards improved overall local authority management, there are strong grounds for believing that the area management school of argument has lacked precision of definition, and may in fact be peripheral to a viable urban policy.

The methodology of area management has been founded essentially on three strands of thought: official government initiatives, the contributions of independent observers and the influence of the neighbourhood council movement. A variety of government reports, for example, have expressed interest in some form of localised administration. Seebohm wanted decentralised local, purpose-built buildings to cater for all social services:[28] the 'one-door' approach. Bains[29] in England and Patterson[30] in Scotland saw the value of area offices as part of local authority reorganisation within which a variety of departments might have officials dealing with local issues, thereby providing a sort of information point for the public. Legislation on housing too, notably advice contained in circulars explaining HAA legislation,[31] suggest that one particularly effective way of implementation would be through a decentralised local presence, perhaps in a demonstration house. Within recent years too, the D of E has become interested in monitoring more thoroughgoing forms of area management, which it sees as being an effective way of adapting local authorities to the needs of specific areas, with the added advantages of better communications between local authorities and residents, and of introducing improved and cheaper services.[32] These advantages had to some extent already been examined within both elements of the Six Towns Studies. The Sunderland Study, for instance, looked at the sort of neighbourhood organisation which might be set up to administer local authority policies,[33] and IAS were specifically commissioned in part to examine the concept of area management and what its implications might be for an authority. Certainly one retrospective evaluation of the Six Towns experiment concludes that a common theme emerging from them 'is the need for a "total approach" to the problems of an area and linked with this, the idea of "area management" '.[34]

Growing interest within government circles as to the possibilities of area management has clearly been paralleled, even caused by, a very definite intellectual trend in favour of the approach. Donnison, in the early 1970s, for instance, in discussing the micropolitics of London suggested that local area teams might well be set up, possibly with central government funding, to avoid too overt a local authority influence.[35] More recent contributions by Kershaw, suggesting a 'ward watch' approach with far greater involvement of local councillors in the problems of their wards,[36] by Harvey Cox, promoting local centres to co-ordinate service delivery and planning,[37] and by a working party into the future of planning advocating area management as a means of strengthening the role of the councillor at ward and neighbourhood level[38] are three out of very many clear manifestations of the growing influence of the methodology. And specifically with regard to deprived inner city locations, Falk and Martinos suggest the setting up of Social Priority Areas where all available discriminatory programmes might be co-ordinated within an Action Plan prepared by a multi-disciplinary team within a local office.[39]

There also has been a third institutional trend which has done much to stimulate the diffusion of area management techniques: the movement towards neighbourhood or community councils. In Scotland the Wheatley Commission[40] and the subsequent Local Government Act allowed for the creation of community councils which would present the views of communities to the local authority, which in turn was required to 'take action in the interests of that community as appears to be expedient and practicable.'[41] In England the emphasis has been placed on neighbourhood councils, which in a consultation paper in 1974 the D of E considered might organise self-help projects, represent the needs of a community to the local authority, and assume some administrative responsibility, within a very flexible legislative framework.[42] Responses from the Association for Neighbourhood Councils indicated that the official D of E initiative was seen as inadequate and that neighbourhood councils should be formally elected, legally defined, and to have the right to raise finance.[43] Quite clearly this response indicated a desire to establish a form of decentralised local government which, potentially at least, would be far more powerful than central government envisaged.

But whatever the detailed form of localised management being considered, it seems quite clear that there has been a substantial intellectual and institutional trend towards decentralised administration. There are generally agreed advantages in adopting this approach, many of which emanate from a sentiment that local authorities have become too large, remote, centralised and disorganised to deal with local issues effectively. As Boatswain comments, 'the greatest danger to the continued existence of democratic local government is the local authority itself.'[44] And to avoid this self-inflicted injury, area management is alternatively seen as a means of encouraging democratic vitality between councillors and the public, and councillors and the rest of the authority; of improving the co-ordination and delivery of services; of creating a two-way information service with residents; of monitoring policy operating at the local level; of creating a forum for interested parties; of ensuring an areal input into forms of centralised management such as corporate planning; of seeing the effects of capital programmes imposed from above, which might make less sense at the local level; and potentially, through the creation of area programme and budgeting systems, of introducing a genuinely de-

centralised approach to financial implementation.[45] It is not surprising that with such a litany of virtues area management has received considerable attention, both in general terms as a means of
extending and improving local government but also, more specifically, as a technique for reducing urban deprivation. But will it?
Two basic sets of problems emerge, relating both to a lack of definition as to what area management means and to more deeply rooted
theoretical objections to the whole process.

Area management can mean whatever an authority wishes it to
mean, and as Simkins has pointed out, it can in practice be anything
from a decentralised administration of services through to the
opposite end of the spectrum, where elected local representatives
would have full legal and financial powers to implement local policy.[46]
The whole issue remains so open because systems of area management vary tremendously in at least four respects: in the size of the
area being administered, in political accountability, over the position
of resident involvement and over the status of other agencies.

The question of optimum size of areas being administered has
clearly caused problems, for as the Liverpool IAS points out, it needs
to be large enough to allow for real decision making and to warrant
political and financial powers, but small enough to ensure that residents are aware of its existence and consider it truly local, one of the
main points of the exercise in the first place.[47] But to achieve this
balance may be distinctly tricky. For a start, improved management
at the centre will mean that some services retain a strong centralised
focus. As the Lambeth IAS says, 'some services, generally those
where a complex of specialisms is more efficiently provided in one
place, need to cover large areas and this necessarily precludes them
being locally available to all but those immediately in their environment.'[48] It might well be argued too that strong centralised powers
should remain anyway, to ensure that resource allocation is directed
centrally to those areas and individuals most in need. Furthermore,
if an entire authority were to be divided into area management teams
and governed in this way, would this mean any more than simply
introducing an additional level of government? In such a case no
area would hold sway over any other, and the chances are that power
would remain at the centre, with area management committees
becoming impotent talking shops.

This might happen in any event, whichever system of geographical
division is employed, because there is no guarantee at all that powers
over financial resources will actually be granted to area committees.

A variety of systems have been suggested for incorporating local committees into the overall authority structure: the Liverpool IAS, for instance, suggests that this might happen through subcommittees reporting to the central Policy and Finance Committee, on the basis of either each area having a committee or all areas responsible to one committee,[49] and there have been other approaches based on various relationships between central committees, subcommittees and the council as a whole. But the important issue is not the details of the organisational arrangements, but the existence or otherwise of genuine powers to implement local policy. This in turn will depend upon the representatives of area committees, and on the legal and financial powers devolved to them. If, as seems normal, very limited powers are granted, it needs to be established whether such structures are worth the effort at all, since quite evidently they are, and will be seen as, impotent. It is hard to imagine then that residents would remain committed, or that the system would reduce the very overt political alienation encountered particularly in older inner city areas. The whole problem may further be compounded, because it has been argued that where local councillors are prepared to become much more ward-conscious, their actual influence at the centre is correspondingly reduced. Certainly Cockburn sees this process in operation in that 'those that remain close to the community may be far from the sources of power.'[50]

And of course whatever power structure is set up, it still begs the question as to how the local community is to be involved. Should residents sit on area committees, and if so how are they to be chosen? How are existing groups to be treated? And if residents are to be elected locally and vote on area committees, will this inevitably reduce the influence of such decentralised structures at the centre? It seems likely. But in a sense these are the problems of success. What happens when apathy sets in as the political irrelevance of many decentralised structures becomes generally apparent?

And finally, there is one other area of confusion within the technical organisation of area management, and that relates to the status of voluntary and private organisations. Various forms of area management have been devised which would contain representatives not only of the major local authority services involved but of all relevant public and private bodies. But this seems naive. Many agencies do not think in spatial terms, and even if they do, the proliferation of different boundaries is a notorious characteristic of British social administration. And returning to the perennial prob-

G

lem, if the committee has little power and probably no financial resources, why should outside agencies bother at all?

Considering these confusions over size and political accountability, and the position of residents and outside bodies, it is not at all surprising that one of the main commentators on local authority management should stress the necessity for all local authorities to establish why they are setting up an area management scheme, how it is to operate, where it is to be located and who it is for.[51] Just as the introduction of corporate planning has brought with it substantial technical problems, so the operation of area management is shrouded in confusion and lack of definition. And similarly, as with the whole drift to improved co-ordination at the centre, area management can be criticised on more fundamental methodological grounds too. This is possible over two issues: the motives behind area management, and its relevance. On the first of these points, it is not unreasonable to interpret area management as an attempt by local authorities, aided and abetted by central government, to co-opt local dissent into governmental processes by establishing elaborate administrative structures to which local residents may well be elected, but to which are granted minimal financial and implementary powers. The whole exercise becomes one of innocuous consensus seeking, with major decisions left at the centre and debate focusing at the local scale on extremely minor questions. It is not, then, surprising to see the whole process evaluated by some activists as a meaningless exercise which should be avoided, and orthodox lobbying, if any, continued through established channels. The Coventry CDP team, for instance, states that more fruitful initiatives are likely to 'come from supporting and servicing local people in making more effective use of the existing channels of representation and from the more fluid organisations which are clearly already active within the local political process'.[52] A further development of this argument would be that all area management exercises are unnecessary because existing organisational arrangements include an areal element, authorities have always known about their poorer localities and have often attempted centrally to allocate additional resources to them. The fact that deprivation has not been eradicated is a reflection not of the lack of an adequate local dimension, but of anodyne policy which would remain feeble irrespective of the administrative scale involved.

For activists in general and sections of the CDP in particular, there is another motive inherent in any introduction of area management: that by adopting this sort of organisation the state can monitor trends within deprived areas in order to know 'what to expect from the ghettos and to have accurate information with which to update the diagnosis of the problems and so produce the next set of policies'.[53] But this interpretation seems to ascribe to local and central government a rationality and uniformity of purpose in which it is hard to believe, and a faith in the willingness of government to change policies which experience suggests is not so. Certainly it is possible to believe that authorities have introduced area management schemes to keep residents in 'active areas' quiet, but hard to envisage that this has been part of a premeditated national exercise in community control.

On the other hand another initiative from the CDP, within the specific context of Coventry, does highlight what is perhaps the most undermining constraint in assuming that area management can improve local government effectiveness and reduce urban deprivation: its irrelevance.[54] The Coventry CDP team in one phase of its development became involved in an attempt at decentralisation which became the local focal point for some improvement in the delivery of services, the dissemination of information, and a centre for political activity. But although these improvements were welcome, they were essentially irrelevant in dealing with the major problems which the team diagnosed for the area: poor housing and low incomes. And this is perhaps the key to the entire debate, for if local authorities as a whole find many problems of urban deprivation beyond their competence, there is even less ground for optimism that basic dysfunctions can be countered at an even smaller scale of administration. For these basic issues, which many would now see as the underpinning causes of urban deprivation, area management is an irrelevance at best and a distracting constraint at worst.

Some commentators, far from seeing possible solutions to urban deprivation at the small scale, have examined the potential of larger new supra-local authority institutions charged with comprehensive powers. Eversley has suggested this sort of approach in the implementation of a social and physical programme for the Docklands,[55] and there have been a number of calls for citywide urban corporations, based on the principle of the new town development corporation.[56] In practice this idea has been granted short shrift, largely because local authorities insist that they are the most suitable agent for dealing with local problems, they have been elected to do this, they have built up strong local ties with individuals and groups which might not be respected in any new organisation; and because of the legal and financial constraints which would be involved in setting up such a corporation.[57] But how valid are these objections? Local authorities have proved remarkably inept at reducing deprivation, and with the present division in responsibilities even within single conurbations, it takes an enormous act of faith to believe that administrative and legal structures will be adequate to counteract structural transformations in employment and other markets. Development corporations might not be over-democratic in operation, but then local authorities can be just as autocratic; and anyway, faced with massive urban decay, how important is that elusive spirit 'democracy'?

No, in fact the concept of a body such as a development corporation deserves greater consideration than has been the case, for two obvious reasons. First, it would be concerned with the administration of a far larger area than is the remit of existing authorities, which is significant because so many problems at the inner city scale have citywide or regional implications; and second, an organisation such as this would by its very nature involve the application of much more powerful policies and additional resources to inner city areas. Development corporations as usually understood in Britain have tremendous powers to acquire and develop land, and because of their capacity to purchase at existing use costs and to regain some developmental surplus, they have been very effective and in many cases profitable institutions. In effect they would be ideal in tackling problems such as overspill, the development of new manufacturing and service infrastructure, the purchase of vacant land and so on, functions which local authorities have traditionally not undertaken effectively.

Of course, development corporations will not come to be: they would tread on far too many political toes and would represent too great a fixed commitment in financial and legal terms for central government to accept. But if political calls to regenerate inner city localities meant just that, and they had a higher priority within central government thinking than is the case, there are many reasons for imagining that local authorities would not be the best agent to achieve these ends. Development corporations, on the other hand, introduce a new element into the debate by, of necessity, providing both more powerful policy tools and far greater potential resources within a larger administrative unit. They would not, of course, be as democratic as local authorities, but they would be far more effective. The impression remains that the excuse of their lack of complete electoral accountability is a smokescreen thrown out to cover a central government unwillingness to countenance what looks too much like a blank cheque.

NOTES TO CHAPTER 9

1 See, for instance, J. Bennington, 'Coventry CDP and the Government's Poverty Programme', in Coventry CDP Final Report Part II, 1975, p. 4.
2 See Terms of Reference in all three studies.
3 See, for instance, policy guidelines laid down in IAS, Summaries of Consultant's Final Reports, 1977.
4 See *Hansard*, Vol. 877, 18.7.1974, where CCPs are envisaged as attempts to improve central and local authority management and co-ordination.
5 HMSO, Report of the Committee on the Management of Local Government, 1967, Vol. I, par. 132.
6 HMSO, Report of the Committee on the Staffing of Local Government, 1967, par. 296.
7 HMSO, Report of the Committee on Local Authority and Allied Personal Services, 1968, pars. 79–82.
8 HMSO, *The New Local Authorities*, 1972, par. 2.3.
9 See, for instance, D of E Circular 14/75, 1.1975, par. 39.
10 D of E, *Management Networks*, 1971.
11 J. Stewart, 1971, p. 21.
12 R. Greenwood and J. Stewart, 1974, p. 2.
13 See, for example, T. Eddison, 1975.
14 Shelter Neighbourhood Action Project, 1972, p. 17.
15 J. Stewart, K. Spencer and B. Webster, pp. 14–15.
16 IAS, Liverpool IAS, Summary of the Final Report, 1977, p. 12.
17 The following section is aided substantially by J. Stewart, K. Spencer and B. Webster (as 15); M. Burchnall *et al.*, 1975; J. Bennington, 'Local Government becomes Big Business—Corporate Management and the Politics of Urban Problems', in Coventry CDP (as 1); and T. Eddison, 'Corporate Planning', in T. Hancock (ed.), 1976.
18 B. Cullingworth, 'Social Problems of Cities', in J. Brand and M. Cox, 1974, p. 14.
19 J. Stewart, K. Spencer and B. Webster (as 15), p. 21.
20 T. Eddison (as 17), p. 117.
21 Coventry CDP Final Report, Part I, 1975, pp. 38–9.
22 Shelter Neighbourhood Action Project (as 14), p. 173.
23 J. Dearlove, 1973, p. 231.
24 NCDP, *The Poverty of the Improvement Programme*, 1975, pp. 22–3.
25 IAS, Birmingham IAS, Summary of the Final Report, 1977, par. 52.
26 IAS (as 16), par. 48.
27 See, for example, M. Burchnall *et al.* (as 17), par. 5.8: '. . . whatever model of future development is accepted (of decentralised administration) however, it becomes clear that some form of locally based organisation is needed to articulate local needs and gain information.'
28 HMSO (as 7), pars. 580–90.
29 HMSO (as 8), pars. 5.78–5.82.

30 HMSO, *The New Scottish Local Authorities*, 1973, par. 6.16.
31 D of E Circular 14/75 (as 9), par. 39.
32 Most obviously through the Area Management Trials.
33 D of E, *The Sunderland Study*, 1973, Vol. II, pp. 138–47.
34 A. Buchanan, 1975, p. 380.
35 D. Donnison, 'Micropolitics of The City', in D. Donnison and D. Eversley (eds.), 1973, p. 400.
36 P. Kershaw, 1975.
37 W. Harvey Cox, 1976, p. 83.
38 RTPI, *Planning and the Future*, 1976, par. 67.
39 N. Falk and H. Martinos, 1975, p. 21.
40 HMSO, Royal Commission on Local Government in Scotland, 1969, Ch. 26.
41 Local Government (Scotland) Act, 1973, IV.
42 D of E, *Neighbourhood Councils in England*, 1974.
43 Association of Neighbourhood Councils, 1974; and B. Dixey, *A Guide to Neighbourhood Councils*; for an expansion of the experience of neighbourhood councils in Lambeth, see L. Freeman, 1973.
44 A. Boatswain, 1975, p. 273.
45 As outlined in R. Hambleton, 1976; IAS/LI/3, 1973; and especially M. Stewart (ed.), 1974 and 1975.
46 A. Simkins, 1975, p. 390.
47 IAS/LI/3 (as 45), p. 4.
48 IAS/LA/3, 1974, par. 7.8.
49 IAS/LI/3 (as 45), p. 9.
50 C. Cockburn, 'Urban Government', in G. Cherry (ed.), 1974.
51 M. Stewart (ed.), 1975, Sec. 3, par. 1.
52 Coventry CDP (as 21), p. 75.
53 CDP, *Gilding the Ghetto*, 1977, p. 57.
54 Coventry CDP (as 21), pp. 26–7.
55 D. Eversley, 1975B, p. 18.
56 For instance, E. Brooks, 1975, p. 361; M. Hook, 1977; T. Hancock, 1977; C. Couch, 1977.
57 See, for example, IAS/LI/12, 1976, pp. 31–2.

Chapter 10

PLANNING AND THE COMMUNITY

Few inner city commentators, political or academic, dare to pro-
nounce on the issue without in some way invoking the value of the
'community'. But take these three points of view: Falk, for instance,
in discussing the problems of inner city manufacturing decline considers that it is not enough to blame capitalism, 'as a large part of
the problem lies in the failure of the community, represented by the
local authority, to take over the responsibilities and role of the private
developer';[1] or the Birmingham IAS team's recommendation 'that
community organisation in inner areas be actively encouraged with
the aim of greater community self-reliance and so that residents may
influence decisions which affect their lives';[2] or the position of one
member of the CDP who sees that the most important achievement
in inner city regeneration would be to get local people to make
decisions, whatever they are, thus 'giving the community counter-
vailing powers against those external forces which limit its choice';[3]
three approaches to the perennial problem of what is the community
and how, even whether, it should be used in inner city regeneration.
But they are three very different approaches, and really there is no
single concept which has given rise to so much ill defined, disparate
and utopian thinking. The three quite arbitrarily chosen comments
above suggest, for instance, that the concept can imply either the
local authority, which may assume its mantle as 'the community' or
encourage resident groups to become integrated into some local
decision making processes; or extraneously organised, politically
orientated bodies operating on behalf of the local populace, willing
and able to fight proposals emerging from all outside agencies
including the local authority. In effect, of course, the three positions
are part of an entire spectrum covering the complex relationship
between government and governed, ranging on the one side from an

assumption that the local authority is the community through to the other extreme where in some sense the authority is seen to act, if not always, at least often, in a manner inimical to many residents. But how valid are these positions?

'Participation' is a relatively recent notion, and there are still traces of an older methodology within the urban programme which assumes that in some way the community and the local authority are in practice virtually synonymous. UA, for instance, can be seen to fall into this category in that the authority becomes the vetting agent for all voluntary bodies, although in practice many of the latter would not want such a close relationship; early assumptions within the CDP programme, too, perceived the cause of poverty to be a lack of communication between the community and the providing authority, each apparently with similar objectives.[4] Both the CCP and the UG also assumed that the authority should in some way plan for the entire community under its administration, that its objectives and policies, although possibly subject to minimal public review, were best for the community and above dissension by being somehow 'objective'. Similar sorts of sentiment can be perceived in official reports of the late 1960s and early 1970s, nowhere better perhaps than in the Bains report where the 'community approach' is seen essentially as the co-ordination of policies for different local government departments, other statutory bodies and voluntary agencies.[5]

Now clearly there are advantages in pursuing urban policy on the assumption that the authority is the community, not least of course for the authority itself. Objectives and their corresponding policies are perceived as basically correct, or if modifications are needed, these can be carried out at the pace and to the wishes of local politicians and administrators. Conflict with the community is effectively ruled out in any formal sense, although of course that is not to say that the community itself in various guises might not reject authority attitudes. The time consuming and potentially destructive process of consultation and participation is avoided, wholesale changes eschewed.

But not surprisingly, over the last decade or so this approach has been widely undermined, both by trends towards greater participation within government itself and from the increasingly vociferous community action movement. It is not hard to see why. For a start one basic cause is that the policies which authorities have pursued, legacies of which still remain, simply have not reduced urban deprivation. Wholesale redevelopment policies removing residential, industrial, and commercial uses have come increasingly to characterise local authority activities, and have resulted in widespread blighting and general dissatisfaction. Very few authorities, on the other hand, have until recently been concerned with alternative inner city policies characterised by, for instance, rehabilitation orientated housing programmes or more entrepreneurial attitudes to not just housing, but industry and commerce too. But in the light of what has in the past been done in the name of 'planning' it is hardly surprising to see generally hostile attitudes on the part of residents towards authorities.

Of course one of the constraints has been that authorities have perceived problems in a different way to residents, and have not always been able to respond to them in what might seem to the outsider a commonsensical way. Take housing, for instance: everyone, inside and outside local government, might feel that redevelopment ought to be reduced and a far greater emphasis placed on improvement. But authorities may simply not be in a position to transfer finance from one sector to another, nor may there be anything like enough in the way of total resources allocated to the overall problem from central government. This shortcoming assumes in turn, of course, that central government itself is in a position to provide extra finance; but IMF loans and tighter belts all round eventually mean fewer rehabilitated houses everywhere. The strong British tradition of government anyway carries with it assumptions that local authorities, if they pulled their finger out, could do more. But one lesson from the CDP, and to a lesser extent the IAS, is that under present legal and financial constraints authorities may simply be incapable of undertaking desirable policies: they do not have the power.

Here then is a basic contradiction in assuming that the authority is the community: the latter requires resources for housing and other social infrastructure, and it needs employment bases. But authorities may simply be incapable of intervening in these markets, either because central government imposes restraints, or because there are not the legal and financial means to carry out policy modifications.

It might well be argued, too, that an attitude which saw the authority as the community is too paternalistic by far, and plays down the innate capacities of individuals and groups within society. There are any number of activities, one might suggest, that can be carried out at least as well by non-official bodies as by any formally structured official agency. In assuming that the authority has to organise and implement all social and environmental policy, an enormous pool of voluntary activity may be lost.

It would, however, be wrong to assume that many urban experiments, or indeed politicians and administrators dealing with urban problems in general, would now advocate an authority-community symbiosis. Different sectoral goals, objectives and organisational abilities are increasingly acknowledged and given outlet through various forms of participation or consultation procedures. This is the methodology rooted in Skeffington:[6] permissive, based on representations from the public, encouraged through devices such as community development officers or informal community forums. Now, in fact, since that committee presented its findings ten years ago there has been a substantial development in the methodology of participation. Especially at the local level, there has been the steady development of areally decentralised administrations, sometimes with local resident representation, sometimes with a locally determined budget. Most planning processes would now contain a substantial element of both consultation—that is, informing residents as to likely proposals —and participation—that is, involving the local community in some degree of decision making. It should be stressed, however, that still there are many authorities not over-enamoured of the whole idea of participation, largely because of conflicts and delays, sometimes to little purpose, that the process entails. Hence in practice, 'participation' can range from telling residents what is going to happen to asking them to make decisions as to whether anything should happen at all.

Now it is this, admittedly broad, classification which has dominated thinking in the IAS, and to a lesser extent the CDP. Decisions are still seen as being made by relevant authorities, but these can be carried out more sensitively, can be better communicated to local residents and might often anyway be decentralised to local committees of both members and residents. Thus, from the Birmingham IAS team, there are recommendations for improved participation techniques and some resident involvement in the management of HAAs;[7] the Liverpool team calls for area management to respond locally to the needs of the community;[8] and the Oldham CDP adopts an organisational structure consisting of local politicians, CDP members and representatives from local community groups.[9] All of these approaches can be seen as manifestations of improved 'participation'. Indeed it is reasonable to suggest that both the major urban initiatives, certainly the IAS, have assumed that the standard participation model generally operative to varying degrees within most urban authorities should remain: essentially power stays with the elected council, although residents are informed of its strategic decisions and may well be involved in the implementation of them, especially at the local level of say the HAA, GIA or area plan. There may, too, be some development of a two-way information process with ideas and proposals at the local level being assimilated at the central core of the authority.

Now in effect the current, vital debates about 'community involvement' revolve around the basic issue of whether this model of 'participation' outlined above is sufficient, or whether in practice, explicitly or otherwise, it is no more than a political con-trick in which community groups are enmeshed in order to bargain with authorities over what are almost always minimal points. Is orthodox 'participation' enough? Should it be intensified? Is it too much?

What might be called the orthodox line of 'participation', tracing its descent from Skeffington, has been very adept at creating new structures for involving local residents, perhaps nowhere more so than in London, where the GLC has set up forums and Steering Groups to deal with tricky local plans as at Covent Garden[10] and in Swinbrook.[11] The advantages of this approach should not be underrated. It helps local politicians and bureaucrats to understand local problems, and how authority policies work out at this scale; it can give some indication as to which policies are preferred by local residents and how ideas being mulled around in council might be received; it helps to stimulate local projects; it can generate local community organisation; it can stop unpopular proposals. Certainly, some commentators of the similar process in America consider that participation has become an important thread in helping to create 'novel connections between citizens and elected officials, the emergence of neglected citizens, less élitist relations between professionals and citizens'.[12] Less thoroughgoing reform in Britain has led to correspondingly fewer changes. But these have occurred, although clearly for some they have been either too much or not at all enough.

From one side of the spectrum have come criticisms to the effect that participation is a delaying and unnecessary process, which tends to encourage blight by proposing too many potential land use policies, and is anyway an unsatisfactory way of reducing what may be very complex issues to two or three 'solutions'.[13] The logical extension of this argument would be that authorities possess the necessary political legitimacy, backed by professional experience, and that there is no better forum through which to make decisions.

But most criticisms of the orthodox participation approach have come from the opposite point of view and have suggested that local authorities have not involved the public anything like enough in decision making processes, even those of a very local nature which would most sensibly be made by residents. Partly it seems that this may be due to planners and other administrators believing, or at least acting as if they believed, that many issues are simply too complicated for residents to understand. Now to some extent this may be true, not so much because of technical matters contained within the evaluation of projects but because legal, financial and administrative constraints militate against so many ostensibly viable policy options. But, it is argued, there seems no reason why these constraints could not be outlined to the public. The whole mechanism of participation is often all too evidently seen as inadequate, with proposals late in being presented, many initial decisions made anyway and, on the whole, limited possibilities for change in authority attitudes set firmly against radical modifications in preselected strategies. Dennis, discussing the position of resident participation in one housing department, summed up much anti-authority sentiment by suggesting that a personal 'intrusion' was 'regarded in some quarters as at best irrelevant, and as likely indeed to bring harm to both (the participant) and others'.[14]

This comment in itself highlights one further aspect of the debate: the fact that different departments have disparate ideas about the principle and details of participation. Authorities still, in the main, remain fragmented in policy implementation, despite the fact that few doubt the interactive nature of deprivation. But usually participation exercises involve few departments, and normally last a very limited time. If the idea is to create an administrative structure, it is argued, within which residents are able to make their individual and collective opinions known, it seems essential that a permanent and corporate response should be elicited from the authority, as a starter, and from both central agencies and other public bodies ultimately, distant though that position might seem.[15]

But it should not be imagined that all criticisms of the standard participation model centre on more technical issues, since there is a very substantial undercurrent of thought which would see all forms of local authority inspired participation procedures as either fraudulent or irrelevant. This argument is based initially in the premise that 'participation' is such a vague catch-all concept that really it can mean all things to all authorities. It can certainly imply genuine community involvement in decision making, both as to general strategy and in the implementation of it. But, as seen by many radical commentators, this rarely happens. Instead 'participation' is perceived as a process which provides information to an authority about working-class attitudes, and at the same time conveniently co-opts dissent by embroiling local activists in the complex and normally frustrating web of urban government. Essentially, then, 'participation' is seen not at all as a means of providing a platform for minorities but rather becomes a process which, whilst it might placate a few consciences, still cements traditional power structures. It has not led to discussions about who makes what decisions about which problems, but rather has become a means through which the politician and professional—normally a planner, since they have been much more involved with the whole participation movement than other professional groups—can 'educate' the public into appreciating the active constraints on local government; although in radical arguments, such constraints are envisaged as more apparent than real.

But furthermore, this public being 'educated' is not at all equal, some commentators would have it, despite the fact that orthodox models of 'participation' tend to suggest this. These traditional models assume a pluralistic environment, in fact, within which different groups will come to some sort of acceptable compromise through normal democratic channels, perhaps gingered up through, say, community forums or area management steering groups to ensure that everyone has a fair say. But a radical interpretation would reject this out of hand. Different groups do not have the same degree of political consciousness, the same organisational ability, the same access to resources, the same connections with established local political channels.[16] Participation becomes a farce, since the generally less organised working class is simply not in a position to present as articulated or politically powerful a position as middle-class groups.

To some extent the difference in bargaining powers between different groups has been appreciated by local government, and attempts made within orthodox participation models to accommodate this dysfunction through means such as advocacy.[17] This position holds that planners and other professionals should be introduced, either officially or otherwise, into certain communities where they would build up a dossier of potential needs and possible ameliorative measures and would, through their knowledge of resource allocating bodies, act as advocates for residents of that particular locality. At the same time an advocate would attempt to instil capacities for self-fulfilment and local organisational ability to aid communities to achieve a permanent and internally sustained political consciousness. To some limited extent, the drift towards officially sponsored advocacy has taken the heat out of the community debate, but in fact not as much as might be imagined in Britain, partly, no doubt, because there are so few such systems operative and partly because they still assume a close interaction between the community and authority. And into the apparent void advocacy has been unable to fill have jumped the community activists, strongly represented of course within the CDP.

To community activists attempts at participation within local authority structures appear inadequate: discussions are normally too late, few fundamental issues are ever discussed and ultimate control remains with elected representatives. Moreover, whatever modifications, by the nature of things minor, are being discussed, they will not normally benefit the less organised, less articulate and less well educated working classes. For one activist certainly, the position seems to be that there is only ever any point in continuing debates 'as long as they evoke a well intentioned and serious response from the government, and all too often the concern of government is to talk out demands, knowing full well that delay and procrastination affect the continued viability of community action.'[18] Delay is encouraged in part by co-opting dissent into official administrative structures which successfully contain action within the bounds acceptable to 'the system' and limit changes to a few, apparently hard earned, but in effect meaningless victories. Not surprisingly, as community activists see it, there is a notorious apathy concerning local government, and a widespread sentiment that councillors do not represent their residents, but are hand in glove with developers and businessmen.

It is, therefore, activists argue, simply an inappropriate position to become enmeshed in official pluralistic organisations which, in an ensnaring network of meetings and committees, will frankly inhibit any discussion of basic issues. So if working within the system does not work, then clearly for some, action outside it remains the only alternative. On the one hand this action might be of the kind which helps to equip minorities to achieve a more powerful bargaining position with outside agencies, through better organisation, a fuller understanding as to the roles and structures of relevant bodies and the optimisation of internal material and individual resources, but within an overall operational framework which accepts the existence of continued resource shortage and the primacy of elected bodies over certain decisions.[19] But there is a further and more radical development of this position: the strategy of direct conflict action.[20] Here collective community objectives are devised, aimed at stimulating strong political working-class organisation so as to achieve solidarity in the face of trends within employment, housing and education markets likely to militate directly against communities in older urban areas. Resources will probably continue to be in limited supply, it is considered, whichever government agent they come from, and it will be essential for poorer communities to organise and fight for what is available. And if the immediate programme is to be organisation and political control, later tactics will need to include direct action, confrontation and the integration of smaller geographical groups into larger city- and nationwide federations. The whole debate about the relationship between the governed and government is thus seen, as for instance Bailey suggests, 'not about participation at all but about control'.[21]

And it is this position which has been advocated to an increasing extent by the CDP. In the Forward Plan for 1975–6, for instance, the projects suggest that attempts to influence policy in isolation from working-class action would be misplaced. What was needed was an attempt to 'provide information and resources so that groups can formulate their own demands and press directly for change'[22] without becoming embroiled in fatuous 'participation' schemes. This nationally devised objective can be seen paralleled in the approach of some of the local teams: Coventry, for instance, promoting the organisation of active political groups bridging the gap between the neighbourhood and the factory floor.[23] And the advantages of community action should not be minimised: it has done much to highlight the extent of deprivation and frustration, it has energised some authorities, stimulated voluntary and community aid.[24] But at the same time, the ideas and concepts behind community action as expounded by some CDP teams and other commentators should not be allowed to pass easily into the accepted canon. There are in fact a number of reasons to imagine that this position is far too simple and based on questionable premises.

1. Community action obviously assumes that communities exist. But do they? Areally, surely not to any noticeable degree, except in certain well (too well?) documented cases. Certainly it is relevant here to note the conclusions emerging from the Lambeth IAS, which

specifically examined this issue in relation to the possibilities of establishing local area management structures but concluded that their study area at least is 'in the minds of most of its residents, not composed of a number of distinct and readily identifiable communities'.[25] Indeed in the spatial sense, one man's community is probably unidentifiable to another. As Stewart suggests, communities cannot be seen either as areas within which interactions take place or as bases to which certain people belong.[26] The whole notion of geographical communities seems rooted in a somewhat anti-urban appreciation of the apparently successful community spirit engendered in rural society. Any urban communities, on the other hand, tend to be of the non-spatial kind, and relate to common cultural, economic or educational links.

2. That is not at all to say that temporary areal alliances have not been and cannot be, formulated, since empirical evidence provides many examples of this happening. But this tends to occur when direct external pressures are applied to certain areas, stimulating the creation of temporary alliances often encouraged by radical 'passers by'.[27] This, inevitably, then raises the issue of how representative specific groups may be within certain localities. Sometimes it is clear that widespread opposition (not so often approval) might exist for a certain proposal, but equally there usually remain divisions within resident groups. The whole drift towards perceiving social interaction in conflict rather than consensus terms is surely right; but why does the model suddenly revert at the level of the assumed, or even real, community? Consensus no more operates at the small scale on a permanent basis than it does for society as a whole.

3. One argument put forward by community activists is that professional 'ethics' and mystiques are engendered by groups such as planners, and other administrators too, in an attempt to carve out an exclusive and apparently very technical area of operation. Thus Davies, talking about the North-East, sees that one of the aims of the would-be profession is 'to convert its customers into clients and in so doing stake out an exclusive area of discourse in which those persons trained in the skills and induced into the mysteries of the trade can claim a monopoly of wisdom and proficiency'.[28] But for activists, this monopoly of wisdom and experience is in practice a fraud, since frequently issues are far simpler than professionals would paint them, and comprehensible to a far wider range of people than is normally

allowed. In fact for some activists, the community is capable of understanding issues and taking decisions over a whole range of topics which have been hived off to professional groups. One commentator, for instance, saw the possibility of the community taking decisions over education, leisure and housing facilities.[29]

But is this position at all tenable? Of course, professions have been far too hermetic in the past and there is evidence of growing and healthy scepticism about the prognostications of many such groups. But two points should be made here. First, to some extent, certainly within planning, there have been increasingly evident attempts to present a more open and comprehensible picture of issues, policies and their implications. Second but more important is the fact that although planning, and probably other professions too, are not as complicated or as technical as might have been indicated in the past, there is a common body of knowledge and experience which anyone bent on understanding or criticising planning matters would need to know. It is on the whole not at all difficult to comprehend what is involved, but it needs to be known. One might well argue that planning is mainly about administrative, legal and financial constraints, and not much about principles or techniques. But planning, like other professions, has to operate within a defined governmental structure, the shortcomings of which are irrelevant to this debate. There would be such constraints however 'good' or 'bad' planning might be. Most people might be able to understand and comment on planning issues given time and experience, but then planning is only one aspect of urban government. What about the social services, architects, engineers, housing and education departments? No doubt many of their operational guidelines are basically simple too, but how realistic is it to imagine each and every 'community' having experts in each of these and other professions—legal, financial and medical, for instance—which will at some time impinge on urban government?

4. There is one activity which planners, and indeed all governmental administrators, have become increasingly involved with in recent years: the equitable distribution of limited, often diminishing, resources. These resources might be for housing, education, social services, leisure, any public run service in fact. Now as indicated elsewhere, attempts to define small areas towards which a policy of positive discrimination should apply is fraught with technical and methodological problems. But even allowing for these constraints,

decisions about how much and where still have to be made, and not preferably by local communities, for more in one place brings with it the inevitable unhappy corollary elsewhere. This sort of decision needs to be taken at national level to establish which regions or cities should receive additional resources, and at local authority level to decide which communities should be favoured. Once additional resources have been allocated to districts, then afterwards it will in most cases be possible to allow a considerable degree of self-determination as to how this should be spent. But the initial decision as to which areas should be favoured must remain a centrally implemented process, because it is not reasonable to expect individual groups to act in a disinterested fashion, and because relatively poor areas may be the least well organised and it is no answer 'to the problem of making government responsive, to make it vulnerable to the pressure of those who merely shout the loudest'.[30]

5. The whole relationship, anyway, between community activists and the local authority remains ambiguous. The former like to believe in conspiracy theories in which authorities are seen as creating and implementing policies directly inimical to the 'community'. But this assumes authorities are able, let alone willing, to do this. But why should they be? It would be hard to argue that local politicians are fired with the desire to hurt local residents in a consciously determined fashion. Their methods might well be counterproductive, but are surely never maliciously intentioned. On the other hand, local politicians dislike activists, partly because of the latters' consistently underdeveloped exposition of objectives, down even to the level of their knowing whether they wish to be left alone or exactly the opposite.[31] Moreover, concerted conflict action on the part of activists will in any event create contrary forces within local authorities,[32] such as the establishment of rival local structures, or politicians stressing the vulnerability of less organised groups in 'non-active' parts of their administration. And local politicians have, of course, the final undeniable remit: they are elected, they stand up to be counted, they are political masters. Electoral turnouts may be low, interest in local politics negligible, but at the end of the day they are and should remain accountable. If activists do not like it, they too should stand and rely on their own real or imagined electoral support.

6. Even if greater political autonomy were given to communities,

assuming they can be defined, what actually can be done at that local level of presumably a few thousand, or even tens of thousands of, people? Evidence from a variety of sources, including somewhat ironically the CDP itself, suggests that very little in the way of basic policy changes can be implemented at this scale, since to an ever increasing extent deprivation is perceived as causally related to changing structural conditions, especially economic ones. From the CDP have come statements indicating that whilst self-help is a desirable ideal, 'it frequently cannot tackle issues of major importance which are decided by higher authorities in distant decision making centres.'[33] Other commentators, Cullingworth[34] and Eversley[35] for example have supported similar conclusions. The latter, within the London context, points out that communities cannot prevent blight, attract jobs, build roads, improve bus services, or release land. One might equally add: improve education, widen training facilities, change regional policy, build houses on any large scale. The list is almost endless. Once structural changes are seen as prime causes of urban deprivation, of necessity political discussion and political change must move up geographical and governmental scales too.

7. Now community activists have responded to the criticisms that local groups cannot induce changes at that scale by advocating the national organisation of areal groups with certain defined and commonly agreed objectives. There have been calls for instance, for 'overall policy objectives capable of unifying all slum dwellers in their common interests',[36] through nationally structured political and social organisations,[37] possibly tied to those existing political organisations concerned with the basic issues of urban equity. Clearly the CDP, in this context, saw its aim as devising national perspectives based on the findings of the local teams in an attempt to stimulate the development of working-class action and pressure on the widest possible front.

But how realistic is this approach? It implies that political initiatives can be created which are nationally based on the differing experiences of local communities. This might be possible on certain specific issues such as, say, the level of supplementary benefits, but even then these are rarely likely to take on the status of national crusades. This position anyway assumes that working-class groups have common interests, but the attitudes of, say, skilled men in Bristol and unskilled ex-dockers in Liverpool may not at all coincide.

It ignores too the unusual, and to activists frustrating, phenomenon of the working class Tory voter, and as so many assumptions behind any national platform would be of an overtly left wing nature, this discrepancy might prove somewhat undermining. And even if national organisations were to be created, they would at some point have to come to the table and bargain. But this is exactly what activists in local groups have tried to avoid as far as possible, since as they see it the process leads to compromise, shifting principles and the co-option of dissent.

'Encouraging the community' has become one of incontrovertible *sine qua nons* of urban planning: no speech, report, plan would be complete without it. And yet clearly the entire notion of 'community' can imply many different things ranging from the paternalistic, where the authority assumes it is the community, to the anarchic, which assumes that the authority and the community are permanently antagonistic. But the latter position, currently widely held, seems open to criticisms relating to the definition, power and accountability of community groups. The Liverpool IAS team are surely right in this context to evalute community action as an overrated response to the failures of understanding and provision in local government.[38] The real reason why attempts have been made to organise independently of established local government structures is precisely because the latter have proved so inefficient in dealing with the apparently ever more acute manifestations of urban deprivation. If on the other hand they had proved more successful, even at the expense of reduced local democracy, would there have been the same widespread rejection and contempt for local government in general, and local politicians in particular? It is hard to believe that there would.

But it is frankly unreasonable to pin the blame for urban decline on local government. It has become increasingly clear that it is not solely, or even principally, incompetence that is in question here, but rather powers of authorities, which are being seen as ever more inadequate to cope with nationally and internationally stimulated changes in economic structures that have proved so detrimental to urban areas. On the other hand however, a form of Development Corporation armed with extensive acquisition and developmental powers might become, in a significant way, more powerful in ameliorating urban deprivation than any existing local authority. Or by the same token, so could existing local authorities charged with greater powers and a political willingness to implement measures which, by their very speed and comprehensiveness, would inevitably lead to considerable local opposition. Ultimately it is impossible to reconcile meaningful inner city regeneration with greater community control. All decisions require arbitration between the conflicting claims of different areas. There is no 'correct' answer as to what should happen, or where. But if anything is to happen at all, it must be left to the implementing agency involved to devise a programme and stick with it. To sub-contract policies out to the contradictory aims of different community activists will lead to delay, to compromise and to the fudging of issues. If, as so many inner city reports assert, the prime require-ment is for a political will at both national and local levels to carry out a concerted and comprehensive plan, then ultimately this will require a decision on what should be done for the best of an entire city region, not for a few hundred or even thousand people. Con-flicting claims cannot all be reconciled, and in the light of the deteriorating status of older urban areas, perhaps there should not even be an attempt to do so. Think of a plan for an entire area and stick to it. If the policies are ill-conceived and powers too weak, it will not work, but if it is put out to the specific and inward looking aims of local communities it will certainly not. For despite claims to the contrary,[39] the problems of deprived areas will not be solved at the local level, but at national and regional ones, if at all, and then based on far wider powers than exist at the moment. The community can do no more than ice the cake, if there is any.

NOTES TO CHAPTER 10

1 N. Falk, 1974, p. 192.
2 IAS, Birmingham IAS, Summary of Final Report, 1977, p. 28.
3 G. Green, 'Towards Community Power', in H. Glennerster and S. Hatch, 1974, p. 20.
4 See, for instance, HO, *CDP Objectives and Strategy*, 1970.
5 HMSO, *The New Local Authorities*, 1972, p. 92.
6 HMSO, *People and Planning*, 1969; expanded in D of E Circular 52/72, 1972.
7 See, for instance, IAS/B/7, 1975.
8 See, for instance, IAS, Liverpool IAS, Summary of the Final Report, 1977, p. 15.
9 Oldham MB, Report of the Community Development Project Working Party.
10 D. Blackhurst, 1976.
11 G. Towers, 1975.
12 S. Miller and M. Rein, 'Community Participation: Past and Future', in D. Jones and M. Mayo (eds.), 1975, p. 20.

13   See R. Batley, 1973, for contrasting views, official and otherwise, in one development project.
14   N. Dennis, 1970, p. 347.
15   For development of this argument in one area, see D. Frost and N. Sharman, 1975.
16   This argument is developed in greater detail by D. Harvey, 1973, p. 78.
17   An approach which seems to have become more widely accepted in planning circles. See RTPI, *Planning and the Future*, 1976.
18   J. Dearlove, 'The Control of Change and the Regulation of Community Action', in D. Jones and M. Mayo (as 12), p. 30.
19   This seems to be the position of, say, J. Greve, 'Research and the Community', in D. Jones and M. Mayo (as 12); and D. Thomas, 1976.
20   Which seems to be the position of, say, L. Friedman, 1974; S. Baine, 1975; and R. Bryant, 1972.
21   J. Bailey, 1975, p. 37.
22   NCDP Forward Plan 1975-6, 1975, p. 1.
23   See Coventry CDP Final Report, Part I, 1975, Ch. 7.
24   For an expansion of this point, see R. Holman, 1972.
25   IAS/LA/5, 1974, p. 51.
26   M. Stewart, Introduction to M. Stewart (ed.), 1972, p. 33.
27   This is recognised by community activists: see, for instance, A. Kay, 'Planning and Participation in D. Jones and M. Mayo (eds.), 1974, p. 209: '. . . an initial burst of enthusiasm often gives rise to temporary involvement (particularly in the case of students) and thus vital continuity and commitment are lacking.'
28   J. Davies, 1972, p. 220.
29   J. Rowland, 1973, p. 138.
30   W. Harvey Cox, 1976, p. 181.
31   A point expanded by D. Eversley, 1973, p. 211.
32   A similar state of conflict characterised some American attempts at community action: see, for instance, J. Donovan, 1967. Activists in the UK, too, are quite aware that their own efforts can set up counter-productive forces in local authorities, such as delay or reduced financial commitment: see Calouste Gulbenkian Foundation, 1973.
33   Cumberland CDP, 1973, p. 47; many very similar assertions could be found in national and local CDP publications.
34   J. Cullingworth, Vol. II, 1973, p. 167.
35   D. Eversley, 1975B.
36   R. Silburn, 'The potential and Limitation of Community Action', in D. Bull (ed.) 1971; similarly R. Pahl has suggested that some action groups may be 'the forerunners of more organised locality-based associations concerned with the basic issues of urban equity'; 1975, p. 178.
37   As advocated by M. Mayo, 'Community Development: A Radical Alternative', in R. Bailey and M. Brake (eds.), 1975.
38   IAS/LI/12, 1976, p. 27.

39 See, for instance, N. Deakin and C. Ungerson, 'Beyond the Ghetto: The Illusion of Choice', in D. Donnison and D. Eversley, 1973, p. 237: '. . . ultimately the solutions of many of the problems of deprived areas must come from below, from the inhabitants, they cannot be imposed from above.'

Chapter 11

POVERTY, POLICY AND REALITY

Central government has proceeded over the last decade or so to instigate a series of urban projects aimed at eradicating, or at least moderating, urban deprivation. True, not all of the schemes were initiated on the premise that they should examine and explore the totality of urban influences: some, indeed, were much more specific in their intent. But collectively they add up to a programme of action and research which officialdom ostensibly believed would go some way towards understanding urban deprivation, or symptoms of it, in selected localities, and which would in turn provide more general conclusions and lessons applicable to inner areas as a whole. The findings of these initiatives have been extensively assimilated at the central level and an explicit inner city policy formulated based upon them. But has the urban programme presented a coherent, consistent and believable analysis of what urban deprivation is all about? Will inner city policy based upon it actually work? And—the stage beyond—should it?

The urban programme as it developed in the ten years after 1967 has clearly evolved in a markedly dynamic way. Many of the early premises which underpinned the structure of UA have gradually, although by no means universally, been discredited. In the late sixties it was quite possible to embark on an urban programme assuming, for instance, that small, identifiable pockets of deprivation existed; that improved co-ordination by government bodies could make substantial inroads into the generation of deprivation; that the community contained inherent individual and collective talents which could be tapped to ameliorate internally created disadvantage; and that the basic cause of deprivation related in some way to deleterious cultures of poverty. It is a reflection of the value of the urban programme, and specifically of the more radical findings of the IAS and the CDP,

214

that these assumptions could not now be widely and uncritically accepted.

Instead these later projects developed different, but intellectually consistent theories, sometimes assimilated from other sources, to explain urban deprivation and its continued generation. To a large extent, these new frameworks have invoked structural arguments which perceive urban decay as a symptom of changing economic bases within an era of national and international slump—changes which have militated most evidently against the relatively unorganised urban working class. True, other factors may need to be called in to explain the totality of inner area decline and the worsening economic and political status of some inner area residents.[1] Educational disadvantage can cement early inequalities; public resources might not fairly discriminate between the deprived and those who are not; life cycles can stimulate periods of relative poverty for individual families; cultures of poverty no doubt do operate in some localities. But these forces cannot be perceived as accounting either individually or collectively for the extent of poverty in Britain in the late seventies. Certainly they cannot be ignored; and many of them anyway interact with, and can be seen as part of, structuralist hypotheses. But it is the latter which must form the keystone of future discussions as to the direction and purpose of deprivation programmes. And for that metamorphosis both the IAS and, especially, the CDP must take most of the credit.

However, such an intellectual transformation inevitably brings in its wake severe operational implications. It implies, for instance, that much of the urban programme is redundant. Traditionally, it has operated on the assumption that deleterious cultures of poverty acted on residents of small, deprived areas. Possibly they do, but these processes cannot be invoked as exclusively, or even largely, responsible for deprivation. Projects operating within this framework must now surely be seen as essentially diversionary in that they deflect concern from structures to individuals, from expensive to cheap solutions. Ideal, of course, for the politician in that they obtain 'a high return in publicity ... from a minimal commitment to expenditure'[2]—but essentially, as the later urban programme itself established, irrelevant. And there is the irony: the urban programme wrote its own obituary.

But if the urban initiatives have rejected small-scale experiments as an exclusive answer to the issues of urban poverty, what sort of policies need to be evolved? More radical protagonists would advocate greater political organisation and hence, ultimately, control on the part of urban working classes, a control which would need to direct, or at least influence, the spatial and structural organisation of British industry so that its expansions, contractions, mergers and rationalisations were undertaken in a socially just manner and for the benefit of existing workforces.

But not all those commentators prepared to accept the validity of structuralist arguments necessarily see advances through sectoral conflicts. In America, for example, analysts who see basic causes of poverty as inherent in capitalist industrial systems nevertheless admit the possibility of improvements without advocating the destruction of capitalism since, like every other social ideology 'it has had to make compromises with reality.'[3] In Britain, too, it is quite possible to perceive advances through moderating rather than attacking capitalist structures. Partnerships, state intervention, institutional investment within older urban industrial bases, recent changes in government economic and financial planning which attempt to benefit inner city areas generally, can all be seen as attempts by capitalist systems to reduce the antisocial, even unacceptable, consequences of their operation, in the specific spatial context of the inner city.

Administratively, too, there are pragmatic avenues which the social scientist and social policy maker can explore, even when operating within the wider context of the primacy of structural influences. There is a growing awareness, for instance, on the part of those involved with the administration of social policies of all kinds of the need to avoid previous tendencies to see, among other things, spatial poverty as generically different to child poverty, or homelessness, or the poverty of the single parent, or the inadequacy of state benefits. Structuralist arguments, whilst clearly not likely to explain the totality of individual circumstance, still nevertheless provide a basic and common explanatory framework. Sectoral and spatial poverties are rooted in similar processes, and experiments such as the urban programme have done much to show their common distribution at the local level and causative links at the national.

But if structuralist arguments are employed to explain urban deprivation, and advances in ameliorating it ascribed largely to nationally implemented policies, can anything be done at the local scale? For those who have addressed themselves to this problem, it seems that there can.[4] Local-scale independent projects can provide valuable physical and social infrastructure, can influence local politicians and parties, can generate greater community and political consciousness, can emphasize social injustices and—perhaps most important—can highlight the effects, intentional and otherwise, of national policies at the local scale. And furthermore, within local administrations, a wider appreciation of the power of structural forces can lead to positive advances: in the field of local economic planning, for example. Certainly, a wider acceptance of the importance of national and international economic forces need not be paralleled by growing sentiments of fatuity at the local scale. Urban deprivation clearly cannot be understood, even less ameliorated, at this scale; but a fuller appreciation of the effects of structuralist forces, of the validity of government policy and of the viability of locally devised and implemented schemes still need to be obtained at this more detailed scale.

Of course, what the urban programme has said about the effects of structuralist forces and the extent to which they can be countered at national and local scales is clearly different to what has actually been proposed in the government's new inner city policies. True, some of the recommendations emerging from the later, more comprehensive studies, notably the CDP and the IAS, have been implemented in full or in part. Local authorities, for example, are likely to have wider economic planning powers, there is to be a new inner city dimension to government expenditure, and in particular UA is to be extended in quantity and direction, especially in the partnership authorities. New towns are to be cut back too, and instructed to take more of the urban disadvantaged. And, of course, central government still retains the power to do much more, for instance in the control of industry through its powers of grant investment, partnership agreements and social investment through the NEB.

But this collection of actual and potential powers should not deceive us into thinking that the inner city programme will work, and urban environments be regenerated, for there remain inconsistencies between the sorts of policy modifications which elements of the urban programme have identified as essential and those which central government proposes to implement. The perennial problem of land, for instance, remains very much to the fore.[5] Valuations for inner city sites still relate to the relatively small number of transactions being undertaken at historically high and inflated prices, generally between public bodies not prepared to reduce paper assets by accepting lower, more realistic prices. The result is a stagnant, and yet paradoxically expensive, market which the Community Land Act, because of limited political and financial commitment to it, has been unable to moderate. But as long as inner city land prices remain so high, comparative costs between these and other locations will remain invidious to the older urban areas, so that economic expansion there becomes very unlikely and decentralisation further encouraged. And, of course, if inner city regeneration ever were to occur spontaneously, local authorities, unless able to acquire and develop land more easily, would once again largely miss out on any wealth created.

But it is not just that central government has steered clear of simply the land issue in its apparently new inner city dimension. No discussion of the viability of official urban policy could ignore the question of the scale and organisation of financial resources, for instance. The urban programme itself is to be granted more than the magical £1,000m in the next decade. That might appear substantial, and it is certainly substantially greater than the funds allocated to the programme in the past. But still it is peanuts. Central government expenditure by the mid-seventies was running at over £35,000m;[6] the Rate Support Grant alone was averaging out at over £8,000m;[7] the 1976 spending cuts introduced in one year expenditure reductions several times greater than funds allocated to the urban programme for a decade.[8]

Of course it is not that urban authorities anyway receive, or expect to receive, very much in the way of financial resources through the urban programme, since over 60 per cent of their expenditure is met from the Rate Support Grant. Now in fact, in recent years the cities have received more than their fair share of this centrally allocated capital because of the operation of the needs element, which attempts to even out differences between areas in the amounts they have to spend to provide similar levels of services. But then, quite clearly, cities normally need additional support because of the generally higher *per capita* dependency on local authority services in cities, because of the need to renovate what is often outdated infrastructure, because urban residents tend to pay higher rates, because so little private investment is occurring in cities, and because of the additional expenditure which any regenerative programme will inevitably entail. And yet it would be difficult to argue that the needs element in the Rate Support Grant does in practice actually compensate the urban authorities for their additional expenditure. Of course there are political problems. The non-urban authorities obviously resent any allocative bias, and anyway because of the legal necessity imposed on

authorities to provide certain services, central government is unlikely ever to create too much of a pro-city emphasis. Thus, if the
cities are not only to maintain, but even improve, existing services
and undertake additional development programmes within a financial
environment hostile to private investment, it will probably have to be
accepted that available resources are not sufficient. And yet this must
remain the central issue, for 'without an initial injection of resources
and a sustained commitment to increase investment over the next
few years, there will be little improvement in the circumstances of
those living in relatively depressed areas.'[9]

This discussion of the relative merits of centrally devised urban
initiatives has concentrated largely, as indeed has the government,
on the intrinsically urban aspects of policy. And yet there are strong
grounds to suggest that precisely because so much of the official
debate has centred on these, thus ignoring wider spatial and theoretical frameworks, it is doomed to fail. In particular—and these have
been lessons gleaned from the urban programme as much as from
anywhere—urban policies must be linked to wider regional, national
and international processes, and urban poverty needs to be defined
in relation to, and amalgamated within, more general theories of
relative deprivation, and indeed of relative affluence.

Cities have decayed because their economic bases have declined, in
some cases remarkably rapidly. This has happened largely because of
financial and spatial changes within national and international economic markets which have encouraged the larger, sometimes multi-
national, firms to thrive, especially in the cheaper national labour
markets, and in—from their point of view at any rate—better industrial, usually suburban locations. And the corollary of this is
that many older, smaller and often inner city firms have been
'rationalised', which normally means at best relocation, or more
often closure. This twin system of economic merger and spatial
relocation is basic to the decline of cities, and yet it has received
minimal coverage from official sources.

In the case of the former process—economic mergers and rationalisations—this is hardly surprising. Government economic strategy
in Britain has encouraged the rationalisation of existing firms and the
development here of the major multinational corporations. This might
have made economic sense, although there are strong arguments that
financial centralisation brings diseconomies in its wake, but from the
point of view of the inner city it has been a disastrous policy. Inner
city firms have been acquired, 'rationalised', and therefore usually

closed, as the larger firms set about purchasing or removing these potential competitors and stripping their assets. But existing inner area workforces were rarely offered the opportunity of alternative employment, and indeed the heavy social costs which industrial closure inevitably brings were, to a large extent, borne not by the company concerned, but through public expenditure in the way of increased state benefits. Central government could have negotiated more socially equitable procedures through, say, powers of financial provision and partnership agreements. But it elected not to do so, and it is unlikely that it ever will to any substantial extent: its primary objective of long-term manufacturing growth will ensure that. But it still remains disingenuous to formulate an urban policy which largely ignores the widespread effects of industrial amalgamation that have clearly been so influential in accentuating urban decline. And without central government direction, a CDP commentator who examined this issue is surely right to see the growth, especially, of the multi-national corporation showing loyalty to neither country, region nor town as presenting 'a daunting and unprecedented challenge'.[10] And it is a challenge which the new inner city dimension does not even acknowledge, despite the fact that the later urban programme, upon which the new initiatives are heavily dependent, clearly identified the importance of the process and its effects.

It is, however, impossible in the British context to discuss the influence of economic centralisation without a consideration of regional policy. Simply because regional policy has concentrated on providing extremely favourable financial incentives to the expanding, usually footloose, firm, it has implicitly subsidised the efficient, often relatively new, often larger and sometimes international firm at the expense of the older, smaller, often urban concern. Perhaps it was right to do so; but the cost, certainly the cost to the cities, has been tremendous. Of course, decentralisation has become a characteristic of many urban functions in many countries. But in Britain it has been accentuated and favoured by a regional policy which stimulated the migration of expanding firms from the older urban cores to the suburban locations of the Assisted Areas. It did not, on the whole, help older urban firms wishing to expand *in situ*, a discrepancy not helped by planning policies and lack of equity finance which militated against urban expansion proposals anyway. Nor did it direct migrating firms to the older parts of the Assisted Areas, where the largest unemployment pools existed. It did not impose a sectorally specific procedure whereby certain industries could have been directed to certain locations. Instead, it provided large amounts of public capital in an unrefined spatial and sectoral package to enable larger, more affluent firms to optimise their profits. It accelerated the massive decentralisation of the cities, especially in the South and Midlands, and it provided minimal compensation in the way of additional inner area employment facilities in the Assisted Areas. Regional policy has caused more destruction to the economic bases of cities than the anodyne economic policies proposed for urban authorities are ever likely to repair.

To some extent these discrepancies have been recognised recently, and there are, for instance, to be some minor modifications to the IDC policy. But that is hardly the point. Most IDCs have in fact been granted in the past. The real reasons for urban economic degeneration relate to economic and financial patterns which have encouraged the closure or decentralisation of older firms, aided by regional policy, and which have created a generally unfavourable environment for the expansion of existing city firms or the creation of new ones. If the government was at all serious about its inner city policy, it would need to introduce more interventionist policies to restrict some mergers and closures, to impose planning agreements covering future developments of firms, and to obtain a better deal from its regional policy through a more sectorally and spatially specific policy which aimed at helping existing firms as much as the relatively small amounts of mobile industry. For, as Holland has pointed out in an analysis of capital investment in Britain, local solutions to problems of the cities 'will not work unless related to the wider spatial distribution of resources in the economy. And in the twentieth century, despite new policies, the capitalist firm remains largely free to determine the location of investment, jobs and income.'[11] Here again, of course, the imponderable dilemma looms large: will central government impose restrictions on private investment which might undermine its global policy of economic regeneration? But then that is no excuse for officialdom to present an urban programme divorced from the economic realities of the private market, and pretend that it can work.

It is important here not to forget that the new urban policy not only divorces urban problems from their ultimate spatial scales, but also attempts to separate urban poverty from deprivation and privilege generally. And yet clearly, the urban experiments showed the connections. True, the rate of economic decline might accentuate the extent and generation of poverty in urban areas but, alternatively, deprivation should not be seen as a specifically urban phenomenon. It has a far wider and more random spatial spread than has in the past been imagined, or indeed is reflected in the new urban dimension. And it is distributed in such a way largely because the processes of economic contraction and declining public wealth, which define deprivation, occur throughout the country. To highlight particular urban areas, then, and attempt to improve poverty there—as the partnership schemes propose, for instance—can be seen as a misguided, *ad hoc* response to a much wider problem. In terms of actually attempting to reduce day-to-day poverty, as opposed to trying to regenerate urban economic bases, it would be far more sensible to raise supplementary or unemployment benefits nationally. It would be far more effective in reaching those who must generally be regarded as poor.

But then that raises another problem, for poverty is not an absolute criterion but relative to deprivation and wealth elsewhere. Can a British urban programme be welcomed when, relative to world rankings, most of those regarded as poor here would be relatively well off elsewhere?[12] And more pertinently, can an urban policy attempt to deal with the incidence of deprivation without attacking intrinsic inequalities in British social and economic structures? Education, housing and employment markets contain rigidities and dysfunctions which militate against wider social mobility, and which still uphold an influential élite with considerable powers over the generation and distribution of public and private resources. To one commentator at least, 'a direct reduction in the power and resources of the privileged minority is required.'[13] And this may be particularly apt, because as the urban experiments, notably the CDP, pointed out, deprivation does not imply simply a material disadvantage, but also a political and an organisational one which tends to produce a generally disorganised, often uninformed, working class. As seen by the CDP, this deficiency needed to be remedied through an urban programme which encouraged the development of working-class political consciousness. But again, not surprisingly, there has been a deafening official silence on this issue too.

And it is this selectivity on the part of the new urban dimension which is undoubtedly its main shortcoming. It has an enormous analytical and prescriptive base, relating to every conceivable aspect of urban structures, upon which to formulate its policies. The CDP and IAS, in particular, presented a comprehensive analysis of what was happening in urban localities and why such processes were operating. Of course, not all the prescriptive solutions proposed were ever likely to gather much support in Whitehall. But what the urban experiments did reveal is that urban problems cannot be treated in isolation, but are part of wider national and international structural changes. Now how, or if even whether, these processes should be countered is a different issue; but for central government to accept the primary importance of urban economic decline, and not, in anything other than the most marginal manner, attempt to introduce policies likely to moderate the forces responsible for the contraction is simply fraudulent. As it stands the new urban policy will make only a minimal difference to the general fate of cities. Central government politicians would only need to read their own experiments to find that out.

But does it matter that the new urban policy is unlikely to work? Does it matter that cities probably will continue to decline in size and diminish in importance? For many commentators, of course, it does matter.[14] The decay in urban environments is seen by them as a major social and economic problem. Decentralisation takes away the skilled and the ambitious workers, the more efficient and profitable firms. It is a regressive process in that those who remain, generally the poorer, are faced with higher costs and rates, diminishing investment bases, reduced employment opportunities, decaying infrastructure and deteriorating services. On the other hand, new public and private investment tends to locate in the new and expanded towns and the new suburban and ex-urban sites generally. And as long as private commerce and industry continues to decentralise, as the D of I sees its policy in largely aspatial terms, and as the Treasury perceives cheaper development solutions in the new towns as opposed to the traditionally expensive cities, then urban decay will continue. But still to many, it remains an unacceptable reflection of market forces, and it should be combated. How, of course, is a different matter. Some want to encourage community action and enterprise in the cities, some want major industrial regeneration, some want radical political changes, some massive new financial investments. But collectively most of them would agree with the position of the National Council of Social Service, for whom 'it is questionable whether society can afford the increasing long-term burden which would follow from inaction, and in purely economic terms, whether we can allow suboptimal use of resources.'[15]

There are, however, contrary arguments. Partly these relate to the general sentiment that the plight of inner cities has been wildly and

H

dangerously exaggerated. Perhaps the best testament to this position is the Study of the Inner Areas of Conurbations undertaken by the D of E, and very quickly forgotten by it.[16] This is perhaps the most optimistic appraisal of older urban areas made in recent years. Basically, the Study compares the inner parts of conurbations with other areas of the city regions, and concludes that social polarisation is not as marked as had been imagined, employment prospects may be better there than in other locations, housing standards have improved markedly and that in general the only sector 'where there appears to have been a deterioration in the level of provision in the inner areas compared with the outer areas is local authority finance'.

Organisations such as the TCPA,[17] and other independent observers too,[18] have expanded on the findings of the Study and have devised and justified a general programme of decentralisation. To them it seems apparent that inner cities are not in the predicament that is sometimes stated, and that the 'urban dimension' approach devised by central government to overcome the inner city problem is badly conceived, will have unanticipated effects in cities if it should be even marginally successful, and unwisely attempts to counteract what are sensible and acceptable modes of demographic and economic decentralisation.

To these commentators it seems apparent that decentralisation of people and jobs is the basic characteristic of cities in virtually all advanced, industrialised countries. People leave because of the perceived advantages of suburban life, and jobs move out for well attested economic reasons. It is futile and expensive for central government to formulate an urban policy, because it will ultimately prove to be an expensive irrelevance. Only a relatively small sector of the population, and only certain specific economic functions, actually wish to retain or acquire inner city status. In trying to prevent the centrifugal forces at work, government is introducing a socially unpopular and economically foolhardy policy. What it should be trying to do is to encourage the relocation of industry to better and hence more profitable sites, and to combine this with more socially just policies which allow all socio-economic groups the opportunity to acquire or rent accommodation in suburban or ex-urban zones. This will mean an active policy of stimulating greater and not, as has recently happened, reduced decentralised investment. But if such a transformation in policy were to be introduced, both the city hinterlands and the older urban areas would benefit. In the case of the former, better, and better planned, facilities would be provided for those who wish to relocate. And from the point of view of the older cities the benefits would be manifold. Demographic and industrial densities would be reduced, thus improving the quality of life for those remaining and reducing the competitive demand on urban land which has done much to stimulate the present artificially high costs. With lower land prices and lower densities, better, larger and cheaper dwellings could be provided by both public and private sectors.

New economic bases would need to be introduced too since, according to Hall for instance, 'we need to plan for an orderly reorientation of our space economy, whereby each part of the urban system does the things that it is best suited to do.'[19] Adopting a long-term strategy such as this might well involve taking some admittedly hard decisions. A large proportion of the existing manufacturing base would move out. But on the other hand, inner cities might adopt other economic functions. Craft industries, tourism, administrative and educational enterprises, research and development, and innovative projects might all thrive in older urban areas. Of course, if cities were to devise long-term strategies based on these premises there would be very real problems. It would, for instance, be necessary to institutionalise far better administrative systems within housing markets to allow those workers who wish to remain in the manufacturing sector to decentralise with it, and far better retraining arrangements for those wanting to stay in cities. But better this, so the TCPA argument goes, than attempting to introduce a misguided and expensive inner city policy.

And even if, this position points out, the new inner city policy were to be marginally, and almost certainly temporarily, successful, what would the consequences be? Land prices would rise and not fall, since urban space competition would be accentuated. This would in turn lead not to an improvement in standards of urban housing, which so many commentators see as essential, but a deterioration, since unit land costs would rise.[20] And if more industry were to be attracted to older cities, this in turn would create additional congestion and pollution which have been responsible for so many better-off residents leaving cities in the first place. And there would be minimal compensation in the way of additional jobs, since new manufacturing industry, usually heavily capital intensive, requires limited labour, and very little of this unskilled. Certainly, per unit of space, the older, city based industries would have provided more jobs. And it is not as if any new industry would be cheap to install. Cities might have an existing physical infrastructure, but it is generally 'in such a state of deterioration that substantial replacement costs would be involved'[21] if it were to absorb new development. Far greater costs would be incurred than for the development of 'green field' sites.

To some extent the position advocated by the TCPA has been seen as a reactionary viewpoint: that in some way policies which undermine the regeneration of cities are not those which should be followed by the Left. But there seems no reason why decentralisation must inevitably be seen as a radically unacceptable solution.[22] Older urban areas are undoubtedly relatively unattractive for many residents of all socio-economic groups, both because of the inherent physical problems that generally exist there and because economic bases have deteriorated so rapidly. Decentralisation, provided that it is undertaken in a socially just manner which irons out spatial and sectoral mismatches between people and companies wishing to go and those able to go, might provide in the long term the most viable and sensible policy.

And certainly as it stands now, the government's inner city policy is neither viable nor sensible. Intellectually it is discredited, torn between the severity of the widely flung degenerative processes its own urban experiments have identified and the economic reality, which some wish to accept and turn to advantage, of acute urban decentralisation. On the one hand, whilst formulating a long-term national economic strategy of manufacturing regeneration, it is not prepared to follow the logic of that programme and accept the unsuitability of urban locations for virtually all manufacturing industry. And on the other hand, faced with the massive analytical and prescriptive contributions from its own urban initiatives, it accepts the validity of the diagnosis, without introducing solutions which are likely to make more than the most minimal impact on the degenerative processes identified. Central government should either have accepted what is perhaps the inevitable, and sought new socially just solutions to generally decongesting urban environments or, alternatively, introduced sufficiently interventionist powers to counteract relevant national and international structural changes. Instead, it formulated a typically British, and almost certainly ineffectual, compromise. And we can say that—and this is perhaps the lasting tribute to the urban programme—because a few urban initiatives were able to investigate in depth inner area structures, able to identify the processes of change, and able to formulate policy recommendations which, collectively, form an informational and intellectual input that no urban debate, still less an urban policy, can ignore.

NOTES TO CHAPTER 11

1   R. Young, 1976.
2   D. Donnison, 1974.
3   E. Eames and J. Goode, 1973, p. 267.
4   R. Hambleton, 1977A; R. Holman, 1973A.
5   M. Allan, 1977.
6   HMSO, Financial Statement and Budget Report 1977–78, 3. 1977.
7   D of E Circular 129/75, 31.12.75.
8   HMSO, *Public Expenditure to 1979–80*, 1976.
9   The Inner City Working Group of the Joint Centre for Regional, Urban and Local Government Studies, 1977, p. 29.
10 I. Harford, 1977, p. 101.
11 S. Holland, 1976, p. 47.
12 P. Townsend, 1974.
13 R. Holman, 1973B.
14 See, for instance, P. Stone, 1975; and D. Eversley, 1975A.
15 The National Council of Social Service, 1977, par. 2.1.
16 D of E, Study of the Inner Areas of Conurbations, 1975.
17 For an expansion of the TCPA argument, see TCPA, 1977; P. Self, 1977; J. Silkin, 1976; W. Strang, 1977; D. Lock, 1977; D. Hall, 1976; M. Ash, 1976.
18 See, for instance, J. Rogaly, 1976.
19 P. Hall, 1977B.
20 G. Lomas, 1974B.
21 M. Brownrigg, 1977.
22 H. Stretton, 1976.

Bibliography

Abrams, M., *Subjective Social Indicators*, Social Trends, No. 4, 1973, HMSO.

Acland, H., 'What is a Bad School? Plowden in Retrospect': I, *New Society*, Vol. 18, No. 467, 9.9.1971.

Allan, M., 'Employment and Land: the Key to Inner City Regeneration', *The Surveyor*, Vol. 149, No. 4435, and Vol. 149, No. 4436, 6.1977.

Amos, F., *Inner Area Study and Local Planning Making Process*, Liverpool City Council Planning Dept Information Booklet.

AJ, The, 'Shoreing Up the Inner City', Editorial, Vol. 164, No. 44, 3.11.1976.

Ash, M., 'Open Letter to the Secretary of State for the Environment', *Journal of the TCPA*, Vol. 44, No. 12, 12.1976.

Association of Metropolitan Authorities, *Cities in Decline. A Report on The Problem of the Old Industrial Cores of the Metropolitan Areas*, 12.1976.

Bailey, J., *Social Theory for Planning*, Routledge and Kegan Paul, 1975.

Bailey, R. and Brake, M. (eds.), *Radical Social Work*, Edward Arnold, 1975.

Baine, S., *Community Action and Local Government*, Occasional Papers on Social Administration, No. 59, G. Bell & Sons, 1975.

Barber, R., *Iron-Ore and After-Boom Time. Depression and Survival in a West Cumbria Town. Cleator Moor 1840–1960*, Cleator Moor Local Studies Group, Cumbria CDP.

Barnes, J. (ed.), Educational Priority, Report of Research Project sponsored by DES/SSRC, Vol. 3, *Curriculum: Innovations in London EPAs*, HMSO, 1975.

Batley, R., 'An Explanation of Non-Participation in Planning', *Policy and Politics*, Vol. 2, No. 2, 12.1973.

Batley, R., *The Neighbourhood Scheme. Cases of Central Government Intervention in Local Deprivation*, CES/RP 19, 11.1975.

Batley, R. and Edwards, J., 'The Urban Programme. A Report on Some Programme Funded Projects', *British Journal of Social Work*, Vol. 4, No. 3, Autumn 1974.

228

Batley, R. and Edwards, J., Urban Programme Research Working Paper No. 11, Dept of Social Policy and Administration, University of Leeds.

Bennington, J., 'Community Development Project', *Social Work Today*, Vol. I, No. 5, 8.1970.

Berthoud, R., 'Where Are London's Poor?', *Greater London Intelligence Quarterly*, No. 36, 9.1976 (A).

Berthoud, R., *The Disadvantages of Inequality. A Study of Social Deprivation*, A PEP Report, Macdonald and Janes, 1976 (B).

Birmingham CDP, *Workers on the Scrap Heap*, 2.1975.

Birmingham CDP, *The Cost of Buying Your Freehold*, 3.1975.

Blackhurst, D., 'Electing a Covent Garden Forum', *Greater London Intelligence Quarterly*, No. 35, 6.1976.

Blake, J., 'Backhand LOB', *Journal of the TCPA*, Vol. 45, Nos. 7–8, 7.8.1977.

Boatswain, A., 'For "Local" read "Area" ', *Municipal and Public Services Journal*, Vol. 83, 28.2.1975.

Bond, N., *The Hillfield Information and Opinion Centre. The Evolution of a Social Agency Controlled by Local Residents*, Coventry CDP Occasional Paper No. 2.

Bond, N., *Knowledge of Rights and Extent of Unmet Needs Amongst Recipients of Supplementary Benefit*, Coventry CDP Occasional Paper No. 4.

Booz Allen and Hamilton, Organisation Recommendations, County Borough of Stockport, 1971.

Bradshaw, J., Taylor Gooby, P. and Lees, R., 'The Batley Welfare Benefits Project', Papers in *Community Studies*, No. 5, Dept of Social Administration and Social Work, University of York, 1976.

Brand, J., 'The Politics of Social Indicators', *The British Journal of Sociology*, Vol. XXVI, No. 1, 3.1975.

Brand, J. and Cox, M. (eds.), *The Urban Crisis. Social Problems and Planning*, RTPI, 1974.

Broady, M. (ed.), *Marginal Regions. Essays on Social Planning*, Bedford Square Press, 1973.

Brooks, E., 'Development Problems of the Inner City. Symposium on Spatial and Social Constraints in the Inner City', *Geographical Journal*, Vol. 141, Part 3, 11.1975.

Brownrigg, M., 'New Town Growth: An Economist's Viewpoint', *The Planner*, Vol. 63, No. 4, 7.1977.

Bryant, R., 'Community Action', *British Journal of Social Work*, Vol. 2, No. 2, Summer 1972.

Buchanan, A., Talking at a Symposium on Spatial and Social Constraints in the Inner City, *Geographical Journal,* Vol. 141, Part 3, 11.1975.

Bull, D. (ed.), *Family Poverty, Programme for the Seventies,* G. Duckworth and Co Ltd, 1971.

Burchnall, M. *et al., History of Urban Aid. Approaches to Urban Management,* Dept of Civic Design, Liverpool, 1975.

Butcher, H., Cole, I. and Glen, A., *Information and Action Services for Rural Areas. A Case Study in West Cumbria,* Papers in Community Studies No. 4, Dept of Social Administration and Social Work, University of York, 1976.

Butterworth, E. and Holman, R. (eds.), *Social Welfare in Modern Britain,* Fontana, 1975.

Calouste Gulbenkian Foundation, The, *Current Issues in Community Work. A Study by The Community Work Group,* Routledge and Kegan Paul, 1973.

Cameron, G., 'Economic Renewal in the Inner City. Glasgow', *The AJ,* Vol. 165, No. 5, 2.2.1977.

Camina, M., 'Local Authorities and the Attraction of Industry', *Progress in Planning,* Vol. 3, Part 2, Pergamon Press, 1974.

Canning Town CDP, *Canning Town to Woolwich. The Aims of Industry? A Study of Industrial Decline in One Community,* 1.1975.

Castle, B., *The Cycle of Deprivation. The Political Challenge,* Paper Presented to a National Study Conference, Manchester University, British Association of Social Workers, 3.1974.

Cherry, G. (ed.), *Urban Planning Problems,* Leonard Hill, 1974.

Cicirelli, U. *et al., The Impact of Head Start on Children's Cognitive and Affective Development,* Westinghouse Learning Corporation, Washington, DC, 1969.

Clark, K. and Flopkins, J., *A Relevant War Against Poverty,* Harper and Row, New York, 1970.

Coates, B., Johnston, R. and Knox, P., *Geography and Inequality,* Oxford University Press, 1977.

Cockburn, C., *The Local State. Management of Cities and People,* Pluto Press, 1977.

Community Action, 'Action Report—The Urban Aid Programme', No. 3, 7/8.1972.

Community Action, 'Urban Aid', No. 10, 9/10.1973.

Community Action, 'Collapsed Community Programme', No. 23, 12.75/1.76.

Corina, L., *Local Government Decision Making,* Papers in Community Studies, No. 2, Dept of Social Administration and Social Work, University of York, 1975.

Corina, L., 'Housing Allocation Policy and Its Effects. A Case Study from Oldham CDP', Papers in *Community Studies*, No. 7, Dept of Social Administration and Social Work, University of York, 1976.

Corina, L., *Oldham CDP. An Assessment of Its Impact and Influence on the Local Authority*, Papers in Community Studies, No. 9, Dept of Social Administration and Social Work, University of York, 1977.

Couch, C., 'Inner Areas Development Agencies', *Journal of the TCPA*, Vol. 45, No. 10, 10.1977.

Coventry City Council, Coventry CDP. Comments of the Coventry City Council on the Final Report, 6.1975.

Coventry CDP, Final Report, Part I, *Coventry and Hillfields. Prosperity and the Persistence of Inequality*, 3.1975.

Coventry CDP, Final Report, Part II, *Background Working Papers*, 5.1975.

Craig, J. and Driver, A., 'The Identification and Comparison of Small Areas of Adverse Social Conditions', *Applied Statistics*, Vol. 21, No. 1, 1972.

Crowther, S., 'The Rotherham Study', *Journal of the TCPA*, Vol. 42, No. 3, 3.1974.

Cullingworth, J. B., *Problems of an Urban Society*, Vol. II, *The Social Context of Planning*, Vol. III (ed.), *Planning for Change*, George Allen and Unwin, 1973.

Cumberland CDP, Initial Study, July 1973.

Davies, J. G., *The Evangelistic Bureaucrat. A Study of a Planning Exercise in Newcastle upon Tyne*, Tavistock Publications, 1972.

Davis, A., McIntosh, N. and Williams, J., *The Management of Deprivation*, Final Report of the Southwark CDP, 1977.

Dearlove, J., *The Politics of Policy in Local Government*, Cambridge University Press, 1973.

Dennis, N., *People and Planning. The Sociology of Housing in Sunderland*, Faber and Faber, 1970.

Dennis, R., *The Decline of Manufacturing Employment in Greater London, 1966–1974*, CES, 9.1976, York.

DES Circular 11/67, *School Building Programme. School Building in EPAs*, 8.1967.

DES Circular 2/73, *Nursery Education*, 1.1973.

D of E Area Management Note 4.9.1974.

D of E Circular 52/72, *Town and Country Planning Act 1971. Part II. Development Plan Proposals. Publicity and Participation*, 6.1972.

D of E Circular 13/75, *Housing Act 1974. Renewal Strategies*, 1.1975.

D of E Circular 14/75, *Housing Act 1974. Parts IV, V, VI*, 1.1975.

D of E Circular 129/75, *The Rate Support Grant Settlement 1976–77*, 12.1975.

D of E Circular 71/77, *Local Government and the Industrial Strategy*, July 1977.

D of E, *The D of E and Its Work. A Factual Note about the Functions of the D of E*, 1975.

D of E, Housing Improvement Group, *Housing Action Areas. A Detailed Examination of Declaration Reports*, 11.1976.

D of E, Housing Services Advisory Group, *The Assessment of Housing Requirements*, 1977.

D of E Inner Area Studies:

IAS/Birmingham (B)/1, Project Report, 2.1974.

IAS/B/4, Interim Review, 7.1975.

IAS/B/5, *Small Heath. A Social Survey*, 7.1975.

IAS/B/7, *Little Green. A Case Study in Urban Renewal*, 10.1975.

IAS/B/8, Fourth Progress Report, 10.1975.

IAS/B/9, *Industrial Employment and Property Availability*, 10.1976.

IAS/B/10, *The Management of Urban Renewal*, 10.1976.

IAS/B/11, *Housing Policies for the Inner City*, 10.1976.

IAS, Birmingham IAS, *Unequal City. A Summary of the Final Report of the IAS*, 1977.

IAS, Final Report of the IAS Birmingham, *Unequal City*, 1977.

IAS/Lambeth (LA)/1, Project Report, 2.1974.

IAS/LA/3, Interim Report on Local Services, 8.1974.

IAS/LA/5, *People, Housing and District*, 12.1974.

IAS/LA/6, *Housing Stress*, 7.1975.

IAS/LA/7, *Policies and Structure*, 7.1975.

IAS/LA/9, *Local Services*, Consumers Sample, 7.1975.

IAS/LA/10, *Poverty and Multiple Deprivation*, 7.1975.

IAS/LA/11, *London's Inner Areas. Problems and Possibilities*, 3.1976.

IAS/LA/14, *Multi-Service Project*, 10.1976.

IAS/LA/15, (Second Report on) *Multiple Deprivation*, 5.1977.

IAS/LA/16, Local Employers' Study, 3.1977.

IAS, Final Report of the IAS Lambeth, *Inner London. Policies of Dispersal and Balance*, 1977.

IAS/Liverpool (LI)/3, Proposals for Area Management, 11.1973.

IAS/LI/9, Area Resources Analysis. District D Tables 1973–74, 3.1976.

IAS/LI/12, Fourth Study Review, 4.1976.

IAS/LI/16, *Housing Management*, 2.1977.

IAS/LI/18, *Single Parent Families*, 6.1977.

IAS, Liverpool IAS, *Change or Decay. A Summary of the Final Report of the IAS*, 1977.

IAS, Final Report of the IAS Liverpool, *Change or Decay*, 1977.

D of E, *Leisure and the Quality of Life. A Report on Four Local Experiments*, Vols. I and II, HMSO, 1977.

D of E, *Management Networks. A Study for Structure Plans*, HMSO, 1971.

D of E, *Quality of Life. Four Local Experiments in the Development of Leisure Activities*, Interim Note on Progress, 7.1975.

D of E, *Neighbourhood Councils in England*, Consultation Paper, 7.1974.

D of E, *Rates and Rateable Values in England and Wales 1975–76*, HMSO, 1976.

D of E, Research Report 10, *British Cities: Urban Population and Employment Trends*, HMSO, 1976.

D of E, Study of the Inner Areas of Conurbations, Vol. I, *Summary and Conclusions*; Vol. II, *Detailed Studies*, 6.1975.

D of E Urban Guidelines:

D of E, The Oldham Study, *Environmental Planning and Management*, Nathaniel Lichfield and Associates with Inbucon/AIC Management Consultants Ltd, HMSO, 1973.

D of E, The Rotherham Study, *A General Approach to Improving the Physical Environment*, Urwick, Orr and Partners in association with Graham Ashworth, HMSO, 1973.

D of E, The Sunderland Study, *Tackling Urban Problems*, Vol. I, *A Basic Handbook*; Vol. II, *A Working Guide*, McKinsey and Co Inc, HMSO, 1973.

DHSS, *The Family in Society. Dimensions of Parenthood*, Seminar, 4.1973.

DHSS, *The Family in Society. Preparation for Parenthood*, HMSO, 1974.

Dixey, B., *A Guide to Neighbourhood Councils*, published by the Association for Neighbourhood Councils.

Docklands Joint Committee, *Work and Industry in East London. A Working Paper for Consultation*, 4.1975.

Docklands Joint Committee, *London Docklands. A Strategic Plan*, 3.1976.

Donnison, D., 'Policies for Priority Areas', *Journal of Social Policy*, Vol. 3, Part 2, 4.1974.

Donnison, D. and Eversley, D. (eds.), *London. Urban Patterns, Problems and Policies. A Study Sponsored by the CES*, Heinemann, 1973.

Donovan, J., *The Politics of Poverty*, Pegasus, New York, 1967.

Dudley MB, *An Experiment in Area Management. The Approach Adopted by Dudley Metropolitan Borough*, 5.1977.

Dumbarton District Community Development Advisory Board, Final Report to the Local Sponsors.

Eames, E. and Goode, J., *Urban Poverty in a Cross-Cultural Context*, Collier Macmillan, 1973.

Economist, The, 'London's Burning! London's Burning! A Survey', Vol. 262, No. 6957, 1.1.1977.

Eddison, T., 'Bains and the "Total" Urban Approach', *Journal of the TCPA*, Vol. 40, No. 10, 10.1972.

Eddison, T., 'Guide Dogs for the D of E', *Journal of the TCPA*, Vol. 41, No. 12, 12.1973.

Eddison, T., *Local Government and Corporate Planning*, Leonard Hill Books (2nd edition) 1975.

Edginton, J., 'The Batley Battle', *New Society*, Vol. 29, No. 622, 5.9.1974.

Edwards, J., *Urban Deprivation and Stress Indices*, CURS University of Birmingham, Working Paper No. 31, 2.1975 (A).

Edwards, J., 'Social Indicators, Urban Deprivation and Positive Discrimination', *Journal of Social Policy*, Vol. 4, Part 3, 7.1975 (B).

Evans, A. with Russell, L., *A Portrait of the London Labour Market. Some Preliminary Sketches*, CES, 9.1976, York.

Eversley, D., 'Rising Costs and Static Incomes. Some Economic Consequences of Regional Planning in London', *Urban Studies*, Vol. 9, 10.1972.

Eversley, D., *The Planner in Society. The Changing Role of a Profession*, Faber and Faber, 1973.

Eversley, D., 'Who will Rescue our Cities?', *Built Environment Quarterly*, Vol. 1, No. 3, 12.1975 (A).

Eversley, D., *The Redevelopment of London's Docklands. A Case Study in Subregional Planning*, CES Occasional Papers, No. 1, 1975 (B).

Falk, N., 'Community as the Developer', *Built Environment*, Vol. 3, No. 4, 4.1974.

Falk, N., 'Conservation. Another Industrial Revolution', *Built Environment Quarterly*, Vol. 1, No. 2, 9.1975.

Falk, N. and Martinos, H., *Inner City*, Fabian Research Series, No. 320, 5.1975.

Fawcett, J., CIUD Working Note 13, *Areas of Housing Deprivation*, D of E, 1.1976.

Field, F., *Unequal Britain. Report on the Cycle of Inequality*, an Arrow Special, 1973.

Flynn, N., *Urban Experiments Ltd. Lessons from the CDP and IAS*, CES, 1.1977, York.

Flynn, N. and Thomas, K., 'Employment and Housing in the Inner City', *Planning*, No. 210, 1.4.1977.

Franklin, M. and Stafford, F., 'Building for Inner City Industry', *The AJ*, Vol. 165, No. 5, 2.2.1977.

Franks, M., 'An Experiment in Inner City Conservation', *Architectural Association Quarterly*, Vol. 7, No. 4, 10/12.1975.

Freeman, L., 'Third Tier Urban Government', *Municipal and Public Services Journal*, Vol. 81, 21.9.1973.

Friedman, L., *The Politics of Radical Community Action*, published by the Association of Community Workers, 10.1974.

Frost, D. and Sharman, N., 'Housing and Community Based Renewal', *Housing Review*, Vol. 24, No. 6, 11/12.1975.

Garrish, S., *Area Management Workshop*, School for Advanced Urban Studies, University of Bristol, 10.1974.

Glennerster, H. and Hatch, S. (eds.), *Positive Discrimination and Inequality*, Fabian Research Series, No. 314, 3.1974.

Goddard, J., 'Office Location in Urban and Regional Development', *Theory and Practice in Geography*, Oxford University Press, 1975.

Goddard, J., 'The Pressures for a Revision of Office Policy', *Journal of the ICPA*, Vol. 45, No. 1, 1.1977.

Gray, J., 'Positive Discrimination in Education. A Review of the British Experience', *Policy and Politics*, Vol. 4, No. 2, 12.1975.

Greenwood, R. and Stewart, J., *Corporate Planning in English Local Government. An Analysis with Readings 1967–72*, Institute of Local Government Studies, University of Birmingham, Charles Knight and Co Ltd, 1974.

Greve, J., *CDP Research Strategy*, CSG/70/2.

Greve, J., *The First Six Projects. A Commentary*, University of Southampton, 1972 (A).

Greve, J., *Assessment and Synthesis of Experience of First Group of Projects*, Report to Consultative Council, CDP/72/24, 27.10.1972(B).

Greve, J., *Towards an Analytical Framework for CDP*, CDP 73/19, 10.1973.

Gripaios, P., 'The End of Decentralisation Policy in London. Some Comments', *Journal of the TCPA*, Vol. 44, No. 10, 10.1976.

Gripaios, P., 'A Closure of Firms in the Inner City. The South East London Case 1970–75', *Regional Studies*, Vol. II, No. 1, 1977 (A).

Gripaios, P., 'Inner City Economic Decline. Some Implications for Regional Planning and Policy', *Planning Outlook*, Vol. 20, No. 1, 1977 (B).

Hall, D., 'Inner City. Sense and Nonsense', *Journal of the TCPA*, Vol. 44, No. 11, 11.1976.

Hall, P., 'The Inner Cities Dilemma', *New Society*, Vol. 39, No. 748, 3.2.1977 (A).

Hall, P., *Green Fields and Grey Areas*, RTPI Annual Conference, 6.1977 (B).

Hall, P., Thomas, R., Gracey, H. and Drewett, R., *The Containment of Urban England*, Vols. I and II, PEP, George Allen and Unwin, 1973.

Halsey, A. (ed.), Educational Priority, Report of Research Project sponsored by DES/SSRC, Vol. I, *Educational Priority. EPA. Problems and Policies*, HMSO, 1972.

Halsey, A., *Educational Disadvantage. Perspectives and Policies*, Report of a Conference convened by the Secretary of State for Education and Science, 16.4.1975.

Hambleton, R., 'Local Planning and Area Management', *The Planner*, Vol. 62, No. 9, 9.1976.

Hambleton, R., 'Policies for Areas', *Local Government Studies* (New Series) Vol. 3, No. 2, 4.1977 (A).

Hambleton, R., 'Urban Policy. A Learning Approach', *The Planner*, Vol. 63, No. 6, 11.1977 (B).

Hancock, T., 'A Total Approach', *Journal of the TCPA*, Vol. 42, No. 3, 3.1974.

Hancock, T. (ed.), *Growth and Change in the Future City Region*, Leonard Hill, 1976.

Hancock, T., 'An Inner City Programme', *Journal of the TCPA*, Vol. 45, No. 2, 2.1977.

Harford, I., 'The Inner City: Whose Urban Crisis?', *The Planner*, Vol. 63, No. 4, 7.1977.

Hargreave, R., 'An Experimental Industrial GIA', *Journal of the TCPA*, Vol. 44, No. 1, 1.1976.

Haringey LB, Report of the Principal Community Development Officer, *A Proposal for Area Management in Haringey*, 6.1975.

Harvey, D., *Social Justice and the City*, Edward Arnold, 1973.

Harvey Cox, W., *Cities. The Public Dimension*, Penguin Books, 1976.

Hatch, S., 'Between Government and Community', *Social Work Today*, Vol. 5, No. 4, 16.5.1974.

Hatch, S. and Sherrott, P., 'Positive Discrimination and the Distribution of Deprivations', *Policy and Politics*, Vol. 1, No. 3, 3.1973.

Hatch, S, Fox, E. and Legg, C., *Research and Reform: The Case of the Southwark CDP 1969-72*, HO, 1977.

Henderson, R., 'Industrial Overspill from Glasgow 1958-1968', *Urban Studies*, Vol. 11, 1974.

Higgins, J., 'A Project that Got Lost', *New Society*, Vol. 28, No. 609, 6.6.1974.

HMSO, *Half Our Future*, Report of the Central Advisory Council for Education (England), Ministry of Education, 1963 (Newsom).

HMSO, Report of the Committee on Housing in Greater London, Cmnd. 2605, 3.1965 (Milner Holland).

HMSO, *Children and Their Primary Schools*, Report of the Central Advisory Council for Education (England), 1967 (Plowden).

HMSO, Report of the Committee on the Management of Local Government, Ministry of Housing and Local Government, 1967 (Maud).

HMSO, Report of the Committee on the Staffing of Local Government, Ministry of Housing and Local Government, 1967 (Mallaby).

HMSO, Report of the Committee on Local Authority and Allied Personal Social Services, Cmnd. 3703, 7.1968 (Seebohm).

HMSO, *People and Planning*, Report of the Committee on Public Participation in Planning, 1969 (Skeffington).

HMSO, Report of the Royal Commission on Local Government in Scotland 1966-69, Cmnd. 4150, 1969 (Wheatley).

HMSO, Report of the Committee of Inquiry on Small Firms, Cmnd. 4811, 11.1971 (Bolton).

HMSO, *The New Local Authorities. Management and Structure*, The Study Group on Local Authority Management Structures, 1972 (Bains).

HMSO, *Education. Framework for Expansion*, Cmnd. 5174, 12.1972.

HMSO, *The New Scottish Local Authorities. Organisation and Management Structures*, 1973 (Patterson).

HMSO, *The Regeneration of British Industry*, Cmnd. 5710, 8.1974.

HMSO, *Educational Disadvantage and the Educational Needs of Immigrants*, Cmnd. 5720, 1974.

HMSO, *An Approach to Industrial Strategy*, Cmnd. 6315, 11.1975.

HMSO, *Public Expenditure to 1979–80*, Cmnd. 6393, 1976.

HMSO, Financial Statement and Budget Report 1977–78, 3.1977.

HMSO, *Policy for the Inner Cities*, Cmnd. 6845, 6.1977.

HO, *CDP Objectives and Strategy* (Revised), 9.1970.

HO, *Notes on the Urban Programme Legislation*, 4.1972.

HO Official Report on CCPs, 1974.

HO Circular 117/70, Urban Programme Circular No. 3, 12.6.1970.

HO Circular 83/74, Urban Programme Circular No. 11, 22.4.1974.

HO Circular 110/75, Urban Programme Circular No. 14, 18.6.1975.

Hollamby, E., 'IAS Reports. Practice Review', *RTPI News*, 6.1977.

Holland, S., *Capital Versus the Regions*, Macmillan, 1976.

Holman, R., 'The Wrong Poverty Programme', *New Society*, Vol. 13, No. 338, 20.3.1969.

Holman, R. (ed.), *Socially Deprived Families in the UK*, Bedford Square Press, 1970.

Holman, R., 'The Urban Programme Appraised', *Race Today*, Vol. 3, No. 7, 7.1971.

Holman, R., *Power for the Powerless. The Role of Community Action*, Community and Race Relations Unit of the British Council of Churches, 1972.

Holman, R., *'Pressure from Below'*, *Municipal and Public Services Journal*, Vol. 81, 16.2.1973 (A).

Holman, R., 'Poverty. Consensus and Alternatives', *British Journal of Social Work*, Vol. 3, No. 4, Winter 1973 (B).

Holman, R., 'The American Poverty Programme 1969–71', *Journal of Social Policy*, Vol. 3, No. 1, 1.1974.

Holman, R. and Hamilton, L., 'The British Urban Programme', *Policy and Politics*, Vol. 2, No. 2, 12.1973.

Holtermann, S., CIUD Working Note No. 5, *The Use of Census Indicators in the Selection of Housing Action Areas*, D of E, 1974.

Holtermann, S., CIUD Working Note No. 6, *Great Britain*, D of E, 1975 (A).

Holtermann, S., 'Areas of Urban Deprivation in Great Britain. An Analysis of the 1971 Census Data', *Social Trends*, No. 6, HMSO, 1975 (B).

Holtermann, S. and Silkin, F., 'Low Economic Activity as an Indicator of Deprivation', *Urban Studies*, Vol. 13, 10.1976.

Hook, M., 'Cost-Effective Housing. Inner City or Green Fields', *The AJ*, Vol. 165, No. 3, 19.1.1977.

Horn, C., Mason, T., Spencer, K., Vielba, C. and Webster, B., Area Management Monitoring Project, First Interim Report, *Area*

Management Objectives and Structures, Institute of Local Government Studies, University of Birmingham, 3.1977.

Huggins, C., 'The Spitalfields Project. A Study of Deprived Area Work in Action', *Built Environment Quarterly*, Vol. 3, No. 1, 3.1977.

Hutchinson, D. and Gibbs, S., 'Three Ways inside Three Towns', *The AJ*, Vol. 161, No. 7, 12.2.1975.

Hutchinson, D. and Gibbs, S., 'Inner Areas. Cultivating an Important Resource', *The AJ*, Vol. 164, No. 39, 29.9.1976.

The Inner City Working Group of the Joint Centre for Regional, Urban and Local Government Studies, *Inner Area Studies. A Contribution to the Debate*, University of Birmingham, 3.1977.

Islington LB, Islington Plan, Fact Pack, *Employment*, 1975.

Jackman, R. and Sellars, M., 'The Distribution of the Rate Support Grant. The Hows and Whys of the New Needs Formula', *CES Review*, No. I, 7.1977.

Jackson, C., *Lambeth Interface. Housing Planning and Community Action in an Inner London Borough*, Suburban Press, 1975.

Jackson, N., *The Urban Future*, University of Birmingham, Urban and Regional Studies No. 3, George Allen and Unwin, 1972.

James, E., *America Against Poverty*, Routledge and Kegan Paul, 1970.

Jones, D. and Mayo, M. (eds.), *Community Work One*, Routledge and Kegan Paul, 1974.

Jones, D. and Mayo, M. (eds.), *Community Work Two*, Routledge and Kegan Paul, 1975.

Jordan, B., *Poor Parents. Social Policy and the 'Cycle of Deprivation'*, Routledge and Kegan Paul, 1974.

Jordan, D., 'How we can Free the Housing Market', *Roof*, Vol. 2, No. 1, 6.1977.

Kershaw, P., 'Community Dialogue', *Municipal and Public Services Journal*, Vol. 83, 18.4.1975.

Kirklees MB, The Six Area Management Schemes, *Area Care in Kirklees*.

Knight, T., CIUD Working Note No. 3, *Report on Census Indicators of Urban Deprivation. North-West Planning Region*, D of E, 7.1974.

Knox, P., 'Social Well-Being. A Spatial Perspective', *Theory and Practice in Geography*, Oxford University Press, 1975.

Krumholz, M., Cogger, J. and Linner, J., 'The Cleveland Policy Planning Report', *Journal of the American Institute of Planners*, Vol. 41, N0. 5, 9.1975.

Lane, D. *et al.*, *Cities in Crisis*, Tory Reform Group, 1976.

Lees, A., 'Merseyside Revitalising an Older Urban Area', *Journal of the TCPA*, Vol. 45, No. 5, 5.1977.

Lees, R. and Smith, G. (eds.), *Action-Research in Community Development*, Routledge and Kegan Paul, 1975.

Lewisham LB, *Employment in Lewisham*, Part 2.

City of Liverpool, Community Development Section, *Programmes for Increasing Community Involvement in the Planning of Local Authority Services*.

City of Liverpool, Report of the Area Executive, *Priority Issues for Area Management in District 'D'*.

Lock, D., 'Shankland's Pony', *Journal of the TCPA*, Vol. 45, No. 3, 3.1977.

Lomas, G., 'Making Towns Better. A Total Approach', *Journal of the TCPA*, Vol. 42, No. 3, 3.1974 (A).

Lomas, G., *The Inner City*, London Council of Social Service, 7.1974 (B).

London Boroughs Association, Joint Working Party on Housing Action Areas, Interim Report, 6.1975.

London Boroughs Association, Housing and Work Committee, Report on the Regeneration of Inner London, 3.1977.

Luttrell, W., *Employment in Greater London. London Under Stress. A Study of the Planning Policies Proposed for London and its Region*, TCPA, 10.1970.

Marris, P. and Rein, M., *Dilemmas of Social Reform. Poverty and Community Action in the US*, (2nd edition) Pelican, 1974.

Massey, D. and Meegan, R., *The Inner City and the International Competitiveness of British Industry, The Employment Implications of the Industrial Reorganisation Corporation*, CES Working Note WN 437, 5.1976.

McGrath, M., *Batley East and West, A CDP Survey*, Papers in Community Studies, No. 6, Department of Social Administration and Social Work, University of York, 1976.

Midwinter, E., *Priority Education. An Account of the Liverpool Project*, Penguin Books, 1972.

Miliband, R., *The State in Capitalist Society. The Analysis of the Western System of Power*, Quartet, 1973.

Ministry of Housing and Local Government Circular 65/69, *Housing Act 1969. Area Improvement*, 9.1969.

Minns, R., 'An Alternative Employment Policy for the GLC', *Journal of the TCPA*, Vol. 43, No. 11, 11.1975.

Minns, R. and Thornley, J., *State Shareholdings. The Role of Local and Regional Authorities*, CES, York, 1.1977 (A).

Minns, R. and Thornley, J., 'Do Local Authorities have a Role in Economic Planning?', *The Planner*, Vol. 63, No. 3, 5.1977 (B).

Moor, N., *Jobs in Jeopardy. A Study of the Job Prospects in Older Industrial Areas*, Report to the CDP on Behalf of the Batley, Benwell, Canning Town and North Shields CDPs, 6.1974.

Moor, N., 'Job Prospects in Older Industrial Areas', *The Planner*, Vol. 61, No. 2, 2.1975.

Morrison, C. (ed.), Educational Priority, Report of Research Project Sponsored by DES/SSRC, Vol. 5. *EPA. A Scottish Study*, HMSO, 1974.

Moynihan, D., *Maximum Feasible Misunderstanding*, The Free Press, New York, 1969.

Myers, M., 'Urban Deprivation and the GLC', *Greater London Intelligence Quarterly*, No. 31, 6.1975.

Nabarro, R., 'New Jobs in Old Cities?', *Built Environment Quarterly*, Vol. 2, No. 4, 12.1976.

Nabarro, R., 'A New Deal for the Inner City?', *The AJ*, Vol. 166, No. 27, 6.7.1977 (A).

Nabarro, R., 'Inner City Economics', *Built Environment Quarterly*, Vol. 3, No. 3, 9.1977 (B).

Nabarro, R. and Watts, C., 'Looking for Work in Liverpool', *New Society*, Vol. 39, No. 746, 20.1.1977.

NCDP Inter-Project Report 1973, CDP Information and Intelligence Unit, 1974.

NCDP, *The Poverty of the Improvement Programme*, CDP Information and Intelligence Unit, 1975.

NCDP Forward Plan 1975–76, CDP Information and Intelligence Unit, 1975.

NCDP, *Profits Against Houses. An Alternative Guide to Housing Finance*, CDP Information and Intelligence Unit, 1976.

NCDP, *The Costs of Industrial Change*, CDP Inter-Project Editorial Team, 1977.

NCDP, *Gilding the Ghetto. The State and Poverty Experiments*, CDP Inter-Project Editorial Team, 1977.

NCDP and Counter-Information Services, *Cutting the Welfare State (Who Profits?)*.

National Council for Social Service, The, *Inner Cities. A Clear Case for Urgent Action*, 3.1977.

National Enterprise Board, The, *Investment Potential in the North-East and North-West of England*, Report by the NEB, 5.1977.

City of Newcastle, *Newcastle's Approach to Priority Areas: The Attack on Stress.*

New Society Editorial, 'Britain's Poverty Programme', Vol. 13, No. 329, 16.1.1969.

New Society Editorial, 'CDPs Writ Larger', Vol. 33, No. 667, 17.7.1975.

New Society, 'Urban Aid', Vol. 34, No. 681, 23.10.1975.

North-West Joint Planning Team, Strategic Plan for the North West 1973, Technical Paper No. 3, *The Urban Environment*, Part 4, *Deprivation and the Inner City*, July 1974.

Oldham MB, Report of the Community Development Project Working Party, 12.8.1976.

Paterson, A. and Inglis, J., 'The Inter-Generational Cycle of Deprivation', *Social Work Today*, Vol. 8, No. 9, 23.11.1976.

Pahl, R., *Whose City? and Further Essays on Urban Society*, Penguin Books, 1975.

Paisley CDP, *Home and Primary School*, 4.1974.

Paisley CDP, Statement to the Deprived Areas Subcommittee on Renfrew District Council, 9.1976.

Payne, J., Educational Priority, Report of Research Sponsored by DES/SSRC, Vol. 2, *EPA. Survey and Statistics*, HMSO, 1970.

Pearce, J., *An Industrial Co-operative Experiment in Cumbria*, Cumbria CDP, Papers in Community Studies, No. 13, Dept of Social Administration and Social Work, University of York, 1977.

Pinker, R., *Social Theory and Social Policy*, Heinemann Educational Books Ltd, 1971.

Pratt, J., 'CDP Planning', *New Society*, Vol. 31, No. 651, 27.3.1975.

Richter, R., *Save Our Cities*, The Calouste Gulbenkian Foundation, 1977.

Rochdale MB, *Industrial Obsolescence. The Rochdale Approach*, 1977.

Rogaly, J., 'Let the Centres of Cities Wither Away', *Financial Times*, 12.10.1976.

Rogers, P. and Smith, C., 'The Local Authority's Role in Economic Development: The Tyne and Wear Act 1976', *Regional Studies*, Vol. 11, No. 3, 1977.

Rowe, A., 'CDP. A Mid-Term Report', *Municipal and Public Services Journal*, Vol. 83, 31.1.1975.

Rowland, J., *Community Decay*, Penguin Special, 1973.

RTPI, *Planning and The Future*, 11.1976.

Rustin, M., 'Whose "Total Approach"?', *Municipal and Public Services Journal*, Vol. 83, 6.6.1975.

Rutter, M. and Madge, N., *Cycles of Disadvantage. A Review of Research*, Heinemann, 1976.

Sackney, C., *The Political Economy of Urban Poverty*, W. W. Norton and Co, New York, 1973.

Scottish Development Dept, Central Planning Research Unit, *Summary Report of an Investigation to Identify Areas of Multiple Deprivation in Glasgow City*, CPRU Working Paper No. 7, 3.1973.

Scottish Education Dept Circular No. 906/SW, No. 11/74, Dundee EPA Report, 7.1974.

Self, P., 'This Time Listen', *Journal of the TCPA*, Vol. 45, No. 5, 5.1977.

Sharp, G. and Rowley, B., *Coventry and Hillfields. Prosperity and the Persistence of Inequality. Reservations* (undated).

Shelter Neighbourhood Action Project, *SNAP. Another Chance for Cities*, 1972.

Shenton, N., *Deneside. A Council Estate*, Oldham CDP Papers in Community Studies No. 8, Dept of Social Administration and Social Work, University of York, 1976.

Shonfield, A. and Shaw, S. (eds.), *Social Indicators and Social Policy*, Heinemann Educational Books, published for the SSRC, 1972.

Shore, P., Secretary of State for the Environment, 'Inner Urban Policy', speech given at Manchester Town Hall, 17.9.1976.

Shore, Peter, Secretary of State for the Environment, 'The Problems of Inner Cities and Housing', speech given at the Annual Conference of the National Housing and Town Planning Council, Brighton, 3.11.1976.

Silkin, F., CIUD Working Note No. 10, *The Conurbations of Great Britain*, D of E, 6.1975.

Silkin, J., 'New Towns and the Inner City', *Journal of the TCPA*, Vol. 44, No. 9, 9.1976.

Simkins, A., 'Towards Area Management', *Municipal and Public Services Journal*, Vol. 83, 21.1.1975.

Slough Estates, *The Inner City. A Location for Industry?*, 1977.

Smith, B., *Employment in Inner City Areas. A Case Study of the Position in Small Heath, Birmingham in 1974*, Paper to a CES Seminar, 6.1975, CURS, University of Birmingham, Working Paper No. 34, 6.1975.

Smith, B., *What Can Birmingham Metropolitan District Council Do that Will Benefit the Employment and Economic Situation in an Inner Area like Small Heath?*, A Personal Assessment to Stimulate Discussion, CURS, University of Birmingham, Working Paper No. 45, 6.1976.

Smith, B., *Economic Problems in the Core of the Old Birmingham Industrial Area*, CURS, University of Birmingham, Working Paper No. 50, 3.1977.

Smith, D., *Industrial Location. An Economic Geographical Analysis*, John Wiley and Sons, 1971.

Smith, G., 'Community Development. Rat Catchers or Theorists', *New Society*, Vol. 27, No. 593, 14.2.1974.

Smith, G. (ed.), Educational Priority, Report of Research Project Sponsored by DES/SSRC, Vol. 4, *A Case Study of the West Riding Project*, HMSO, 1975.

Smith, T. and G., 'Urban First Aid', *New Society*, Vol. 18, No. 483, 30.12.1971.

Southwark Trades Council and J. C. Roberts (Southwark CDP), *Employment in Southwark. A Strategy for the Future*, 5.1976.

Southwark Trades Council, *Strategy for the Surrey Docks*, 4.1977.

South Yorks County, *County Regional Investment Scheme. Funds for Industry*.

Spencer, K., *CCPs*, Institute of Local Government Studies, University of Birmingham, 12.1975.

Spitalfields Project, *Criteria for the Spending of Spitalfields Project Funds*, Summer 1975.

Spitalfields Project Steering Group, Item 6, *Project Schemes Progress and Financial Report*, 6.4.1977.

Spitalfields Project Steering Group, Item 9, *Public Involvement*, 6.4.1977.

Spitalfields Project Steering Group, Item 10, *Authority Involvement*, 6.4.1977.

Spitalfields Project. Two Down Three to Go, Report by the Coordinator of the Spitalfields Project, 5.1977.

SSRC/DHSS Joint Working Party on Transmitted Deprivation, First Report, 8.1974.

Stewart, J. D., *Management in Local Government. A Viewpoint*, Institute of Local Government Studies, University of Birmingham, Charles Knight and Co Ltd, 1971.

Stewart, J. D., Spencer, K. and Webster, B., *Local Government. Approaches to Urban Deprivation*, HO, UDU Occasional Papers No. 1.

Stewart, M. (ed.), *The City. Problems of Planning*, Penguin Books, 1972.

Stewart, M. (ed.), *Area Management Workshops*, School for Advanced Urban Studies, University of Bristol, Session I, 11.1974; and Session II, 2.1975.

Stockport MB, Report of the Director of Administration, Discussion Paper for the First Meeting of Area Committees, 1974.

Stockport MB, Report of the Management Board, Area Organisation, Policy and Resources (General Purposes) Subcommittee, 2.1977.

Stone, P., 'Balancing the Optima', *Built Environment Quarterly*, Vol. 1, No. 3, 12.1975.

Stone, P., *The London Economy and Policies for Manufacturing Industry*, CES, York, 9.1976.

Stott, P., 'The Quality of Life Experiment', *Journal of the TCPA*, Vol. 43, No. 10, 10.1975.

Strang, W., 'The Education of A Secretary of State?', *Journal of the TCPA*, Vol. 45, No. 6, 6.1977.

Stretton, H., *Capitalism, Socialism and the Environment*, Cambridge University Press, 1976.

Sugden, R., *Unskilled and Unemployed in West Cumbria*, Papers in Community Studies, No. 3, Dept of Social Administration and Social Work, University of York, 1975.

Tesco, *Retailing and the Inner City*, 4.1977.

Thomas, D. N., *Organising for Social Change. A Study in the Theory and Practice of Community Work*, National Institute Social Services Library No. 30, George Allen and Unwin, 1976.

Thomas, K., 'The Impact of Renewal on Small Firms', *The Planner*, Vol. 63, No. 2, 3.1977.

Towers, G., 'Swinbrook. Testbed for Participation', *The AJ*, Vol. 161, No. 11, 12.3.1975.

TCPA, *Statement on Inner Cities*, May 1977.

Town Planning Review Editorial, Vol. 46, No. 1, 1975.

Townsend, P., *The Cycle of Deprivation. The History of a Confused Thesis*, Paper presented to a National Study Conference, Manchester University, British Association of Social Workers, 3.1974.

Townsend, P., 'Area Deprivation Policies', *New Statesman*, Vol. 92, No. 2368, 6.8.1976.

Tyrrell, C., Submission to the Layfield Committee of Inquiry into Local Government Finance, CDP Information and Intelligence Unit, 1.1975.

Wandsworth LB, *Employment in Wandsworth*, 8.1972.

Wandsworth LB, Planning and Transport Committee Reports: 7223, 23.9.1975; 7331, 11.11.1975; 7608, 6.4.1976; and 8155, 11.1.1977.

Wandsworth LB, Policy and Resources Committee, *The Community Planning Process and the CCP*, Paper 7557, 9.3.1976.

Webber, R. J., Liverpool Social Area Study, 1971 Data, Final Report, Planning Research Applications Group Technical Papers, TP 14, 12.1975.

Webster, B., *Area Management Workshop*, School for Advanced Urban Studies, University of Bristol, 11.1974.

Wedderburn, D. (ed.), *Poverty, Inequality and Class Structure*, Cambridge University Press, 1974.

Weightman, G., 'The CDP File', *New Society*, Vol. 35, No. 702, 16.3.1976.

Wood, A., 'Making Towns Better', *The AJ*, Vol. 158, No. 47, 21.11.1973.

Young, R., 'The All Embracing Problem of Multiple Deprivation', *Social Work Today*, Vol. 8, No. 9, 30.11.1976.

Index